I N 1967, PRODUCER GEORGE SCHLATTER PITCHED AN idea for a quirky new television show: one inspired by the hippie counterculture, which would take the idea of sit-ins, love-ins, and be-ins, and manifest that politicized, sexualized, consciousness-raising energy into pure comedy. Much to the surprise of NBC executives, *Laugh-In* soon became the #1 show on American TV, and the careers of beloved stars like Lily Tomlin and Goldie Hawn were born.

Still Laughing features never-before-told stories from the creation of one of the most groundbreaking shows in television history. It also recounts the coming-of-age of one of Hollywood's most iconic producers, from his early nightclub days rubbing elbows with mob figures like Mickey Cohen and John Stompanato, to his influential friendships with Judy Garland and Frank Sinatra, for whom George was asked to deliver a eulogy at his funeral decades later.

An inside look at Hollywood in the wake of the cultural upheaval of the '60s and '70s, *Still Laughing* demonstrates the crucial, deeply creative role a working producer plays in bringing a show (and its stars) to life. With spit-fire humor, tireless wit and keen perception, *Still Laughing* tells of the rise of some of comedy's greatest talents, and reveals the actual people cloistered inside larger-than-life celebrity.

Still Laughing

A Life in Comedy

FROM THE CREATOR OF *LAUGH-IN*

c 1996 AL HIRSCHFELD

George Schlatter

as told to Jon Macks

LOS ANGELES, CA

AN UNNAMED PRESS/RARE BIRD JOINT PRODUCTION

www.unnamedpress.com

Hardcover ISBN: 978-1-951213-79-4
Paperback ISBN: 978-1-961884-21-2
Ebook ISBN: 978-1-951213-83-1
Library of Congress Control Number: 2023930728

Jacket design and typeset by Jaya Nicely

Manufactured in the United States of America

Distributed by Publishers Group West

First Paperback Edition
2 4 6 8 10 9 7 5 3 1

To my *lovely* wife, the amazing Jolene, who has put up with me during sixty-five-plus years of more ups and downs than an Otis elevator and who does not approve of some of the contents of this book. Then again, she does not *always* approve of me.

Foreword
by Lily Tomlin

I never thought that television was right for me. I had two chances, and I failed at both. I was in California to do a TV show that had been canceled midseason, so I was preparing myself to go back to New York because the theater was there. I had planned to make a life in the theater, but I did not get very far. On the plus side, nobody really knew about me yet, so I thought there was still a chance.

My agent and my manager kept begging me before I left Los Angeles to take one last meeting with this producer. Well, I didn't want to meet any more producers. I mean, did I really want to do one of my characters while sitting across from them at their desk, watching them shrink back in their chair with a look of "what is this?" on their face?

I'd been there too many times, and I knew how it always played out. Just a few minutes into the meeting, the producer's phone would ring and their secretary would usher me out of the room. Outside on the street, I'd slip into a phone booth sobbing at the rejection and the humiliation. I'd call my agent. He'd say, "Lily, what did you do? They said, they never want you back again." My reputation was being ruined before I even had one.

But, of course, I hadn't planned on meeting George Schlatter. As soon as I saw him, I knew I was in the right place. He was a happy, big bear of a guy who might as well have thrown his arms around me as soon as I walked in. He appreciated every character I showed him. He laughed, he gave me confidence and, most importantly, he hired me.

So, suddenly, I was on *Laugh-In*! And my life changed. George changed my life. Overnight. Literally. Well, first he changed Ernestine's life. She aired on Monday night. On Tuesday, Ernestine was a star. She was a bona fide star. People stopped me everywhere. At a light, people would actually jump out of their cars. People pushing a cart in the market or walking on the beach would say, "you're that new girl." I'm laughing demurely and saying in agreement, "I guess so." And then they'd say, "The girl who does Ernestine, that phone operator, she's a riot." I'd say, "I do Ernestine. I'm the one who does the phone operator." And they'd drive away or walk away or swim away as if they weren't really sure that I was telling the truth.

I've had a career ever since George had me sit down at that switchboard. He gave me a career, a huge career, just as he's given careers to so many others. And all the people he's helped—all the laughs he's given us over the decades—are in the stories in this wonderful book.

On these pages, George brings to life all the people you can see in those iconic photos on the walls in his office. But they're not just images on photographic paper; they're all George's friends, real people whose names happen to be Frank and Judy and Sammy and Dean and Lily and Goldie and Artie and Ruth and Joanne. The humanity and humor that George brought out in them is reflected in every story in these chapters.

And now it's time for you to turn the page and begin reading *Still Laughing: A Life in Comedy*. And be prepared, you're about to enter the world of a legend: George Schlatter.

Preface: Ode to Jolene

(With a few notes about the writing of this book)

O de: Something that shows respect for or celebrates the worth or influence of another.

Jolene Brand Schlatter. How I got her, I don't know. She was a dark-haired, classic beauty, winning contests and working as a model. Her photo was on many Capital Records albums including the famous George Shearing "Black Satin" album and the calypso album by Robert Mitchum.

As you will read later, we met when she became the lead dancer at Ciro's on the Sunset Strip. Jolene was such a favorite of celebrities like writers Harrison Carrol and columnists Louella Parsons and Army Archerd that she was featured with her name on the Ciro's billboard out front on Sunset Boulevard despite the fact that she wasn't that good as a dancer...although she was gorgeous and the whole town was talking about her.

Jolene was an accomplished actress appearing on many television shows. For several years she modeled on Queen for A Day. She appeared as Anna Maria, Zorro's love interest on Disney's Zorro series and as Pink Cloud on Desilu's Guestward Ho. During her run on the Ernie Kovacs Show, often as part of the Nairobi Trio and the Girl in the Bathtub, Jolene developed a love of sight gags and it was she who came up with the catch phrase, "Sock It to Me," for "Laugh-In."

This lovely lady gave up a flourishing career to marry me. She got me out of checkered jackets and white patent leather shoes. She smoothed off the rough edges and made me acceptable in an important, influential circle which enhanced my career. But most importantly, Jolene got me out of Vegas. That story is in the book.

Jolene became involved with charities in Hollywood. She was one of the early members of "Share," which was founded by a group of Hollywood wives including Jeanne (Mrs. Dean) Martin, Ginny (Mrs. Henry) Mancini, (Mrs.) Jeff Chandler, Audrey (Mrs. Billy) Wilder, Janet Leigh and Niele (Mrs. Steve) McQueen. Share's annual "Boomtown Party" was the most sought after ticket in town and raised thousands of dollars for Children's charities. Today she is very supportive of "Homes for Our Troops," which builds specially adapted custom homes for severely injured post-9/11 and later Veterans.

We have now been married 67 years and have two wonderful daughters. Our daughter Maria won an Emmy for producing the Frank Sinatra birthday special and a celebration of Sammy Davis, Jr. She also won an Emmy for producing and writing a Dolly Parton Christmas Special. Our daughter AJ and her husband Kevin own a ranch in Arizona where they bread horses and train young equestrians. They also own a prize-winning Samoyed named Huxton.

Some of Jolene's many other accomplishments and adventures are told in the stories in this book, but I just wanted to publicly thank my girlfriend, roommate and wife who saw something in me that I didn't and our partnership got me where I am today. I want everyone to know how much this woman means to me.

And now for those notes.

Still Laugh-In. It has so many different meanings. Yes, I created *Laugh-In*, and fifty years after it went off the air, it is still considered one of the most influential series in the history of comedy. *Laugh-In* launched the careers of legends like Goldie Hawn, created catchphrases like "sock it to me," rose to become the number one show on television, and probably elected President Nixon. (I am so sorry about that last one. More on that later.) And me? I'm ninety-three and still laughin'. Which is a lot better than the alternative.

Years ago I did an interview where I said I was born in 1932 instead of telling the truth that I was born in 1929. So many people think I just turned ninety when in fact I'm ninety-three. I feel bad and apologize. I should have told a bigger lie and said I was born in 1942.

Anyway, this is my story—a story of a kid from Missouri who ended up working with some of the most fascinating people in the history of show business. Before I take that long dirt nap, I want to share with you the laughs I've had with them, the lies I've told, the events I instigated (which is a classier way of saying the shit I started), and the laws I may have broken. Somehow, for over half a century, whether as their friend, producer, or drinking buddy, I ended up being in the room, in bars, in planes, backstage, and in casinos with the legends of TV, music, and movies.

I could not write this book the way so many of the other career books have been written, where it traces a person's life and career in a strict chronological and very linear manner. My life's best moments come to me in brief episodes where one thing reminds me of something else, where a story about one person makes me think of someone else. It's not logical, but then again, nothing in my career has been logical. The best I could do is to organize by sections. The reason for doing it this way is that when I look back at my life, the things that I remember most vividly are almost always funny moments, people, and experiences. I believe that the human mind does not have the power to retain the sensation of pain—at least mine doesn't. So, the focus of this book will always be the people I've worked with and show business moments and stories that have made me laugh or made other people laugh.

Some sections will be long and may meander all over the place, while others will be really short. Some people you might recognize will have only brief cameos. Others will feature as recurring characters. Some will have me as a supporting actor; others as the lead. And the best part, almost all of what follows is true.

In this book I'd like to take you back with me, to a world of show business that doesn't exist anymore but will never be forgotten, for it is the foundation on which today's television was built. And my wish is simple: that in the end, when you finish this memoir, you too will still be laughin'.

Still Laughing
A Life in Comedy

Part 1
In the Beginning

G rowing up: Although some may say that a ninety-three-year-old who still loves fart jokes never really grew up, my story does go back a ways. I was born in Birmingham, Alabama. All the nurses were somewhat in awe because they say I was born with a perfect "veil." A veil is a kind of thin membrane that certain babies have that covers their head. In the South it is quite a superstitious symbol in voodoo; it is supposed to denote a person with magical powers of perception who is able to see into the future. Obviously, it was bullshit, because at my age I can't even see someone standing ten feet away from me.

Anyhow, shortly after they removed my veil, which if I could see the future I could have predicted they would do, we left Birmingham and moved around all over the country: Indianapolis, Detroit, Peoria, Jacksonville, and eventually we ended up in a small town called East Aurora in New York. East Aurora was so small there was no West Aurora. My father was a salesman, and we lived at the Roycroft Inn, which was built by Elbert Hubbard, who was quite a renowned individual back in the 1800s. I guess it didn't take much to be renowned in East Aurora.

Having grown up moving constantly, it's not strange that I would continue moving as a young man. In this section I'll share a bit about my early years—about Vegas, and how I got out of Vegas alive. I will certainly tell you about the incident with me and the amorous chimps (bet that got your attention) and how amorous George met gorgeous Jolene.

MY WORLD PREMIERE

East Aurora is eighteen miles outside of Buffalo, which was what I liked best about it. Our backyard had a railroad track right behind it, and I can remember hearing those railroad cars going by and counting them until I went to sleep. The railroad is important: it was the site of my first moneymaking scheme. At night we would go out and tape pennies to the track. The train would flatten them, and the next day I'd sell each flat penny for a nickel—some suckers thought a flattened penny was a treasure. I just knew the value of a nickel. Doing that to money in many ways determined my career path. Driven by such impulses, either you become creative and likely end up in show business, or you keep up your illegal moneymaking schemes and end up as Bernie Madoff.

My mother was a concert violinist with a wicked sense of humor. One of my earliest recollections of music was sitting in the first row when my mom was playing a violin solo in front of a huge orchestra. She had me sit there so she could keep an eye on me. Even then I knew she was really good, but what I remember most was looking up and for the first time realizing that my mom had *great* legs. (How about that? Nine years old and perving on my own mom's legs.) Between my early love for music and legs, I was clearly headed to a life in show business.

Eventually, my father bought a farm on Oleander Road, outside of East Aurora. Now *that* is rural. We lived with my mom's mom, Maimi, who was a real character, and her sister, Eileen, and Eileen's daughter on a farm that had a woodstove and a well. We pumped for water and we had chickens, which is better than the other way around. There is no doubt this had an impact on my career—I always made sure *Laugh-In* always had chicken jokes.

My father said for our allowance we could keep anything we made off the farm. So, we raised a lot of corn, picked it, and then walked all the way down the road to try to sell it to farmers who didn't grow corn. If I couldn't get a reasonable price from the first guy, I had to walk all the way back and down to the other end of the road to see if I could sell it to the other guy. That little adventure was where I first learned to negotiate. Those farmers may have had cow shit on their shoes, but they were smart as hell. Ten cents for a dozen ears of corn doesn't sound like much today. It didn't sound like much back then either, so eventually I let my brothers handle the corn business.

My first adventure in show business was in seventh grade. I was playing the Giant in "Jack and the Beanstalk." My big line was "Fi, fie, fo, fum." I had to sit on top of a big stepladder for most of the play, and then I had to come down the stepladder carrying a chicken. By the time I got there, my green felt costume was covered with chicken shit—good practice for a life in show business, as it got me prepared for reading TV critics' reviews.

In grade school I learned to play first clarinet and then sax, but I wasn't thrilled with either. I was the only kid in school who still had a steel clarinet while all the other kids had wood clarinets, so I took up the sax. The cheapest instrument at the music store was a C melody sax. Any musician can tell you there is nothing written for the C melody sax, so whatever I was playing bore no resemblance to what the rest of the orchestra was playing. Let's just say the concert musician gene did not pass down from my mother to me.

Eventually my dad was transferred by the Magic Chef stove company to St. Louis, and we ended up in Webster Groves, Missouri, which is where I went to high school. I was captain of the wrestling team and the football team, but after I had polio, which weakened me for a while and scared off recruiters, I couldn't get into a big football college, so I got a scholarship to a little school in Marshall called Missouri Valley College, which had a legendary football program. Forty-two games without a tie or defeat. Nobody wanted to play us because most members of our team were ex-marines. Some had even been in prison camps. One of the blocking backs had one arm. Another defensive lineman had one eye—he had lost the other one in a German prison camp. A bunch of grown, bearded, mean men who had just gotten out of the Marines and who came back to this little midwestern school on the GI Bill . . . and me. Our team (think of a squad of marines on liberty) would go out on weekends and get drunk and throw hip blocks on small trees. Our helmets and jerseys didn't match when we started out, but the town made so much money off this football team, after one season we became the best dressed bunch of foulmouthed, tobacco-spitting, cigar-sucking, rebel-yelling, beer-drinking, womanizing, practical joking athletes in the Midwest.

I was the littlest guy on the team; I weighed about 175 pounds, and the rest of the team averaged about 230. The good news was that training on beer apparently adds weight. And as the new guy, I'll admit I was the victim of some hazing. My ex-marine teammates took my mattress and tied it with ropes to the rear of a Model T Ford and dragged it around in the snow just for laughs. It was frozen solid for two days. Another morning I woke up with my bed balanced on top of some lockers. I must have been a sound sleeper, or really hungover. Everyone thought that was funny. Today, I agree, it was funny.

I was in pain most of the time from being pounded by these larger animals, but I wound up playing second string on this college team in my freshman year, right up until I got mononucleosis and got shut down for the season. I was a tough kid, but not indestructible. Although over the years, I survived, which proves beyond a shadow of a doubt that alcohol is a preservative.

During the summer after that first year in college, I performed with the St. Louis Municipal Opera. The amphitheater seated fourteen thousand people, and it was the model for all the outdoor theaters that now exist. On lunch breaks and between shows, I ran down to the Grand Theatre to check out one of its five burlesque shows a day. I loved everything about burlesque—later I'll tell you how I turned it into a TV special—but for me the best part was watching the comics, legends in their day like Tommy "Moe" Raft, Billy "Zoot" Reed, Belle Barth, B. S. Pully, Sparky Kaye, and Hank Henry. I learned what "shtick" meant from the very best, which was useful when I ended up in Hollywood.

How I Got from Missouri to Hollywood

At the end of that summer with the opera, I came to California to go on tour with the road show of *The Desert Song*, and I promptly got a throat infection. A singer with a throat infection is like a field goal kicker with a broken foot. So, showing the compassion that most people in the field of entertainment had back then, the road show left without me. I was stranded with no money, no job, no throat, and no scholarship. At that moment I was getting ready to begin my penny-flattening scheme again. Instead, I took three of those precious pennies, bought a three-cent stamp, and wrote to the coach at my former college in Missouri. One letter from him, and George Pepperdine College gave me a football scholarship, sight unseen. Pepperdine had been offered a chance to play Missouri Valley College in the Junior Rose Bowl, but *nobody* would play Missouri Valley. The Pepperdine coach thought if I was good enough to make the Missouri Valley team as a freshman, I'd be good enough for Pepperdine.

Today, Pepperdine has a magnificent campus in Malibu, the mountains on one side, the Pacific on the other. Back then it was in downtown LA on Vermont Avenue overlooking, as I recall, a bar, a cemetery, and car dealership.

Pepperdine and I proved to be an awkward match. It was a Church of Christ school with two mandatory chapel sessions a day. Talk about culture shock—Missouri Valley had two mandatory beer-chugging sessions a day. The powers in charge at Pepperdine were so strict they did not want the students getting laid because it could lead to dancing. That's an old joke, but in many ways, so am I.

My not-so-distant past, however, came back to haunt me. When I was in Missouri, I would go to Kansas City and fight in the American Legion Hall. If you won, you got a radio; if you didn't win, you got bus fare. But even if you did win, you couldn't keep the radio. You sold it back for $25. The radio had about an inch of dust on it. There were some gangsters who ran the fights there, and you had to always give the radio back. (Although they gave you a choice: you could keep the radio and lose your thumb, or keep your thumb and give back the radio.)

In Missouri they considered that amateur, but not at Pepperdine. I was the Jim Thorpe of Pepperdine, busted for my "professional status." One of the guys I had boxed with remembered my name and that I had gotten some money to fight, and so the school canceled my scholarship. Much later, when I became famous, they put me back on the alumni list. Fame (and a check) helped a lot.

Now, while I was attending classes and chapel, I was also dating this little blond singer by the name of Monti Fraser. She had the voice of an angel and a body to die for. She appeared on Ada Leonard's show *Search for Girls*, which was an early version of *Star Search*, and every thirteen weeks they would have the finals. This girl was terrific and won ten weeks in a row. At some point, we agreed that along with the privilege of dating her, I could also become her manager.

The writer of the show was a young man, and we became friendly. At one point he came to me and asked if Monti would agree not to compete for the next few weeks; otherwise they couldn't do the finals since she had been the only winner they had in that cycle. I stupidly agreed, but instead I should have made a long-term management deal on behalf of Monti. Even so, he wanted me to manage him too, but I told him I only had room for one client and that was my little blond singer. He asked me how I made a living, and I said, "Well, every week of the contest she wins a dress. After the show we sell the dress and we split the money."

He was not impressed. Nevertheless, he tried to convince me to sign him. I knew of course he had no future. The writer's name was

Aaron Spelling. If I had stayed with Aaron instead of the blonde, by now I would have seventy shows on the air and own a twelve-acre lot in Beverly Hills with a three-acre house on it. This might have been the first of many bad decisions I have made along the way.

To try to make ends meet, I worked as a tree trimmer, a bricklayer, a cement finisher, a carpenter, and a truck driver. All that led up to me getting a new suit, which in turn led to how the newly suited George Schlatter ended up in show business.

I BECOME AN AGENT

Stay with me on this one. I feel a veering coming on.

It was 1948. I had read a story in the paper about MCA, the gigantic theatrical agency then known as the Music Corporation of America. It sounded interesting, so I applied for a job, groveling my way into a very low-paying gig in the mailroom, word on the street being that everyone who was anyone had spent some time in the MCA mailroom.

I was wearing a gray gabardine suit with a dignified tie, oxblood shoes, and argyle socks. I may have been the only one there not wearing a black mohair suit and black shoes, and stood out like a Republican at the NAACP convention, like a hooker at a convent, like Kanye at a B'nai B'rith meeting. And that, everyone, is the rule of three.

I had been summoned to meet my new boss in the big office at the end of the hall. His name was Larry Barnett. He was big, bald, and bombastic, with a body temperature of a glacier. His personality could prevent global warming. I went into his office and stood there, waiting for Mr. Barnett to get off the phone, when a shockwave of energy went through the building. Frank Sinatra had arrived unannounced. He strode into Barnett's office followed by everyone in the MCA Band and Act Department. I shouldn't have been there, but there was no place to hide, so I just stood right where I was with my mouth open.

Mr. Sinatra said to Mr. Barnett, "Give me the papers."

Mr. Barnett gave Mr. Sinatra the papers.

Mr. Sinatra then asked, "Has the fat man read this?"

He was referring to his lawyer, Mickey Rudin, aka "the fat man." Barnett nodded yes.

"Okay, it's the same deal as before, right?"

When Barnett meekly nodded yes, Sinatra signed three copies of what I was soon to learn was the MCA management contract.

But this contract was different from every other MCA management contract. The big, BIG difference was that on Sinatra's contract, MCA did not collect any commission. Zero—zip—nada—nothing. At this point you may be thinking, *So how did it make any money?*

A little history. MCA had been founded during the big band era representing big bands, orchestras, and singers. They also represented actors, but the actors were under contract to the studios. The big money was in hotels, ballrooms, and nightclubs and in the very beginning of network radio, "coast to coast." The reason MCA was not charging Frank any commissions was because MCA made a lot of money just representing Frank Sinatra. If a hotel wanted to book Frank for a night or a week or get a radio pickup from the hotel, they had to give MCA exclusive representation of their facility. In some places that might be called "extortion"—we called it "negotiation."

Anyway, I was just standing there trying extremely hard not to be noticed when Sinatra signed the contract, looked around the room, and handed the contract to me. The humidity in my boxer shorts soared. (I will give you a second to try to wipe that image out of your mind.) Frank said to me, "Here. You. Handle this."

He turned away, stopped, and looked back at me, smiling. "I have ties older than you," he said. And then he was gone.

That was my first meeting with the Man, the Legend, the Chairman, the Leader of the Rat Pack, Ole Blue Eyes, Cheech, the Crooner, Francis Albert, Mr. Sinatra, and Frank. Over the years, I knew him by all those names, but what is important is that I not only knew the names, but I got to know the man, and as you'll learn in this book, that man played some pretty important leading and supporting roles in my life.

And because of Frank acknowledging my existence, MCA saw my amazing potential and suddenly loved my new suit—so they had me wear the suit while I wrapped window cards in the MCA warehouse on Pico Boulevard. The window cards were used to promote one-nighters for some of the acts MCA represented then, bands led by Jimmy Dorsey, Tommy Dorsey, Spike Jones, Count Basie, Harry James, Xavier Cugat, Freddy Martin, and Merv Griffin, who got his start playing piano for Freddy Martin. While this was going on, the head of publicity of MCA got picked up on a morals rap. He was married to a member of the King family, who were the 1948 version of the Osmonds, but even more clean-cut. After he got busted, I convinced MCA I could wrap cards and do his job for the same amount of money, about $25 a week. But the key: I convinced them to give me a company car I could drive.

Eventually I organized things so I could do that job just in the morning, so I talked to one of the agents and told him I wanted to be an agent in the afternoon. My theory was since I was college age, I could call all the fraternities in town, relate to them as a fellow eighteen-year-old, and find out if they were having a dance. If they had enough money, I sold them one of the MCA bands. If they didn't have enough money, I would put together a nonunion band and book it myself. After all, no one could live on $25 a week, and the penny-flattening business had dried up.

Everything went great until MCA discovered my augmented income ploy. They should have fired me, but instead they gave me some accounts where I would stay out all night selling piano players to little saloons. This didn't seem to be a good idea either, but as long as I was out anyway, I started booking strippers in clubs. This was a lot more fun, and soon I was turning in a lot of commissions.

One day Taft Schreiber, president of MCA, came into the elegant lobby of MCA and saw it was full of strippers. Some of these women didn't look too good at 9:00 at night, but they really looked funky at 9:00 in the morning. This resulted in a serious scolding but also a promotion where they gave me a couple of legitimate clubs to book.

Billy Eckstine had put up the money for one of those clubs. At that time a Black man could not have a liquor license on the Sunset Strip, so it was arranged that a man from Atlantic City who used to run a gambling joint became the front man. It was called the Crescendo, and it became my first "class" account. The owner was Harry Steinman, a character right out of *Guys and Dolls*, and he liked me, so I was invited to the opening night. I escorted my adorable blond singer, and Harry put us at his table for the show. Harry was married to Fran Warren, who was a great singer and a somewhat bawdy lady. Fran was not terribly comfortable sitting next to this beautiful little blond soprano, so at one point in the evening Fran looked at her and said to her rather loudly, "You look like you'd be a bed full of fun."

Without skipping a beat, my little angel face batted her beautiful blue eyes at Fran and flashed her a great smile. In a ringing bel canto voice, she remarked, "You look like you'd suck cocks, but I wasn't going to mention it."

All the various "greeters" in the club immediately reached for these nondescript lumps under their coats while everyone waited in silence to see what Harry's reaction would be after this insult to his wife. Finally, after what seemed to me to be a six-month wait, with everyone staring at Monti, then at Fran, and then at me, Harry Steinman started to laugh and said, "You're right. She does . . . and . . . she does it very well. Thank you." That broke the ice, and I realized that I might survive.

Later on the little blonde married a famous opera singer, which was kind of too bad because she should and could have been a famous opera singer herself. And, by the way, Fran was right, she was a bed full of fun. You just would not believe those high notes.

Yes, There Was Once a Man Named Doodles Weaver

Before I worked with first-name-only legends like Sammy, Frank, and Judy, I worked with a man by the name of Doodles Weaver. He was one of the first clients I had at MCA, only because no one else would touch him.

Doodles was one of the main performers in Spike Jones and His City Slickers. It was Doodles's idea to have a sign painted underneath the tour bus saying YOU HAVE JUST BEEN RUN OVER BY THE SPIKE JONES ORCHESTRA.

Doodles was also the black sheep of the family. His brother was Sylvester "Pat" Weaver, generally accepted as one of the true visionaries of the television industry and the man who ultimately OK'd hiring me at NBC. He was an elegant, awesome man who exuded class and dignity. Doodles was also the uncle of Sigourney Weaver. But I digress.

Doodles did a little nightclub act, but while it was funny, he was just not terribly reliable. I booked him into Billy Gray's Band Box on Fairfax Avenue once. This was where Joel Grey's father, Mickey Katz, played in a show called *My Fairfax Lady*, which was a Yiddish parody of *My Fair Lady*. Doodles played there one night when Mickey was off and called me to complain the dressing room was too cold. By the time I got over there, he had built a small fire on the floor in the middle of the room. This led to a cancellation of that contract.

I finally agreed to help Doodles get a booking up north in Elko, Nevada. The owner of the club was definitely a boom-boom guy, but it was the only job I could find for Doodles, mainly because the fire-in-the-dressing-room story hadn't reached Elko. I eventually convinced the owner, who looked like a combination of the ugliest characters in *Goodfellas* and *The Sopranos*, that Doodles was reliable and that he would be there for rehearsal at 4:00 in the afternoon. The owner (I think his name was something like Jimmy the Cheese, Fat Tony, or Luca Brasi) called me at 4:01, wondering where Doodles was. I told him Doodles was already there and no doubt looking for him. I got another call at five o'clock, no Doodles. Six o'clock, no Doodles. Seven o'clock, no Doodles. At eight o'clock, this mean and ugly boom-boom owner was now ready to see that there would be no George Schlatter. The final call came at 9:00, when he informed me that Doodles Weaver had opened in the club across the street. Evidently what happened was Doodles drove into Elko, saw a sign saying TONIGHT—DOODLES WEAVER FROM SPIKE JONES ORCHESTRA, and below the sign was a nightclub. Doodles went in and asked the owner if he could rehearse. The owner thought this was funny and said sure. Doodles rehearsed and, in fact, did one hell of a show in the wrong club at nine o'clock on a Saturday night. The owner of the club where Doodles was supposed to appear informed me if I ever came to Elko, I would not leave, and my new address would be somewhere in Lake Mead (which means thanks to the drought I would be reappearing about now).

I Invented the Las Vegas Lounge Act

In early 1949, I began working in Las Vegas for law school dropout and speakeasy owner Herman Hover (what a great combination), who had bought Ciro's in West Hollywood and made it the go-to nightclub on the Sunset Strip by booking the biggest names, everyone from Sinatra to Lili St. Cyr. (If you don't know Lili, she was a legendary stripper and is mentioned by name in the *Pal Joey* song "Zip.") Herman cut a deal in Vegas where he and I would select the acts, negotiate for talent, and produce the shows at the Last Frontier Hotel and the Silver Slipper.

A key element of these shows were the chorus girls and showgirls. So there I am, a young man, working with a line of twelve girls at Ciro's, eighteen girls at the Last Frontier, and eight girls at the Silver Slipper. I'm surprised that I am alive today. The hotels had a policy where those girls were required to sit in the lounge after their show until 2:00 A.M. They didn't have to do anything. They also didn't have to do anybody, but they were the best possible kind of window dressing.

The shows in the main room were the big draw, but after midnight, there was not much going on in the lounge except gambling. At the time the government had this stupid 20 percent entertainment tax. If anybody sang or danced, the IRS got 20 percent. You could play records. You could play music. But the minute you *saw* an "entertainer" in the lounge, that kicked on the tax on all food and beverage and perhaps even on gambling. So to avoid the tax, we would all sit with the showgirls in the Gay 90's Bar at the Last Frontier at 1:00 A.M., listening to a piano player. Boring.

Which led to my genius idea. By the way, you will come to realize at least half of my genius ideas turned into disasters. But a few worked out. Here was my idea: I realized that by turning the piano the other way, the gamblers couldn't see the piano player. Because the tax law said you could hear performers but not watch them, I thought the 20 percent entertainment tax wouldn't apply. I finally convinced Jake Kozloff, the owner, to hang drapes up around the Gay 90's Bar so that the gamblers could hear an act but not see it, so we wouldn't get hit with the tax because the gamblers weren't actually "watching" entertainment. Jake reluctantly agreed, and I hired the Mary Kaye Trio to play in the lounge. And that made Las Vegas history, as they became the first performing lounge act.

For a week before the Mary Kaye Trio opened, we let it be known up and down the Strip that every chorus girl in the desert was welcome "free of charge" to visit the Gay 90's Bar and have laughs with the Mary Kaye Trio. The trio went onstage at 1:00 A.M. As you can guess, this was a rather attractive enticement to male gamblers. Music, gambling, and a hundred showgirls. By the third night, you could not move in the Gay 90's Bar, nor could you find space at any one of the gaming tables. It was an overnight smash. I was a hero, but only temporarily.

The third night Jake Kozloff came over to me and said, "Tell the band not to sing." I pointed out to Jake it was a trio, not a band,

and he gave me that same look he did when I told him the Marquis Chimps had an ironclad contract. That story comes later. I was bewildered by his demand, because three nights earlier, you could have shot deer in the casino (which was one of the few things not being shot in Vegas at the time), and now the place was packed and the Last Frontier gambling tables were stacked three deep. So when Jake told me not to have them sing, naturally I asked why. He said, "They are bothering the gamblers." I explained that three nights earlier he didn't have any gamblers. Once again Jake, who had two looks, mean and meaner, gave me that stone-cold, scary stare, and I said, "Oh . . . now I understand."

I went over to the trio and explained that they had to just play and not sing. Of course they were surprised, because singing and doing comedy were what they did for a living. They didn't know how to "just play." They stopped singing and telling jokes. Within an hour the place was empty, and Jake wondered what happened.

I explained to him that the gamblers were there because the girls were there, and the girls were there because the May Kay Trio was there. I said, "Jake we just have to let these people perform."

Then Jake came up with his own great idea. His idea was to tell the trio they could sing one song every fifteen minutes. And then I topped his idea with another of my ideas, which means I had a record two ideas in a month. I explained to the trio that they could do a medley, and if Jake didn't hear applause in between songs, he wouldn't know that it wasn't just one long song.

For two nights, they did medleys. The gamblers came back, but Jake was still confused. He would listen to the Mary Kay Trio sing three or four songs in a medley and complain to me "those are the longest damn songs I ever heard." By the way, if you haven't figured it out by now, if Jake had gone to school with the Marquis Chimps, during tests he would have cheated off the chimps.

In any case, the Last Frontier did not get hit with a 20 percent tax. I did not get hit at all, and Vegas became a late-night mecca for "lounge acts" like Louis Prima and Keely Smith, Don Rickles, and Shecky Greene. So that's how I invented the lounge act.

I DID LAUNDRY AT CIRO'S: LAUNDERING MICKEY COHEN'S MONEY

A confession. I checked the statute of limitations and I'm in the clear. I was friends with legendary mobster Mickey Cohen.

When Mickey came into Ciro's for dinner, he'd ask for a stack of napkins. And by ask, I mean he would make it clear that he wanted a never-ending supply of napkins. And that's because Mickey would take a bite of food, wipe his mouth off, and put the napkin down. Every time was a different napkin. He was obsessively clean, and nobody ever questioned any of his habits, because that could have been fatal. He didn't really answer questions. One day I asked him what time it was, and he pleaded the Fifth.

The FBI tried everything to nail Mickey, and eventually they did. In fact at one point, the FBI had their own garbage truck go to his apartment to pick up his trash. They actually sent a whole truck and two guys. They'd stop in the alley, pick up Mickey Cohen's trash, leave, and then go analyze everything he had discarded. They knew everything about Mickey. They knew what he ate, what he wore, and details of his every habit. Except they didn't know where he got his money. Until now. I'm ninety-three—what are they gonna do, give me life in prison? At this point eighteen months could be a life sentence. So here it is, the confession: he got some of it from me.

Every ten days or so, I would get a delivery from Mickey Cohen's Haberdashery, and I would discreetly "pay" the delivery boy $1,000 in cash in exchange for the contents of the box. The delivery boy would leave, and I would open the box—it was full of tissue paper. There was never anything of any value in the boxes, but the deliveries arrived regularly, and I would buy empty boxes. Hundreds of them. That's where Mickey got some of the money. Was it a payoff?

Was it money being laundered through Ciro's? Long before Bill Clinton, I had a "don't ask, don't tell" policy, which continues today.

I do want to take a moment to dispel the rumor that I worked as a bouncer. I think the word "bouncer" is such an ugly word. Although before I got my position at Ciro's, I was a "greeter" in a small saloon at Slauson Avenue and Crenshaw Boulevard. I prefer to refer to that particular job title as "executive in charge of emergency departures."

Don't Do Me Any Favors

As you have figured, I did not end up in Lake Mead. But I did have friends who probably knew of people who knew people who knew guys who, if not ending up in Lake Mead, ended up living in gated communities for eight to twelve years until paroled.

But let me make it clear, my friend Sidney Korshak, for all the people he knew who knew people who knew guys, was never accused, charged, indicted, or even alleged to have done anything other than function as an attorney and an adviser to these people who knew people etc. Sidney was the ultimate fixer, the lawyer for the Teamsters Union, and despite what they left out in *The Offer*, he was the guy who got Al Pacino released from *The Gang That Couldn't Shoot Straight* and cast in *The Godfather*.

I met Sidney and his wife, Bernice, when I was producing *The Dinah Shore Chevy Show*. I think Sidney put up with me only because he really liked my wife, Jolene, a lot, and because I was the only one of his acquaintances who actually teased him and got away with it. Occasionally, I would get a call from Sidney, in which he would explain that he would like to "go for a walk." I don't know whether Sidney ever met with anyone else in the office, but I know we never met in the office but would occasionally go for a walk. This meant a stroll through the center of Beverly Hills, quietly discussing whatever Sidney had on his mind. It was similar to the discussion that Billy Crystal had with Robert De Niro when they went for a walk in

Analyze This. This meant that no one could have a tape recorder or write down notes. It was just a walk.

Another idiosyncrasy of Sidney's was when he would arrive at a party. He would look at his watch and say, "Wow, can you believe it, it's seven thirty already." He then would look at Bernice, who was a party-loving thrill seeker, and say, "Can we go home now?"

Bernice would explain that they had just arrived and she would like to stay for a few more moments. With each passing hour Sidney's request to depart became a bit more intense, and I don't remember ever having spent a lot of time with Sidney after ten thirty.

In later years it was wonderful to see this once powerful man, who controlled vast union and business operations all over the United States, become a warm, gentle, loving, kind, sweet grandpa. Although I am not too sure about any of the above, other than the loving grandpa part.

I once told Sidney that I had heard that the last guy who had seen Jimmy Hoffa alive was Jacques Cousteau. Sidney just stared at me. I never told any more Hoffa jokes.

Because I worked a lot in Las Vegas, I knew a lot of guys who worked for one of the leading hotels. Periodically, they would come to Los Angeles with their black mohair suits, white-on-white shirts, white-on-white ties, shiny shoes, and short-cropped hair. They would arrive at the office of a hotel patron who had neglected, overlooked, or ignored his debt to the hotel for longer than they thought he should. These debt collectors would walk into the debtor's office without an appointment and announce that they were there to see him. These "visits" were not to collect small amounts of money from small people, but usually an important amount of money from an important patron. Invariably the receptionist, upon discovering that there was no appointment, announced that her boss was not expecting to see them and there was no way they could see the boss at the present time. My friends would then announce that they would only be there for a minute, but that it was not only important but imperative that they see the individual. No amount of receptionist protest ever seemed to postpone this meeting, and they invariably met with 100 percent success in having a very brief meeting with the individual. They would explain that this indebtedness had gone on longer than was acceptable, and they then asked if it was going to be taken care of that day. The individual usually harrumphed a bit and explained that there were some budget problems, but that some funds were due to come in at any moment. My friends would then explain once again that they were not there to negotiate—they were there to leave with the money. Occasionally it required one more explanation of the reason for their visit and an increased emphasis on the words "going to be paid THAT DAY!"

Once it was explained in that manner, they always left with the money in their hands for the full amount. Think of them as IRS agents without the briefcases.

The El Rancho Vegas had different means of collecting from their debtors. It usually entailed a bill arriving in the mail, followed by a second bill arriving in the mail, which was followed in rapid succession by a past due bill, a final bill, and a final notice, and after all of these had arrived, the next day the postman delivered a picture of the debtor's house. The thought that someone had stopped by in a car, in front of his house, perhaps even at a time when his wife or children were leaving, was very effective in collecting any and all past due encumbrances.

I do remember one time when I was asked to do a favor for a friend in the hierarchy of the Las Vegas Mob. "Ask" may be too gentle a term, but I immediately understood that it would be a really good idea for me to complete the task, which of course I did—despite the fact that the only thing as frightening as having these people angry with you was to have them grateful to you.

A few weeks after I did the favor, I had a visitor who explained how grateful my friends were and asked me what it was that I needed. I needed nothing and told him so. I was then asked what it was that I would like. I said, "Nothing. I did what I did because I was a friend and just wanted to help."

There was a long pause, and then my visitor said, "Surely there must be something that you would like or need. We really want to express our appreciation."

I took a long sigh and explained that I needed nothing, I wanted nothing, and I was just glad to have been of help.

The next pause had just a slight hint of exasperation, and my visitor said, "I understand. But who don't you like?"

You cannot believe the kind of chill that can go through you when you understand the impact of such a question. It became even more disturbing when he pointed two fingers at me, smiled, shook my hand, and, before leaving, again pointed two fingers at me. I later found out that this simple hand gesture meant that I had "two hits coming." I never collected on either one of the hits owed me, although there were a few network executives (hereafter known as "suits") whose notes and pain-in-the-ass interference tempted me more than slightly.

Now to be clear, I was not and am not and will not ever be one of these guys. But I knew enough about them when I was in Vegas and working at Ciro's to know I needed someone to keep me on the straight and narrow. Which brings us to Jolene—but first, Mae West.

GO WEST, YOUNG MAN

Herman Hover asked me (no, he *told* me) to book an appearance at Ciro's featuring Mae West This was a tall order. Everyone knew Mae was financially sound and did not need or likely want such a job.

After some difficulty, I was finally able to set up a meeting with Miss West at the Ravenswood, the apartment building she owned in Hancock Park. I waited in a room that was covered entirely with beige: beige drapes, beige carpet, beige fabrics. Light was streaming through a window. Mae suddenly appeared standing on a raised area with the light behind her. I was amazed at how tiny she was. She was in full Mae West bloom, wearing the wig, the makeup, the eyelashes, the dress, and the platform shoes that made her five inches taller.

We sat down, and I explained to her why I thought that an appearance would be an event of historical importance. Mae was reluctant. I explained to her how vital it was to my career that she appear at Ciro's with her act, which featured musclemen and included Mickey Hargitay, who later married Jayne Mansfield. It was not a great act, but it was Mae West. The chorus of beef hunks usually showed up in white tie and tails, with a half dozen wearing what was an early version of Speedos. After a lot of talk, Mae finally agreed that she would do the show, but only if I agreed to appear as one of the chorus of musclemen. I had no choice but to accept Miss West's offer and appear with her on opening night. (I performed as part of her act only that one night. That was enough—for her and for me and for the audience.)

As we closed the deal and I got up to leave her apartment, she said, "Don't get too enthusiastic, young man, and whatever you do, don't fall for me. Let me tell you this . . ." she added, "if you could catch it, you'll never be able to ride it."

Luckily, I didn't. And that's a pretty good life lesson for any people younger than me in show business, which is everybody: don't screw the talent. Literally or figuratively. That's the agent's job.

IF I'M THE BEAST, IT'S TIME TO MEET BEAUTY

At Ciro's I worked with and became good friends with top performers like Peggy Lee, Kay Starr, Mae West, Diahann Carroll, Sophie Tucker, Maurice Chevalier, Pearl Bailey, Xavier Cugat, Katherine Dunham, Lenny Bruce, Tony Martin, Sammy Davis Jr., Nat King Cole, the Mills Brothers, Lena Horne, Harry Belafonte, Buddy Hackett, Alan King, and many, many more. These friends were also contacts, some of whom would eventually help me get started in television. But none counted as the most important person I met at Ciro's. And no, I'm not talking about Sinatra for two reasons: first, I met him earlier than I met the North Star in my life, and second, he was not nearly as good-looking.

Jolene Brand came to an audition to work in the line. Now although Jolene was great looking, she was not the very best dancer. She was good, but I was looking for a lead dancer. So I hired another woman, but the next day Jolene showed up for work and explained to me that the owner had hired her. I was not happy, as my decision had been reversed, my authority undermined, and I looked like a schmuck in front of this beautiful dancer. Somehow, this awkward beginning has led to sixty-six years of marriage.

Jolene was on her way to a great career. She had gone to acting school with Jack Nicholson, and back in those days she posed for record album covers, toured as Miss Rheingold, worked as a top model on *Queen for a Day*, guest starred on *Gunsmoke*, and was under contract to Disney for the Zorro series as Zorro's girlfriend. She put that on the back burner to run my life, our investments, and everything else. My gain was television's loss.

Jolene was also on *The Ernie Kovacs Show*. Through her work with Ernie, we became very friendly with Ernie and his wife, Edie Adams. At one of their parties, which included all the greats and near greats, someone asked Audrey Wilder, wife of Billy Wilder, to sing. She had been a vocalist in the band days and was still exciting to listen to. Billy had heard it all before and was ready to leave, so he went out to get the car while Audrey did her one song. Of course one song led to another. A while later Billy came back and in his heavy accent said, "Aud-zee, engine iss rrrrrunning und you are still zinging."

With that, they left.

One of Jolene's sketches on Ernie's show involved her sitting in a bathtub full of suds while strange and exotic props such as a periscope and individuals and even pets came up through the bottom of the tub. So how does this connect with me? Because Ernie did terrible things to Jolene, including throwing buckets of water on her and countless sight gags, which inspired many of the sight gags on *Laugh-In* and all the "sock it to me" sequences with Judy Carne. Please note that I didn't steal the idea, it's an homage.

Actually "sock it to me" was Jolene's idea. Aretha Franklin had come out with a recording of "Respect." We were riding in the car, and Jolene said we ought to do a "sock it to me" segment ending in a pretty girl getting hit with a pie the way Ernie used to do to her. I didn't really like the idea too much until our five-year-old daughter, Maria, sitting in the back seat, started chanting, "Sock it to me, sock it to me, sock it to me." I dropped off the two girls, went to the studio, and immediately put "sock it to me" into the pilot of *Laugh-In*.

So my point, and I have one, is that not only did I marry the greatest woman in the world, but she became the creative source of some of the most memorable moments on *Laugh-In*.

HOW I BOUGHT A HOUSE FOR SAMMY DAVIS JR.

No, it wasn't a gift. Let me explain. Sammy Davis Jr. wanted to buy a house in Hollywood, but at that point back in the 1960s, no one would sell to a Black person. And it sure didn't help that Sammy was Jewish. Throw in the fact he had one eye and was half Puerto Rican, and there was no chance he was going to be able to buy a house in that neighborhood.. This was not just pre-Zillow; this was pre–Civil Rights Act. To top it off, Sammy was always in trouble with unsavory people. Everyone wanted to spend time with Sammy, but he was "high-maintenance": drugs, booze, broads, cars, cons, hoods, celebrities, porn stars, and politicians (the difference is there are some things porn stars won't do for money). Sammy and I had fun with all of the above, often at the same time. But I digress . . . back to the house.

I knew Sammy from Ciro's, the legendary nightclub where I worked in a variety of roles, most of them legal. Sammy had found a house up north of the Sunset Strip that he loved that once belonged to Judy Garland. Sammy and I worked out a deal where I would buy the house in my name and subsequently transfer it to Sammy. I must admit I was a little nervous, because I had a very small bank account, and this was a very big house. But it was great for me to drive up in a borrowed car, because mine was not that impressive, and fill out escrow papers for a house that I never dreamed I would be invited into, let alone purchase.

Sammy never forgot what I did for him, so any time I ever needed him, he was there for me, including when *Laugh-In* was just starting and we hadn't gotten any ratings yet.

I needed some star power and Sammy was a star with a capital S. When Sammy came by to talk about what he would do on the show, we started reminiscing about Pigmeat Markham, an old-time burlesque comic who was famous for his routine "Here Come da Judge." Sam and I spent a couple of hours doing "Here Come da Judge" crossovers. Later we went onstage and taped them with Sammy wearing a white wig and long robe. That night when people were leaving the studio saying, "Here come da judge," we knew we had a big hit segment, and, indeed, that was when *Laugh-In* took off and became a huge hit.

The day after that episode of *Laugh-In* aired, nine members of the Supreme Court were entering their courtroom when someone uttered the phrase "Here come da judge," and the entire courtroom burst into hysterical laughter. That was back when people actually liked the Supreme Court.

ME, RONALD REAGAN, AND THE CHIMPS

1954. That year I was booking shows at the Last Frontier Hotel in Las Vegas, and legendary Grammy producer Pierre Cossette was booking acts for MCA in Las Vegas. One of Pierre's light bulb moments was to have then B-level movie actor Ronald Reagan do a nightclub act in Vegas. MCA head Lew Wasserman wasn't sure.

Ronald Reagan wasn't sure. But Pierre Cossette was sure, so he convinced Ronald and casino owner Jake Kozloff to let Ronald open in the Last Frontier, which worried me a lot.

Pierre put Ronnie together with a great act of five guys called the Continentals. Pierre immediately told Ronald that I would produce his act and that he could get him a huge price, so we were set to open in the Last Frontier on February 15, 1954.

As we began to rehearse, I couldn't stop thinking about Ronald Reagan working with a chimp in *Bedtime for Bonzo*. If you never saw that movie . . . don't. Combined, that movie and I have no Academy Awards. But Bonzo gave me my own light bulb moment. What if in Reagan's opening act, I used not one ape but five. And luckily, one of the best acts at that time was the Marquis Chimps, and I discovered that they might be available.

The five chimps were so well trained that they were almost human. And they had a hell of a manager and agent. Their contract stipulated that the chimpanzees would do no more and no less than twenty-five minutes per show, two shows a night. Twenty-five minutes exact, and it was *not* negotiable because the act ran exactly twenty-five minutes. Their manager, who was from Australia (but wait, there are no chimps in Australia, go figure), would go into great detail explaining to anyone who booked them why it was so critical to time the act for exactly twenty-five minutes. The way it worked, the chimpanzees would practice during the day, take a nap, go to the bathroom, get dressed, come out onstage, do their twenty-five minutes, come offstage, get undressed, go to the bathroom, have a snack, play, go to the bathroom again, get dressed, come onstage, and do the second performance, which was twenty-five minutes. No more, no less. Twenty-five minutes.

But there was a problem. No show in Vegas was allowed to run over one hour and twenty minutes. This was so the hotel could get the people out of the dining room and back into the casino to gamble. At rehearsal, Ronald Reagan's act ran over an hour, meaning that there was only fifteen minutes left for the other act, which were my chimps who had a signed contract guaranteeing them a twenty-five-minute appearance. Not only that, their contract said there could be no changes: no cuts, deletions, re-routing, alteration, revisions, or any changes in the performance. I should have a contract as detailed as that.

Ronald Reagan rehearsed first as the monkeys were still in their dressing room (the nicer dressing room), and following the rehearsal of Reagan's act, Jake Kozloff came up to me and said, "This show is going to run too long. Cut some time out of the fucking monkeys"—although he didn't say it that nicely.

I nicely explained to Jake that the contract he had signed specifically prohibited any cuts, deletions, re-routing, alteration, revisions, or any changes in the performance. I also explained they were technically chimps and not monkeys. Now understand I was saying this to a gorilla. As I was telling this to Mr. Kozloff, he looked at me in a way that only a Vegas hotel owner can look at you, which says, *I do not want to discuss this—just do it.* He then inquired as to the status of my hearing by saying, "Do you hear good?"

I said, "Of course, Mr. Kozloff."

He said, "Do you understand good?"

I said, "Yes, Mr. Kozloff."

He said, "Cut the fucking monkeys to twelve minutes so I can get those fucking people back to the gambling tables."

I went backstage to Gene Detroy, the chimps' manager, and explained that we had to cut the act to twelve minutes. He took that about as well as Jake Kozloff did when I said the chimps' act couldn't be cut. He said, "Are you crazy? I can't do twelve minutes. Our contract says twenty-five minutes. You know twenty-five minutes. We've always done twenty-five minutes. That's why it's in our contract."

I said, "Well, contract or no, we have to cut the act to twelve minutes."

Gene said, "Let me explain it to you once more, mate. These are not people. They're bleedin' flippin' chimps. They're not actors. They're not singers. They're chimps. The routine is they play all day, they take a nap, seven o'clock they have a snack and go to the bathroom. At seven thirty I get them dressed. We warm up. Seven forty-five we go backstage. We hear the music, and at eight o'clock on the button we walk onstage. We do twenty-five minutes—not twenty-six minutes, not twenty-four minutes—we do twenty-five bleedin' minutes. We take a bow. We come off. Take the chimps out to the truck. Take off their clothes. Put them back in the cage. Feed them their dinner. They play for a while. They go to the bathroom, and at eleven thirty I repeat the whole bloody thing again. Play. Bathroom. Get them dressed. Take them out. Backstage. Twelve o'clock music. Onstage. They do their act. Take a bow. Back out to the truck. Not twenty-six minutes. Not twenty-four minutes. Twenty- five minutes."

I said, "You have chimps, but the owner of the hotel is King Kong and he said twelve minutes."

Gene began his explanation again, an automatic monologue he had been giving for years any time anyone wanted to try to cut his act. So I went back for one more chat with Jake Kozloff. This time he didn't even utter a sound. When I walked into his office, he motioned his head and thumb toward the door, indicating that it would be a real good idea for me to leave. This was a disaster—Jake Kozloff wouldn't budge and the chimps wouldn't budge. Then I came up with the most brilliant idea of my life . . . up to that point in my career. A foolproof idea. I went backstage to the manager and said, "Gene, you are absolutely right, the contract says twenty-five minutes and the chimps can only do twenty-five minutes. I understand and I agree that was our deal. However, the contract does not say where you are going to do the twenty-five minutes."

He said, "It's twenty-five minutes. Don't ask me to do less."

I said, "No, Gene, you're gonna do the twenty-five minutes—only we're gonna do the first thirteen minutes in the hallway . . . and then we'll go onstage and do the last twelve minutes onstage."

He said, "'Ello, mate? I can't do the act in a bleedin' 'allway." Did I mention Gene was Australian, although the chimps were from Kenya?

I said, "The contract doesn't say that you have to be onstage. It only says twenty-five minutes, so tonight we do the first thirteen minutes in the hallway, and then we go onstage for the last twelve minutes of the act."

Well, you can imagine the level of intensity and volume that this discussion reached. Nevertheless, at thirteen minutes to eight, there was Gene, in the hallway, doing the act with the chimps performing in front of a brick wall.

Now, I don't know what your definition of "bizarre" is, but this event clearly defines what "bizarre" means to me. The chimps were somewhat disoriented inasmuch as they had never performed to a wall before, so the act didn't have quite the precision that it usually had, but right exactly at eight o'clock the music started. We opened the door, and Gene Detroy with his five chimps walked out onstage and did the last twelve minutes of their act. The chimps were disoriented, but the audience loved it and didn't know that wasn't the way the act was supposed to look.

When they came offstage, Gene was pissed, the chimps wanted snacks, and I was ecstatic. I told Gene everybody enjoyed it. He said, "Enjoy this," pointing to a body part that he thought deserved my attention, and he walked off with his furry family of chimpanzees. He took off their clothes. Put them in their cages. The chimps had a little dinner. Played. Went to the bathroom. Rested and got ready. Gene came backstage and explained to me that he just couldn't do it again for the second show. I said, "Gene, there is no other way." And, at thirteen minutes till midnight, we began the act in the hallway, performing to the wall. Again, it was bizarre, but by now the chimps were a little bit used to it, and promptly at midnight the orchestra played and Gene and the chimps went onstage and did the last twelve minutes of the act. The audience loved it. They went off, and Ronald Reagan came on with the Continentals with a George Schlatter–produced act of songs, dances, and snappy patter. Success!!!!!

The second night we repeated the process; the third night was even smoother, and by the fourth night the chimps were totally acclimated, Ronald Reagan was comfortable, and even Jake Kozloff was as happy as a casino owner can be. Which means on a 1 to 10 scale, with 10 being the happiest, he was level 3.

On the fifth night at exactly five minutes to eight, an enormous guard came backstage and explained to me that Mr. Reagan had some friends coming who were going to arrive late, and they would like to hold up the show for fifteen minutes. I raced backstage to explain this to Gene Detroy, who was in the middle of his hallway performance. I told him we had to hold the show. While the chimps were performing their bizarre brick wall routine, Gene explained to me, yet once more, "These are not actors, these are not singers or dancers or people. These are chimps, and it would be impossible for them to now stop the show and resume it fifteen minutes later. We do the show top to bottom, twenty-five minutes, no cuts, no changes, no alterations, and we normally don't work in front of a fucking wall." They went on to complete their thirteen-minute hallway performance. It was now 7:59:45.

The guard explained to me once again we would start the show at 8:15, instead of 8:00. But the chimps, who had adjusted to the hallway performance leading into their performance onstage, now were ready to go onstage. So I did the only thing I could. I locked the stage door, so they could not get onstage until Ronald Reagan's friends had arrived.

Pandemonium. The chimps tried to get onstage, and when that didn't work, they tried to complete the act backstage as they had been doing for the first four nights of their performance.

At approximately ten after eight, the guard came backstage and said they were ready for the chimps.

I opened the door so that the chimpanzees could go onstage. The chimps ran on to huge applause. The problem was it was now 8:12, and there were five crazed chimps who had completed their twenty-five-minute act backstage and it was playtime. They started roaming around loose in the main dining room of the Last Frontier Hotel. They were swinging from the chandeliers, running around, riding the bicycle that was supposed to be used in the show, but now they were riding it on the floor. They were totally disoriented. The conductor of the orchestra wore a shaving lotion called Aramis that had an odor of sandalwood, which had enormous appeal to the largest one of the chimps. The conductor had been doing flirtatious bits with the chimp the first four nights, but now the chimp was loose and was ready to pursue this liaison with him. The rest of the chimps sat down in the audience. The biggest chimp actually went out into the house, sat down at a table, downed a fifth of Jack Daniel's, and smoked a cigar, while the other chimps visited other tables, eating some of the food and doing bits with the customers. They were in the lights. They were in the rafters. On the curtains. On the conductor. They were everywhere. The audience was hysterical. One of the chimps did indeed follow his previous routine of getting undressed and relieved himself in the corner of the bandstand, the aroma of which wafted through the entire Last Frontier Hotel and mingled with the overpowering smell of Aramis and a chimp in heat. Finally, Gene Detroy was able to regroup four of his chimps. The orchestra played Ronald Reagan's walk-on music (it wasn't yet "Hail to the Chief") as Gene pulled his final chimp off the orchestra leader, while the announcer said, "And now, ladies and gentlemen, here is the star of the show. Ronald Reagan."

Some men might have quit show business. Not me. I went backstage to calm Gene Detroy as he was trying to calm the chimps, who were trying to get back onstage because they had just had a great time, and the big one seriously wanted to consummate his relationship with the orchestra conductor. The same enormous guard came through the stage door and said, "Schlatter, Mr. Kozloff would like to see you. Now."

I had a lot of bad news that night, but this news was perhaps the most disturbing of all. I knew I had to go and see Jake Kozloff and I knew this was not going to be a happy experience. With great fear and trepidation, I walked through the curtains and up to the back of the house, where Mr. Kozloff was seated in a booth with his head on his hands down on the table. At that point, I was not concerned about Ronald Reagan or the chimps or Gene: I was mostly concerned with the fact that I had not written out a will.

With Ronald Reagan going through his snappy opening patter song, Jake Kozloff lifted his head off the table, and I could see that he had been crying. His eyes were red, there were tears streaming down his cheeks, and I was prepared to get ventilated, or at best to lose some fingers. Suddenly, I realized that Jake was not crying tears of grief; he had been laughing so hard that he was totally out of control. He told me that was the funniest thing he had ever seen in his life and to forget the rest of the act—just have the chimps do that for the next show.

There was no way to explain to Mr. Kozloff that the chimps did not normally do that. The chimps were not trained to do that, and the idea of going back to Gene Detroy now, who had just barely succeeded in getting the chimps back into their cages, was indeed a daunting task. Since Mr. Kozloff's request was a rather firm one, I tried to discuss it with Gene Detroy. He never even responded to me, as he was too busy cleaning chimp shit off their costumes and trying to reestablish some sort of authority. He just screamed, "Go away. I never want to see you again."

I went back out front and told Mr. Kozloff that we had indeed discussed his suggestion, but that it might be very difficult to pull off because of the dangerous aspect of chimps roaming around. I finally convinced him that we were better off with the chimps doing the full twenty-five minutes and asking Ronald Reagan to cut a few minutes out of his act and not allowing the chimps to go out into the audience, as the insurance rates would soar should one of the chimps decide to become amorously involved with the wife of one of the high rollers. Jake immediately saw the value in this and for the rest of the engagement allowed the act to stay as it was.

Postscript: I heard the orchestra conductor got divorced soon after that. I hope it wasn't because of the chimp.

JOLENE AND THE 1960 ELECTION

My parents were hardline, right-wing conservatives. In fact, they raised so much money for the Republican Party that when Richard Nixon came to Orange County for a political rally, they sat on the dais directly behind the Nixons. How I ended up as someone who leaned so far left he was in danger of falling down, I'll never know.

My dad was the type that when he would listen to fights on the radio when Joe Louis was champion, he would root for Tony Galento, Tami Mauriello, and Billy Conn, basically an endless group of white hopefuls, who all wound up with their toes pointing toward the ceiling of the arena. Coincidence he rooted for them over Joe? Let's just say he saw things somewhat differently from how I did.

And if my dad's pet peeve was Black heavyweight champions, my mother's pet peeve was Catholicism. She was an avowed Christian Scientist. When I had polio, she did not believe there was anything wrong with me and convinced me of the fact. And I made a full recovery. Despite that, Drs. Salk and Sabin did not concur. If Mom had been around in 2020, she would have told Dr. Fauci we need *P-R-A-Y-E-R*, not *M-R-N-A* vaccines.

At another time my whole upper body was burned in a gasoline explosion. My mom said the burns and scars would eventually disappear, and they did. Mom's belief in Christian Science got her through some extremely trying times and got me through them too.

Imagine me bringing Jolene home. She was raised in a rather strict Catholic household and attended Catholic school, she was of Spanish heritage, her family adored John F. Kennedy and Franklin Delano Roosevelt, and she had worked as a dancer in Las Vegas. And I'm bringing her to meet my right-wing anti-Catholic parents.

So when I took her to Sunday dinner at my folks' house, I had warned her in advance what she was about to enter into. I knew my brothers would absolutely love Jolene because she was beautiful, talented, and funny. But I did have to warn her about my father, who would sometimes forget to take his hand off the sofa cushion before one of his sons' girlfriends would sit down. He'd also some-how, when he put his arm around these young women, manage to have a hand either go too far around the side or dangle precariously over the shoulder. We have a name for that kind of man nowadays: studio executive.

My version of *Guess Who's Coming to Dinner* took place during the heated Nixon vs. Kennedy election, so we definitely had two different political philosophies represented at that dinner. After some very surface chitchat, we all sat down at the table to eat, and as I expected, the conversation got around to politics, Catholicism, and John F. Kennedy jokes. One of the jokes I remember that my mother particularly enjoyed was about the fact that America was gathering up all the used bowling balls to make a rosary for Our Lady of the Harbor. This was interspersed with numerous pope jokes, nun jokes, and other references to the Kennedys. At some point, Jolene smiled sweetly, looked at my parents, and said, "It's just like the Republicans say about Richard Nixon . . . no one can lick our Dick."

I am sure fans of comedy have seen what they call a "spit take." That was what my father did. My brothers fell off their chairs. My mother asked, "What does that mean? What does that mean?"

Turns out "dick licking" had not yet become the subject of con-versation at the Schlatter dinner table. Probably not in the Schlatter parents' bedroom either. At that very moment, my brothers loved Jolene. My father held off a glimmer of hope that he could leave his hand on the sofa cushion a little bit longer, and my mother eventually came around and thought, for a Catholic girl, Jolene was not half bad.

Leaving Las Vegas

It's simple. I left Las Vegas for love. I wanted to marry Jolene, and although she was not totally against the idea, she explained that if we were going to get married, I would have to promise to get out of Ciro's, the Last Frontier, and the Silver Slipper and away from all my shady friends in Las Vegas, the Copa, and the other nightspots that I frequented. She was right, because at that point, a number of my contacts in that area had suggested to me that I had a very promising career and could make a good living as a "representative" of that element. If you're not sure what I mean, watch *The Godfather* and the scenes with Moe Greene.

Jolene realized this and said there was no way she wanted to be part of this. I immediately said, "No problem." A lot of people owed me favors, and it would be a matter of a few phone calls and I could be anything I wanted to be. She suggested I try television. I said, "That would be terrific. I'll become a television director and producer. In the meantime, let's get married."

And we did.

We were married at Herman Hover's home. The only other couple who had been married there were Jeanne and Dean Martin. We had a huge reception at Ciro's with all the young Hollywood personalities, and we were joined by Hedda Hopper, Louella Parsons, Mitzi Gaynor, Pearl Bailey, Sidney Skolsky, and a lot of members of the Hollywood press. Jolene's mom and stepdad were there, as were my own parents. My mom was so thrilled to meet Louella Parsons that she spilled champagne on her.

Sixty-six years later, they're the two best decisions I ever made: marrying Jolene and going into television. Which brings me to . . .

Part 2

I Want to Be a Producer

W ith apologies to Mel Brooks . . .

I want to be a producer
With a hit show on TV.
I want to be a producer
Drinks with Sinatra at Patsy's.

Just like Leo Bloom, I wanted to be a producer. And I was lucky. I got in on the ground floor of the early days of variety television. No experience necessary—we were making it up as we went along. During that time, I learned the business, got to work with the legends, and, perhaps most important, determined that when a producer tells a little lie, it's not perjury when it is done for the greater good of the show. I also became somewhat adept at coming up with "lightning bolt" ideas on the spot, many of which did not quite work out the way I anticipated.

So how does one become a producer? Where does one get the skills? I guess there are colleges for it. Or to quote the great philosopher Yogi Berra, "You can observe a lot just by watching."

For me, it can be traced back to my days hitting the local carnivals. When I was in high school and during my first year at Missouri Valley College, I used to attend little carnivals that would come through the small surrounding towns. Every carnival had a wrestler and a boxer. My brother and I would show up and enter the ring, because we got $25 if we could go three minutes with the wrestler or three one-minute rounds with the boxer. It was a way to make a few dollars, except by the third night, when they realized who we were, they tended to get a little grumpy. That's when the carny folk would teach us a lesson by bringing in a couple of ringers. I learned every dirty trick in three rounds with a salty old sailor: thumbs to the eye, elbows and forearms to the face, head butts, toe stomps. That was the first lesson in preparing for a life as a producer.

What I loved most about hanging out at carnivals was the side-show and its pitchmen. They were exciting. The midway was at the center of the carnival, but the real action was at the sideshow, with characters so totally corrupt they fascinated me.

Ed McMahon worked as a pitchman on the Atlantic City board-walk, and that is where he perfected the sincerity and honesty that convinced me and countless others to buy a garage full of magazines by telling us that we "may already be a winner." Pure carny come-on. Ed's boardwalk pitch went something like this:

> Come see the flora and fauna of the fabric of America. If you want your Ferris wheel, if you want your merry-go-round for the kiddies, if you want to throw balls at bottles, you stay in the center aisle. However, if you want to walk in wood chips and saw dust to see life in the raw, if you get my drift, wander over here to the sideshow where the big show is happening. During the stay of the carnival right here in your wonderful metropolis, city, town, or community, the management has authorized me to make available to you, at an unbelievably reasonable price, this ceridium-tipped fountain pen that will last your lifetime. If it ever dries out, chips, bends, or breaks, you return it with your twenty dollars to cover handling and postage, and we will replace it free of any charge to you.

Twenty dollars for postage? But I saw people fall for it. Then again, people voted for Trump—the ultimate carny pitchman.

Another favorite pitch I remember was this:

> Walk right up, ladies and gentlemen, take two steps forward, your body will naturally follow. For ten cents, one thin dime, one-tenth of a dollar, come into the big tent and see JoJo the Dogface Boy, who, from the neck up, is as normal as you or me, but from the neck down this boy has the skin of an alligator . . . and this poor boy must remain submerged in a tank of ice water for twenty-three hours a day . . . Hold on a minute . . . By golly . . . Folks, you are in luck today— JoJo is about to come out of the water for one of his few brief visits to dry land. If we get into the tent right away, you'll be able to see JoJo. Please take notice that JoJo has the skin of a cold-blooded man-eating reptile, which entraps this poor young man in a tomb of ice water. Walk right up . . . but don't get too close . . . It's the big show and it is only ten cents, so for two dimes you can bring a friend.

Diana the Gen-u-ine Hermaphrodite also comes to mind: "Diana is half man, half woman, a person possessing both sexes combined in the one body, as she will prove by daringly revealing those two sexes at the same time."

So where does this lead to? No influence gets forgotten—no part of the buffalo goes unused. My point, and I have one, is that I probably ended up as a television producer because of my love of carnies. In both businesses you get to provide entertainment while telling small lies to people who want to hear them.

I'm going to take you through some of the shows I produced or directed, starting with *The Dinah Shore Chevy Show* and all the way up through my work on a number of presidential inaugurals. Because two series in particular deserve a special place on their own (*Laugh-In* and *Real People*), they will follow separately.

GEORGE BURNS, THE SCHLATTER WHISPERER

One of the first shows I did with Dinah Shore had Nat King Cole, Ginger Rogers, Al Hirt, and George Burns as guest stars. I was the new kid on the show, the entire staff having been hired before I got there, which was not great, because many of them had been there for years, and I was coming in as the hotshot "savior." Talk about being nervous. The humidity in my Speedos soared right up and off the chart.

George Burns understood that I was under a lot of pressure, and he helped me. There was a slight age difference between us, as I was in my twenties and George was 253 years old. But he was the Yoda to my young Luke, and he taught me the ways of the show business force. He would stand next to me during rehearsals, camera blockings, dress rehearsals, and even during the show. Quietly, he would make suggestions under his breath. I took every suggestion he made and relayed it to the cast as if it were my own. By the end of that first show, the staff, the crew, the cast, NBC, and Dinah all thought I was a genius. George knew better and never said a word.

Years later, I was producing a show with George called *The Meaning of Life*. We showed up at his house to tape the introductions and got everything on cue cards. George's manager, Irving Fein, who was also 253 years old and who also was Jack Benny's manager, came to me and said, "George, we have a problem. Mr. Burns cannot read those cue cards."

I asked, "Why? Are they too big . . . too small?"

Irving said, "You don't understand. George Burns cannot read any cue cards."

This of course was a stunning bit of information, considering the years George Burns had spent in radio and television. We trashed the cue cards and had George make up the introductions, which were better than what we had originally written.

Another time I worked with George was on a Goldie Hawn special. We lowered George on a cloud while we played the theme from *Star Wars*. He and Goldie talked, and then they did a soft-shoe. George, who loved to rehearse and who never changed the steps of his dance routine for the last forty years of his life, had carefully laid out a piece for him and Goldie to do, which was a routine he and Gracie Allen did together. George wanted to know if Goldie would like to rehearse it, and I explained that Goldie would love to rehearse and spend time with him, but I didn't think they should over-rehearse it. That way we could keep the spontaneity and keep it from getting stale. In fact, I preferred no rehearsal at all because that was when Goldie was at her absolute best, but we did give them minimal rehearsal time and then got ready to tape it.

We rolled tape. Goldie and George did the song and performed the soft-shoe routine. They then went into their talk portion and then back to the song again. George had done this routine maybe a thousand times. When George heard Goldie reading the same words that he had heard before from Gracie, the look of surprise and adoration on his face was something to behold. In his eyes, Goldie was Gracie reborn.

Because I would never say "cut" when Goldie was performing, we went through the entire piece, with an audience, to the very end. I then kept the tape going, which included Goldie saying, "Oh, George, I'm so sorry, could we do it again?"

We did three more takes, eventually getting the song, the dance, and the patter to where she thought it was perfect. I told Goldie that I loved it, and then she asked George if he was happy. Everybody was happy. Goldie then turned to me and said, "You're going to use the first take, aren't you?"

I said, "Absolutely, Goldie. This is no time to reinvent show business."

THE DAY I THREATENED MILTON BERLE

The Dinah Shore Chevy Show was the first time I worked with Milton Berle. I scheduled a meeting with Milton, and moments after he walked into my office to discuss the show, he dropped his pants while explaining to me he had terrible hemorrhoids and desperately needed a suppository.

I don't care who you are, where you are, what you've done, or what you may have seen—if you saw Milton Berle drop his pants, you'd be in awe of a schvantz that was rivaled only by Niagara Falls or the Pyramids of Giza. Dan Rowan was a six-foot-one prick and Milton's was bigger.

I recovered from this anaconda sighting, and for the next five days, every time I'd talk to Berle, he would look at me, ask me how old I was, and give me a slap on the cheek. The night before we did the live show, he did it again, and I very quietly and respectfully explained to Milton that although I was still in my twenties and didn't know as much about show business as he did, I was reasonably certain that if he slapped me on the cheek one more time, I would knock him on his ass so hard that he wouldn't be able to take a crap for a week. From that moment on there was no more slapping . . . but to this day when I think of Berle, all I can say is "What a prick."

Judy Garland and the Fake "Energy" Pills

In late 1962, CBS announced that Judy Garland was going to do a series. I was a big fan of Judy, and I was 100 percent convinced I was the perfect person to produce this. This was my thought process: I had been very successful producing the Dinah Shore series, and it had been training to produce a show for Judy. Kind of like saying playing checkers with your best friend is good preparation for chess with Garry Kasparov. It's not. But with the arrogance and confidence of youth, I drove Mike Dann, head of programming at CBS, and Judy's agents/managers, David Begelman and Freddie Fields, crazy with calls, letters, meetings, and recommendations. I even chased Mike Dann down Beverly Boulevard one day, yelling at him, "Don't screw this up." Despite that, they hired me, even though I had never met Judy. Although I had seen *The Wizard of Oz*. Twice. (Fun fact: Jay Leno told me he got bored the first time he watched it and shut it off after ten minutes, so he never knew it turned to color.)

I didn't know how to audition for Judy Garland, so I thought I shouldn't meet her until it was 100 percent set that I was going to do the show. Eventually the deal was cut, and I headed to New York to finally meet her. I was in the office at 9:00 one night. Mike Dann called me and said, "Could you come down for a minute." Like with most of these guys, it was not a request but an order. I had been there since about 8:00 in the morning, so I really looked raggedy. Even on my best day I tend to look raggedy. Nevertheless, I went down to Mike's office, and there was Judy. As you can imagine it was a bit of a jolt, because it wasn't at all the way I wanted to meet her. I wasn't wearing what I wanted to wear, I hadn't shaved, I had prepared nothing to say. She just kind of looked at me for what seemed like an hour. You could just see her mind analyzing every single follicle, and finally she said, "So here we are."

I will never know why, but I said, "I don't care what you may have heard about me, there is no truth to the rumor that I'm difficult."

She laughed and said, "You really are not difficult."

I said, "No, I don't care what you've heard," which caused her to suggest we leave and go have a drink.

When Mike Dann came back in, having arranged this summit meeting, he was stunned that two minutes after I'd met Judy, we were headed for 21, where, as I recall, we spent quite a bit of time that first night. I was introduced to a new beverage, Blue Nun Liebfraumilch with an innocent little novitiate on the label. We had a lot of it.

In our first meeting we really didn't discuss much about what the show would be, we just kind of got to know each other. At least she got to know the one me and I got to know a little bit about one of the many Judys. Judy was very intense. When you'd sit and talk to Judy, you felt that you were the only person in the world who she was interested in hearing from or about.

Judy also had a habit of touching you when you talked to her; she needed some kind of physical contact. This concerned CBS for some reason. They didn't like the fact that Judy always grabbed at people. She was a clinger—she'd touch your arm, she'd touch your knee, whatever. Fine. Considering how many times networks tried to grab me by the balls, her touching my arm was no big deal. Plus over time I found out that if when you talked to Judy you reached over and touched her back, it relaxed her, and she became much calmer. If CBS had an HR department back then, they would have fired both of us for excessive touching. Anyway, back to the bar at 21.

We sat there a long time that night, and eventually we started talking about her show. I asked her, "Why are you doing a TV variety show?" She said because she needed the money and because she had done everything else. I told her that this kind of TV is a different experience. It's a lot of work and it's not at all like doing movies. This was like working without a net. She loved that.

I felt that we had to do it like a live event, because the most comfortable place for Judy was onstage at a concert. She said that was fine. No endless retakes as she had done so often in films. That night, as I became more aware of this woman and what she was, I realized that we could do a lot more comedy than we had previously planned. I don't think I have ever met anyone who liked to laugh as much as Judy. That had become a necessary element of her life, and certainly it became a necessary part of our relationship.

A lot of people were afraid of Judy; at that time, I didn't know why. I mean, after all, this tiny, tiny, little woman generated great love, great passion, great devotion, and loyalty. Over time I learned they were afraid of her because when she walked into a room there was a force field of energy; every encounter with Judy Garland was a test, it was like she was trying to find out something about you. That comes from having seen it all and done it all. She had a bullshit alarm with a hair trigger. One trick or phony comment and she could strike like a cobra or a python . . . and I don't mean Monty. So I knew the key to making this work was a lot of laughter, a lot of touching, complete honesty, and surrounding her with a very special team. So like Yul Brynner in *The Magnificent Seven*, I went about hiring the pros.

First was Mort Lindsey, who'd worked with Judy in New York. I figured he'd be great, as we needed a person who was classically oriented as well as theatrically knowledgeable.

I realized that Judy needed to take a unique and maybe a new approach to music, so I called Mel Tormé. His vocal arrangements had always been distinctive and exciting and challenging, even for Judy Garland. So I called him up and said, "Hello, Bunky [I had known Mel when we were at Ciro's]. I've got a really good gig for you, pal. I'm going to produce *The Judy Garland Show*."

He said, "Wonderful, I really want to sing with Judy." I then informed him that was only part of it, because I wanted him to write for Judy. Mel got really upset. He said, "I only write for myself."

I said, "Well, welcome to the new world, Bunky, you're gonna write for Judy Garland."

He said, "I don't think so."

I said, "Don't fool around with me, I'm late for an appointment, so let's just get this out of the way—you're going to write for Judy, and that's pretty much it. Please don't make me hurt you."

So it was arranged that Mel would do a couple of guest shots on the show, but he would do her vocal routines, which he did brilliantly.

We then brought in Jack Elliott, who started out on the show as a rehearsal pianist, but he was a brilliant, brilliant musician, and he eventually became quite a well-known conductor in his own right. We also had Johnny Bradford, the Waldman brothers, and some other pro variety writers. All of them were multitalented—they could write jokes as well as music. And having writers like that was a key for Judy, not only to make her laugh, but because they would be interesting to her. And that was crucial, because she could get bored in a nanosecond, and when she got bored, that door closed, and boy, you better be on the inside when it did.

Judy wanted Edith Head to do the costumes, so I went to meet with Edith Head, whose name I repeat because it always makes me laugh. Her first question was to ask me when we were going to tape the show. I said, "Well, we're going to do this in the fall."

She said, "Oh, that's impossible, we need time. We're going to need costume tests."

I said, "No, I don't think you understand. We're going to just make her clothes and that's what she's going to wear."

Edith actually aged in front of my eyes and said that was impossible, and she demanded to have camera tests first.

I said, "Miss Head, say hello to the world of television."

This did not go over well, so goodbye, Miss Head.

Judy was not easy for anyone to dress because she was so tiny. We wanted her to look taller and have a shape. There was a young assistant costume designer named Bob Mackie who worked with a very well-known and successful designer, Ray Aghayan. I felt he was really bright, so I set up a meeting with Ray, Bob, and Judy. Judy really liked them a lot, and Bob started to design some clothes for her right there in the meeting. The minute she put his designs on Judy was comfortable, and Bob was a star. That one show launched Bob Mackie on his brilliant and ongoing career.

My next challenge with Judy was to come up with a way to keep her loose. Since she loved to laugh, from day one I made sure outrageous things happened onstage and in the office, a lot like I did with Frank Sinatra and the Sands casino ad (which I'll get to later). Judy would arrive in the office, and we always had planned some kind of funny event. We wore costumes, we put up banners, funny delivery boys arrived, we had animal acts in the hall. Somebody would walk in and make a silly sound or even deliver an obscene package, and she would laugh—and when she laughed, it broke that coil, it broke that spring that would build up and become the tension that everybody was afraid of.

Now there was another challenge before we launched the show. CBS in its wisdom decided it didn't need to have a dressing room for Judy. Danny Kaye, who also had a show on at this time, had this luxurious penthouse to dress in, and yet CBS wanted Judy dressing in a closet somewhere. So I said, "Why don't we put a trailer on the side of CBS, on that walkway that goes around?" Now there were all kinds of building ordinances and city codes to deal with, but eventually we got a big house trailer, and we lifted it in with a crane. We put it right there at the end of that hallway and decorated it. Coming out of that trailer, you went down some steps, and there was her makeup room, candy-striped with a calliope cover over it. There were pictures from her past that were hung around. From that room, we painted a yellow brick road down the hallway. So when she came out of her makeup room, she went down this yellow brick right into the studio. The first day she saw that she was just blown away. She saw the trailer first, then she saw the makeup room and the yellow brick road. She was as happy as any performer I have ever seen. Another problem solved.

But the biggest challenge was the fact that Judy felt that she achieved her performance high through medication. We cut that out altogether. I got into her medicine cabinet, and I took those capsules, dumped them out, and put sugar in them. She got the same high from that sugar pill. Now they have a name for this . . . bipolar. Her, not me.

We got the first show all ready, rehearsed and ready to tape. She was happy with her trailer and the candy-striped makeup room and the sugar-filled "energy capsules." And I knew that when Judy came down that hall on this yellow brick road and hit that studio, the audience would go crazy the moment they saw her. And to make it even more of a "special," I decided we really had to make her premiere into a major show business event, because, well, this was not Snooky Lanson, this was Judy Garland. You'll learn more about Snooky later. So opening night we put together a very large celebrity/press party. That caused a problem with CBS. When the suits there heard that we planned a party, they went nuts. They made it clear they did not want a party at the first taping in case Judy didn't show up and people found out. I said, "If Judy Garland doesn't show up for her first taping, trust me, people will hear about it. The fact that we are depending on her and relying on her as a dependable performer will impress her." And it did. She showed up, we taped that first show in one hour, and it was just perfect. Everybody in the audience was ecstatic. CBS was so pleased they took credit for the party. They didn't pay for it, but what the hell.

To make sure Judy felt at home on her first show, our first guest star was Mickey Rooney. They had grown up together, and as children they were dependent upon each other. When they were young, they'd work on four or five films at the same time. They'd meet on set in the morning with no idea which film they were doing, nor did they have time to prepare for it. They would shoot a scene from movie one, and then the next day, scenes from movie four. They had to arrive at 5:00 in the morning ready to go, and that meant they had to go to bed early. To get them to go to bed early when they were so keyed up, the studio gave them milk, then later warm milk, and then started with the pills. They had a bigger wheel of pills at age sixteen than I do now, and I'm ninety-three. Thank you, Louis B. Mayer. I think MGM stood for Must Give Medication.

I wish we had had videotape facilities then, to tape that first meeting between Mickey and Judy, because that should have been a television special. They met, they hugged, they loved, they laughed, they even cried, they talked about what they went through as kids.

The approach I took to Judy was that she was a very special performer with many facets, so every performer we put with Judy showed another facet of her—which is what we tried to do by booking Mickey Rooney, Tony Bennett, Count Basie, Lena Horne, Nat King Cole, Dick Shawn, her daughter Liza, and a very young Barbra Streisand. Every one of those guest stars showed a different side of Judy. We decided each show would be a special event, and it was, like her show with Lena where Judy sang Lena, and Lena sang Judy—that is a classic show business moment.

Once CBS became pretty sure Judy was going to show up, they became more involved and had opinions and "notes." But they were consistent: not one note made any sense. Like when they said they wanted Judy to be the girl next door. There are only two people in the world who live next door to anybody like that, and it's the two people who lived on either side of Judy. The "girl next door" was not the girl CBS bought. I told them, "I didn't buy this show. I will deliver this show, I did not buy it. There is no way under the sun that Judy Garland is going to become the girl next door," and she never did. But it did cause some tension, because CBS did not want this electricity, this vibration, this aura of event, when she walked into the room and people would stand up and cheer. Seeing Judy was a religious experience for her passionate fans. CBS wanted it much more relaxed, much more laid-back. They wanted it more "homey," like what I had done with Dinah Shore. The suits wanted her to come out like Danny Kaye and just chat and have a warm kind of a thing.

Okay, that's what you asked for, here's my idea.

We brought out a big steamer trunk onstage, and in the steamer truck we put a lot of Judy's personal memorabilia. We then had Judy come out and stand at this trunk and just tell stories. It was not written, it was not prepared, and we would do two or three of these stories, which would lead into her closing story. One of my favorites was on the second show, when she stood up at this trunk and told the story about the day she was fired from *Annie Get Your Gun*. The executives at MGM were all terrified of her, so they sent a notice down to Judy that she had been fired. It was Friday afternoon of a holiday weekend, and everyone had gone. As Judy told it, "Here I was dressed as an Indian, with war paint, and I had been fired. So I stormed through the old Thalberg Building with a tomahawk, looking for any of the MGM executives that had fired me." Not exactly the girl-next-door story.

Shows like Dinah's were all finely honed and stitched, and every word had been prepared and rehearsed. Judy was not that girl. With Judy you hoped for the accident, because Judy's best moments, many times, were accidents. One of her best came about when CBS told us that they wanted Judy to go to New York to appear at the affiliate dinner at the Waldorf Astoria. This interrupted what we were doing, but it was absolutely necessary that she do it. She didn't want to do it. I said, "Judy, this is your new life. This is television. You're going to have to do some of these things." So she said all right.

Heading back east on the plane, she was really nervous. She kept repeating, "What am I going to say, what am I going to do? These are the affiliates, these are my bosses, and I know what they've heard."

I said, "Well, you're just going to walk out, and they're going to love you."

And then we came up with something to let her own the moment. While on the plane we wrote a parody of "Call Me Irresponsible." That night the Waldorf Astoria ballroom was full of executives and affiliate heads, all wondering whether Judy would show up. As she walked out onstage to a huge standing ovation, she got her heel caught in the tiniest hole and she couldn't get it out. So she took off her shoes and walked down to the apron barefoot, and the audience went crazy. When the music came down, she sang:

Call me irresponsible,
Call me unreliable,
Call me undependable too.
Have my foolish alibis bored you?
I won't take a powder, I can't afford to . . .

The ovation lasted five minutes.

The Time Judy Garland Tried to Kill Me

I knew that doing a television show was going to push Judy Garland's attention span into another level—a very, very tense, dangerous level. Which meant that at any time she could explode in rehearsal and become the Judy Garland everyone was afraid of. It happened early on when I was producing her variety show, when she started yelling about the lights and sound. I had to do something, so I started singing "Over the Rainbow." Of course, everyone in the place froze . . . and she froze . . . I froze. She looked at me and said, "What the hell are you doing?"

And I said, "I just thought that if you were going to produce, I would sing."

This did not have the effect I hoped for. She got really upset, and she stomped off the stage. She blasted up her little yellow brick road, stormed into her trailer, and slammed the door. And I thought maybe I'd gone a little too far. Maybe? Anyway, I ran right after her and I went in her trailer. I didn't know what to say, so I got up on her coffee table, and I held a match under the sprinkler. A logical thing to do. Who hasn't done that? And she said, "Now what are you doing?"

I said, "If you don't apologize to me, I'll drown you."

She screamed, "Apologize to you, you asshole? You embarrassed me in front of the crew. What do you mean you're going to sing 'Over the Rainbow'?" She was ranting.

I said, "Judy, it's going to take another thirty seconds for this sprinkler to go off, so you better apologize."

Since she didn't want her trailer destroyed, she said, "All right, all right, I'm sorry, I'm sorry. Asshole" (she loved that word).

Considering I had won, I said, "See that it doesn't happen again." Big mistake.

As I got down off the coffee table, she pulled a lamp out of the wall and chased me down the steps, through her candy-striped makeup room, and down her little yellow brick road, yelling, "I'll get you, I'll get you, you son of a bitch, I'll get you. Asshole!!!" And of course it struck me as funny: I'm being chased down the hall by America's little girl and sweetheart, and she is swinging a lamp to try to kill me. It struck her as funny too, and we both laughed. We fell down on her yellow brick road laughing. Then we went back into the studio. The whole experience maybe lasted under three minutes.

Now that we had recovered from me singing "Over the Rainbow," Judy figured she was going to test me again. She had another blowup and yelled, "Fuck you, George, I'm not going to do this," just to see what I would do. I was ready for her. We had prepared an audiotape of explosions and machine guns and crashing bells and sirens and screams. It was terrifying to listen to this. So, when she got mad and started ranting and raving, I had them play this tape really loud. Of course the tape scared everybody in the studio. Maybe I had forgotten to tell the crew. Judy fell down on the floor and started screaming, "My God, they're shooting at me."

When the tape ended, I said, "All right, cut the tape."

And she looked at me—she was really mad now—and said, "You scared me, YOU ASSHOLE!"

I said, "You scare me too . . . So . . . Judy. Don't fool with me . . . I have an army."

And then she laughed again. Break that coil—break that coil. Laugh—tremble—laugh.

But the all-time best way to get her to relax involved flatulence. She loved fart jokes. A good fart joke would absolutely cause her to lose it. One day she got mad at me onstage, and I played a long, loud selection of farts. The biggest and loudest farts anyone ever heard, and they were edited to play a melody. Forget about it. She almost couldn't sing that night. I mean she just tore her throat out, screaming and hollering and pounding on the stage. And I said, "Judy, please don't test me anymore. Do you know what I had to eat to make that recording? I am exhausted."

To the day she died, she had a copy of that tape, which she said was the most treasured memento of our relationship. Sometimes she would call the house at 3:00 A.M. and just play that tape.

DECORATING LIZA'S ROOM

On Judy Garland's third show we booked her daughter Liza Minnelli. But there was a problem. Not about song choice or wardrobe. The problem was Judy had told Liza that she'd redone her room at the house, but somehow, she had forgotten to mention it to any of us. Or to anyone. That is, until the moment Judy pulled me aside and said, "Oh my God, I told Liza that I'd redecorate her room and I didn't."

So Gary Smith, who was our set designer, and I went out to a store and bought wicker furniture and white curtains, wicker picture frames and a white shag rug. We went out to Judy's house, and we redid Liza's room from 10:00 in the morning until she arrived at 6:00 that night. And as Liza came in the front door, the movers were all going out the back. Liza now had a wonderful white wicker bedroom. And Judy carried it off when she saw her: "Oh, darling, I knew you would like it, we'd been working on it for months." Liza, if you are reading this, you're welcome.

When Liza came in to rehearse for her appearance on the show, there was electricity in the air. This was, I think, the first time that they had sung together on American television. For the set we made these huge blowups of Liza as a little girl, but I didn't show them to Judy beforehand, because Judy's initial natural reaction to a situation like this was pure gold, and if you could capture it, it was magic. When Judy walked out and saw these huge twelve-foot blowups of Liza as a baby, it put a quality in her voice that was a combination of pride, pain, love, and joy. She sang the song "Liza" like nobody had ever heard it before. Both of them were touched by it. They cried, the audience cried, I cried, even CBS cried. And suits never cry.

Judy was intensely proud of Liza, but when they sang together, they were fiercely competitive. Each sang louder than the other and hit notes higher than the other. There was none of Judy taking it easy because it was her little girl. Once you started singing with Judy, she took no prisoners. I don't care who it was, Judy would have upstaged the pope. It was interesting to watch the two of them, because although they were mother and child, given Judy's personality and Liza's maturity, it was hard to tell which was which. It was Liza the mother, then it was Liza the child. Liza put Judy on her lap, and Judy became the little girl and Liza bounced her mom on her knees. Two fragile stars, two immense talents.

FIRED, DISMISSED, PINK-SLIPPED

We had taped five Judy shows, and the sixth show was going to be Nat King Cole and Jack Carter. Before the taping, CBS kept hitting me again and again with the notes about her being the girl next door. I wanted to do what was best for Judy and the show, but at the same time I knew by doing so I was giving the middle flying fickle finger to the suits.

We had a big meeting at CBS where they made their position clear, and I made my position clear. The next day I was walking down the hall on the way to the rehearsal with Nat King Cole and Jack Carter, when Judy's managers, Freddie Fields and David Begelman, stopped me in the hall and said they needed to talk to me.

I said, "Not now, I'm late. I have to get to rehearsal."

And they said, "No, you don't, you've been fired."

I think there were a few reasons this happened—mainly, of course, because CBS wanted a Judy who didn't exist. I think I sealed my fate on the day we met with Hunt Stromberg Jr., an executive at CBS. It was Hunt, Judy, and me at lunch, and he started on this girl-next-door thing. He said, "Judes [and I went, *Uh-oh!*], we know what you have to do to fix the show."

Judy looked at him and looked at me and said, "Hunts, I wasn't aware that the show needed fixing."

And he said, "No, Judes, listen, babe, I don't have much time here. So let me explain to you what we want to do." He said, "You need a family."

She said, "I have a family."

He said, "Don't kid around, Judes, I'm serious. You need a family, you need Ken Murray, Bob Denver, Marion Lorne, and Cara Williams, a very pretty young girl. That will give you a family, and that will be what we want with this girl next door."

Silence from Judy. Eyes blazing. At which point I explained to Hunt that I didn't think the meeting had gone very well and I thought perhaps he should go out on Fairfax and play in the traffic for a while. I think at that moment he was already mentally writing my dismissal notice.

The suits said they didn't think I took their wishes seriously enough. Not true. I didn't take their wishes at all seriously. And I was mad. We had done five shows in six weeks, we were on budget, we were on time, and the work was sensational. And then I was dismissed, and I didn't know why, the industry didn't know why, Judy didn't know why, but then they changed the show and brought in Norman Jewison.

Norman, who was a movie genius, was not a variety TV guy. So when he walked in and looked at the shows we had done, he told CBS, "I don't know why I'm here. This is exactly what I would do with her, this is exactly what I think Judy Garland should be doing." This disappointed CBS, because they were paying him all this money and his first act was to tell them that they had made a mistake.

When Judy and I met the afternoon after I had been fired, I said, "Hey, Judy, look, here's the thing. You're gonna have to go with them, that's the system."

And she said, "No, I'm gonna walk out with you, I'm not gonna be there, I don't want to do the show."

I said, "You really have to do the show. We've built up a new Judy Garland, and you can't just destroy that by walking out."

She did stay and I left. The only thing I told CBS was that when they brought me back, they were going to have to pay me more money than they paid Norman Jewison. Which leads me to . . .

LET'S TALK ABOUT THE ELEPHANT (NOT) IN THE ROOM

When I was fired from *The Judy Garland Show*, I was making $7,500 a show, and CBS replaced me with Norman Jewison, whom they were paying $15,000 a show. About a year later CBS decided at the last minute that they needed me to do a new series starring Steve Lawrence, based loosely upon a special I had done with Steve at NBC called *NBC Follies*. The deal was made for the right amount of money, and I was happy . . . for a moment.

The Steve Lawrence Show had to be done in New York because Steve lived there, and CBS wanted some New York programming after Jackie Gleason moved his show to Florida. In addition, CBS needed something to put in the Ed Sullivan Theater. What I didn't realize was that our show would eventually be the last black-and-white show on CBS and that it was going to be scheduled on an evening against Andy Williams and Dean Martin on NBC, with both shows in color. So let me sum things up: I had Steve Lawrence, who was less well-known than the competition; I had less money to work with and less time to prepare; the show was in black and white instead of color; and it was filmed in New York, where guest stars were not as easy to book as they were in Hollywood. But I was young and stupid, so I thought I could do anything. I told CBS, "What the hell, we can pull it off if we are just a bit outrageous." By the way, now I am old and still stupid enough to think I can do anything.

Even though I had all those challenges, what I had in my favor was the fact that Steve could really sing and was charming and very funny, so people liked him and wanted to work with him. But I still could not get a guest for the first show.

Out of desperation I called Lucille Ball. I knew Lucy and Desi from back when I was managing Ciro's. She and Desi came in all the time, and we all became friends. Later, when I was producing *The Dinah Shore Chevy Show*, she convinced me to hire her son's teen band, Dino, Desi, and Billy, to appear on the show. So she owed me a favor.

I told her that Steve and his wife, Eydie Gormé, were big fans of hers, and it would really help them get started if she would make an appearance on the show. And to reel her in, I mentioned that we would like to take all the stunts that Lucy had ever done and put them into one videotape package to introduce her on the show. Okay, that interested her. She then wanted to know how I was going to follow that. And I said, "With you and Steve coming through Shubert Alley on a Saturday night singing 'Together' on a pink elephant, and then you arrive in the studio on the elephant wearing a top hat, tails, and silk net stockings" (Lucy would wear that, not the elephant). This appealed to Lucy because she loved schtick and she really loved to show her legs. I must admit at that point, I had no idea if there was a pink elephant in New York, or what trouble we would get into bringing it through Shubert Alley and into the studio, or how we would even shoot it, but Lucy committed to do the show, Shubert Alley, elephant, song, silk stockings, and all. So we went ahead with the plans.

I did eventually get a permit, upon the assurance that we wouldn't play the music too loud and that we would wait until the area had cleared out at 1:00 A.M. to shoot. But when we got there to tape their opening, it looked like it might start raining, which would ruin the sign we had with STEVE LOVES LUCY. And more important to Lucy, it would get her hair wet. As far as I know the elephant was fine no matter what time we shot. So I decided instead of going at 1:00 A.M., we would shoot the number at 11:00 P.M., just as the theaters were breaking. As you can imagine, this two-hour change of plans caused a commotion among New York's finest. Commotion, hell, it was a near riot. At 11:00 P.M., just as the crowds left the theaters, there was a pink elephant with Steve Lawrence and Lucille Ball on top and huge speakers blaring "Together" as they came through Shubert Alley. It was wonderful, and we got the number finished before midnight. Of course, at this point, the police were looking for the guy who had jumped the gun and who was responsible for all the commotion . . . and by the way, the elephant had diarrhea.

That was a really big problem. The elephant must have had a street vendor hot dog.

As the police stared at the mess, they wanted to take me to jail, but I wouldn't go without Lucy, and she wouldn't go without the elephant. While the cops were discussing this dilemma of whether they had a cell big enough for the elephant and me, I got in a side door at Sardi's and sat there until six in the morning, when it was safe to leave the area without spending some time in the slammer.

The picture and story of Steve, Lucy, and the elephant hit every paper around the country, and overnight *The Steve Lawrence Show* became a new kind of "happening," and it was much easier to book people like Bobby Darin, Tony Bennett, Anthony Newley, Diahann Carroll, and all the other guest stars whom we had been unable to convince to perform up until then.

ANOTHER REASON CBS HATES ME

In the '60s, CBS purchased three specials with Meredith Willson, who was famous for having written *The Music Man* and other Broadway musicals. Because Meredith was so identified with "Seventy-Six Trombones," the finale of our first show included hundreds of kids from every high school marching band we could find in Los Angeles, starting out with three kids walking up the driveway with a flag and ending with bands going off far into the distance, all playing "Seventy-Six Trombones." It was a hell of a finale.

Naturally, with television philosophy being "if some is good, too much is better," CBS decided we needed another big finale for the third show. I explained that you could not top "Seventy-Six Trombones" unless you wanted to go out and hire one thousand marines. As I said it, I realized that it was not a bad idea.

So we met with the Marine Corps, who explained that getting one thousand marines together in the middle of summer was not an easy assignment. This led me to suggest we fill in the gaps with the National Guard. This Marine colonel in charge looked at me like I was the enemy, and at that point, I guess I was. Nevertheless, it was agreed that on Saturday morning, at eight o'clock, eleven hundred marines would arrive at CBS from Camp Pendleton and do calisthenics in time with another march that Meredith Willson had written, this one for President Kennedy's fitness campaign. Meredith named this song "Chicken Fat," and the idea was to do exercises to get rid of chicken fat. Let's just say it didn't go to number one on the *Billboard* charts.

Because a number like this couldn't just happen by accident, we had sent a choreographer to Camp Pendleton to rehearse them. His name was Billy Foster, and he eventually became quite a well-known director and, as a matter of fact, shot the pilot of *Laugh-In*.

We had built a big scaffold on the parade grounds for Billy to stand on to give the marines instructions and teach them the calisthenics he had choreographed. Billy had a slight speech impediment and could not pronounce the letter *R* without it sounding like a *W*. Billy was straight, but when he said, "All wight, you mawines, wet's do it now," eleven hundred guys looked at him like he was from outer space.

Anyway, the "mawines ahwived" at CBS for the shoot and got ready to do their calisthenics, push-ups, and high-intensity exercises in 100-degree heat. Confession: Although we had figured out how to serve lunch to eleven hundred marines, I had not given much thought to the inadequacies of the CBS bathroom facilities needed to accommodate eleven hundred marines during a ten-minute bathroom break.

But marines are creative, and they devised on the spot a number of ways to solve their bathroom problems. When we got the bill, it turns out they did $50,000 in damage to the CBS facilities. And when CBS employees came to work on Monday, there was a strong aroma of human waste wafting throughout every corner of the office building. The entire structure had to be fumigated. Most of the trees, shrubs, and plants on and surrounding CBS property died within a few days.

It gets better. Part of the finale was to reveal the marines and bands everywhere while the entire front of CBS was a giant flag. No one, meaning me, contemplated the fact that if it was windy, the flag might blow up against the building and leave some very patriotic red, white, and blue stains. Between the damage to the air-conditioning, the aroma of the CBS executive offices, the dead flora, and the requirement that the front of the building be repainted, it was not my finest hour. Just another reason CBS hates me.

AL HIRT AND I KILLED A MAN

Although Judy Garland didn't end up killing me, I did kill a man. But it wasn't my fault. In the early 1960s, NBC wanted to do a show plugging Rockefeller Center, and they wanted to shoot the show from the RCA Building so the viewers could see the area surrounding the center. I was very young and very arrogant, which is redundant, and I was the only producer who thought this idea stood any chance of being pulled off. So I got the gig. That was their mistake, not mine. I staged songs, dances, and acts on the ice rink, on the roof, in the lobby, in the restaurants, in Studio 8H, in the makeup rooms, in the shops, and on the streets. We even had a conga line down Fiftieth Street chanting, "There was no other sweller than Rockefeller." We had performers all over, including a big finale celebrating Easter in which the full cast came walking up the promenade in front of the ice rink and the Prometheus statue.

The show starred our host, Robert Goulet, who was costarring with Julie Andrews in *Camelot* at the time. We also had world-famous ice skater Dick Button perform an Olympic ice ballet, the Radio City Music Hall Rockettes, plus other acts, singers, and dancers. Nancy Walker did a comedy number about the "fourth girl in the second row at the Radio City Music Hall." For that era, it was a star-studded lineup.

We were getting ready to tape the show, and Chrysler suddenly decided they needed one more act. Again, I had a problem: I didn't have any more physical locations to stage any more acts.

I was walking back to the Warwick hotel from NBC when I heard a rivet gun. I looked up and saw the new Sperry Rand Building, which at that point was just gray cement and orange steel. I thought that would be a great place for a number. So the next day I called Al Hirt in New Orleans. Al's nickname was Jumbo. He weighed 310 pounds and was six-foot-three with a big beard and a great smile, and he played a trumpet that would have made Herb Alpert want to sit in the sax section. I loved him for two reasons: his talent and the fact that he made me look like a jockey. I told him I had a great idea for a number, and Al agreed to come up from New Orleans with his six-piece Dixieland band and do the show.

When Al arrived, we did a prerecord of "South Rampart Street Parade," and then Al asked what studio we would be in. I said, "We're not really going to be in a studio, but meet me on the corner of Sixth and Fifty-Third. And by the way, dress warm."

At seven the next morning, we met in front of Radio City Music Hall and walked over one block to the building next to the Sperry Rand Building. We took an elevator up and went through an office, out a window, up a stepladder, across a rooftop, and up another stepladder, and we were at our "location." Al did not look thrilled, especially after he saw I had arranged Al's band on the lip of the eighth floor of the Sperry Rand Building, with cameras set up across the street on the roof of Radio City Music Hall. The idea was to hear a rivet gun, which turned into a snare drum as we panned down off the steel and glass of the Time and Life Building and revealed the incomplete building, a building that you could see all the way through since it was all orange girders and cement floor. There we would see Al Hirt and his band wearing striped jackets with straw hats playing "South Rampart Street Parade." It was a great idea.

Admittedly Al was a little nervous, because he had just had to go out windows and up ladders, which is not easy when you are three hundred pounds. He was also afraid of heights, and it was a little cooler (32 degrees) than I had hoped it would be. Maybe a little colder than I promised him it would be. Our director, Clark

Jones, was across the street with two film cameras and loud playback speakers. We were ready to get this opening shot, after which we would break and reset the cameras. Shooting in that area was like shooting in the Grand Canyon. We had only so many minutes of light until the sun would move behind the building. It was essential that we get this opening master shot.

We rehearsed it a couple of times. It was a Sunday morning. There were the St. Patrick's Cathedral church bells ringing at one end of the street and our prerecorded "South Rampart Street Parade" blasting away at the other. The shot really looked great, and we were ready to go for a take. We had just said, "Roll 'em," when we turned around and saw the night watchman and the foreman running up to see what was going on. It seems we had gotten permission, but not everyone had been made aware of what we were doing. The foreman was really pissed off and was menacingly carrying a two-by-four, as foremen back then liked to do. He and the watchman were both panting because they had run up eight flights of stairs and ladders; they were panting like Al Hirt climbing one flight of stairs. I explained what we were doing and showed them the permit. We were getting ready for another take when I turned around and saw that the night watchman was lying down right in our shot.

Al Hirt's manager, Jerry Purcell, had been a fireman and a para-medic. He announced that the man was having a heart attack. While we had someone run downstairs and call for an ambulance, Jerry Purcell proceeded to give the night watchman mouth-to-mouth resuscitation. Shortly it became quite evident that the night watch-man had gone on to his next gig. It seems the run up the eight flights was just too much for him.

The fire department arrived with sirens and bells screaming in competition with St. Patrick's Easter bells. The paramedics ran up the eight flights and looked like they too were going to have heart attacks. They proceeded to also try to revive the night watchman. Finally, they gave up and covered him with a pink blanket. Evidently with the fire department, pink meant dead and gray meant damaged.

I saw that pink blanket and where the night watchman was lying, and I said, "We would like to move him." This was not acceptable because the law was clear that he could not be moved until the coroner arrived to pronounce him dead. Same thing in *The Wizard of Oz*: they couldn't move the Wicked Witch of the East until the coroner of Munchkinland pronounced her "really dead." Which is different from *The Princess Bride*, where Miracle Max explained how you can be "mostly dead." But I digress.

Looking at the guy, you knew he was going no place on his own, and I was then told that the coroner was at the track that day. The police officer was really insistent that the body could not be moved. I then asked, "Could he at least be covered by a gray blanket?" because he was in the shot, and we had only a few minutes more of light left and the pink would show up on camera. This sounds cold, but I was under time pressure, because Al Hirt had to make a plane that afternoon and was not available after that. This was my last chance to get the shot or NBC would put a pink blanket over me. So they put a gray blanket over him so we could keep filming.

It gets worse. Al's piano player was scared of heights and was terrified to be out on the lip of this building. Al's mouth kept freezing to the trumpet because it was so cold. Ever see that scene in *A Christmas Story* where that kid's tongue freezes to the pole? That was Al. So, now, here's the scene: I have Clark Jones with two film cameras and loud playback speakers on the roof of Radio City Music Hall. I have a dead watchman covered with a pink blanket, which is covered by a gray blanket, lying in the shot behind Al Hirt. I have Al Hirt, in a straw hat and a striped blazer, with a frozen mouthpiece, and a panicky piano player, and church bells clanging away at one end of the street and "South Rampart Street Parade" blasting away at the other end of the street while I am losing light fast. But the good news: we were now ready to roll film again to get the opening shot.

Just as I was about to call "roll 'em," the family of the watchman arrived. They too had come up eight flights and were out of breath.

It looked like we might lose one or two of them. It seems the whole family had been together because it was the old guy's birthday. The policeman on guard asked me if I could stop the music, and I explained to him that Al was playing in sync to the prerecord and that I had to get the shot before we lost light. I then realized how futile it was explaining lip sync and sunlight to a police officer. He asked me if we could at least turn the music down a little, which we did. I'm surprised he didn't ask if Al could throw in "Taps."

Right before Al performed the opening music of "South Rampart Street Parade," he explained to me that he was from New Orleans, where they took dead people very seriously, and that this was just wrong. I tried to calm Al by explaining to him that the watchman had told me "South Rampart Street Parade" was his favorite number and that he would have wanted it that way. We finally did get the opening shot finished, and we broke for lunch.

When we came back from lunch, there was the corpse, the police officer, and the family still praying, with our cameras set up to finish the number. By then we had gotten a little bit used to working around the body being there, and we almost tripped over him a few times. As we were shooting the rest of the number, the vice president of Chrysler arrived wearing a homburg hat and a long black overcoat with a velvet collar. He went immediately to NBC executive Lester Gottlieb to see how it was going, and of course, he noticed the body. He asked, "What is that?" Lester told Mr. Chrysler that "that" was a body.

When the Chrysler suit wanted to know why we had a body in the shot, Lester tried to explain it to him as best he could but suggested that he not discuss it with me right away because it would only upset me. We finished the number.

After he was done playing, Al Hirt explained to me that our future negotiations would be somewhat different from this one. Al chugged down the stairs to catch his plane back to New Orleans. Lester Gottlieb ushered the man from Chrysler down the ladder, across the roof, and through the window while explaining to him that the body wasn't really in the shot, which of course was a lie. That's what people in show business do. When it comes to our shows, we would rather climb a tree and tell a lie than stand on the ground and tell the truth.

(Years later when I was producing a musical special with Nat King Cole, George Burns, Ginger Rogers, and Dinah Shore, one of the guest stars was Al Hirt. Al's contract came back with a rider attached to it explaining that if I was involved, Mr. Hirt must work indoors, on the floor, and that everybody else on the show would be alive and healthy throughout the taping. The contract went into great detail that if during Mr. Hirt's performance anyone had a heart attack, Al could immediately leave and go back to New Orleans. This contract had almost as many stipulations as the Marquis Chimps contract.)

Eventually we were faced with the representatives of Chrysler wanting to see the tape to be sure you could not see the night watchman. On a large screen you most certainly could see him. So as I rolled the tape for them, I stood in front of the picture pointing to another area while my dark blue suit made it almost impossible to see the dead watchman. When the show went on the air, of course, you couldn't actually or easily make it out unless you knew where to look. I knew where to look. It certainly was not my proudest moment. But the watchman would have wanted it that way.

The last time I saw Al was in New Orleans. It was about 3:00 A.M., and Al was playing his last set. I sent him a note onstage. A waiter took it up. The note said, "The night watchman is still alive." Al read the note in the middle of the set, put his trumpet down, and started screaming, "Schlatter, you son of a bitch."

CUE THE FUCKING BUNNY BALLOONS

On that same special where Al Hirt and I killed the night watchman, I got a brilliant idea that if we put detergent in the fountain at the RCA Building, it would fill up the area with bubbles, which would have made one hell of a look, to have the entire Rockefeller Center ice rink covered in bubbles with colored lights on them. We had two five-gallon drums of detergent ready to go, but by then we were constantly accompanied by security people from the RCA Building, who strongly resisted any attempt to make the statue of Prometheus in the fountain into a gigantic bubble machine, especially as it would have been disrespectful to a dead night watchman.

I did get permission to paint the ice red, which really had a great look to it for the finale, with the entire cast coming up those stairs and walking up the promenade as hundreds of these giant bunny balloons rose majestically from the red ice and up the front of the RCA Building. It was a one-take-only shot, and it had to be timed so that there was no wind and so that the cast hit their mark on the promenade, singing "In Your Easter Bonnet," with the balloons being released behind them. Obviously, this had to be very meticulously staged. We'd rehearsed it for two weeks, using different weights on the balloons, so that five hundred balloons would fill the area as the big moment arrived.

Clark Jones was in the control truck, and I was behind him, nervous as hell that we were going to miss one of the big shots in the show. We got started once, and as the cast approached the failsafe mark, it got windy, so we stopped. We tried again and again, and each time, the wind came up just as we were going to release the bunny balloons. The fifth time, the wind died down, and it was absolutely calm. The cast walked up singing "In Your Easter Bonnet," and it appeared to me that they were about to cross the line where they couldn't go back, so I calmly suggested to Clark over the headset to cue the bunny balloons. Nothing. Once again, I told Clark to cue the bunny balloons. Nothing. By then I was frantic. I yelled, "CUE the FUCKING BUNNY BALLOONS!" Of course, at that moment, Clark had hit the announce button to notify the crew, and me screaming "Cue the fucking bunny balloons!" rang throughout all of Rockefeller Center's Easter celebration. When I came out of the truck, all the employees in the RCA Building pointed at me.

I thought they were about to yell at me for saying "Cue the fucking bunny balloons," but instead, one said, "There's the nutcase who killed the night watchman."

We edited all night that night to get the show ready in time, and when we came out of the RCA Building at six o'clock in the morning, I went by the ice rink. It was still red because they had not figured out any way to get the ice up without staining the cement underneath it. The area was totally deserted except for one homeless guy, looking at the rink, finishing off the remains of a bottle of wine in a paper bag. I couldn't resist, so I went by him and said, "Man, you should have been here, it was really a hell of an accident." Then I went back to the Warwick hotel, where my wife said, "Don't tell me any more stories that involve people dying."

A WILD WINTERS NIGHT

It took me years to sell Jonathan Winters's special, called *A Wild Winters Night*. It took years because Jonathan was a tad crazy, and yet we pushed it through and were finally ready to shoot in late November 1963—and then President Kennedy was assassinated. Everything was put on hold. No one wanted to work, no one wanted to think, everyone was numb.

A week later, we arrived at the studio not having rehearsed *anything*. Nothing was working, and we were headed for a total disaster. Out of total desperation, I got the prop people to round up every prop and object in the CBS building and put them all on a long table in front of the backings of three of the set pieces. I then told Art Carney and Jonathan Winters to just play for about an hour. Each one would pick up a prop and improvise. They would do sight gags. They would become different characters and exchange lines. I ended up shooting the whole thing with no idea what we were doing or why.

My plan was to take this very funny material and edit the bits together in a series of jump cuts, an endless barrage of sight gags, jokes, takes, looks, and moves, and cut back and forth between

Jonathan and Art. It made no sense, and it didn't look like anything that had ever been on the air, but it was funny. And that counts.

When we previewed it for CBS, the execs laughed like crazy and then asked the natural question about how I was going to edit it together for the show. I said, "That's exactly how we're going to put it for the show." We had just sat in a screening where fifteen people laughed hysterically, so why couldn't we air it like that? Actually, the show was to air in two days, so they had no choice but to air the tape as is. As I left the meeting, CBS once more explained to me that I would never work for them again, but the show did go on the air, as is, with all the jump cuts. It was television without a net and even won a TV Guide Award as the Top Variety Show. Good training for what was to come in my career.

Jonathan Winters Shows My Wife His Rocks

One night my wife and I went to dinner at Jonathan Winters's house. After dinner he asked Jolene if she would like to see his rocks. Jolene looked at me with a *what the hell does that mean?* look. But with some trepidation she followed Jonathan into the next room, and there was a floor-to-ceiling bookcase that had nothing in it but rocks. And Jonathan went through the entire collection, showing them to Jolene and saying, "I got this one in Arizona. Oh, here's another one, this I got in Maine." He showed Jolene rocks that had nothing to distinguish one from the other. He went through the whole collection wondering how long Jolene was going to stay with him, and she stayed with him until he ran out of rocks. I love her for many things, but that night made me love her even more, because anyone else would have said, *What? Are you crazy?*

I'm the Reason Stages Are Raised Thirty-Six Inches

In 1964, I had been signed to do six Danny Thomas specials for Timex. Danny Thomas was one of the most brilliant nightclub performers

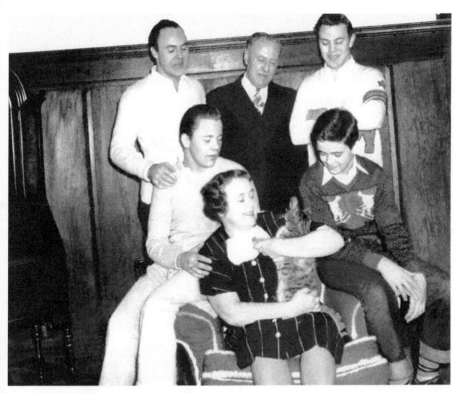

The four Schlatter boys with Mom & Dad

A very young George

A still young George

Ronald Reagan tries Vegas

Jonathan Winters and George

The famous Ciro's with Jolene Brand on the marque

Jolene and Ernie Kovacs

Jolene Schlatter begins her career as a model

George escorts Judy Garland to a rehearsal for her TV series

The scene of *The Steve Lawrence Show* featuring Schlatter, Lucille Ball, and Steve Lawrence who were all arrested in New York's Shubert Alley for causing public disturbance and leaving two tons of elephant memorabilia in the street.

Lucille Ball, Steve Lawrence & George — before they were arrested

The Joke Wall — what the audience saw

The Joke Wall — what they didn't see

John Wayne as a Bunny

Dan Rowan and Dick Martin

Laugh-In cast photo

Laugh-In cast photo for Nixon

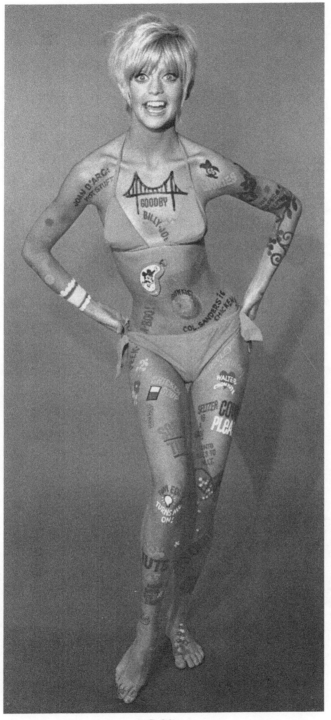

Goldie

Kirk Douglas

Jack Benny

Arte Johnson

Ringo Starr

Lily and George

in the world and the personal protégé and favorite of Abe Lastfogel, head of the William Morris Agency. He was Abe's favorite because he made Abe a lot of money. It's amazing! By some coincidence, every agent's favorite is the guy who can make him the most money. William Morris had built a huge empire with Danny Thomas and Sheldon Leonard, who also produced sitcoms including *The Danny Thomas Show, That Girl, The Andy Griffith Show,* and a lot of others. As a result, Danny was vastly wealthy. Not Bezos wealthy, but not bad. Then again, Bezos never made me laugh. Danny built a home in the Hollywood Hills that had its own chapel in it. When you sat in his dining room, which was circular with a gigantic circular table, at the top of the circle he had Lebanese warriors looking over a wall as if they were watching you. Danny also had a twelve-foot carving of *The Last Supper,* and to me, all the disciples looked like Danny. Even Jesus had a big nose. Apparently one of Jesus's miracles was not cosmetic surgery.

Everyone thought Danny was Jewish, but he actually was a devout Catholic, except for one trip I made with him to Las Vegas. As Danny got on the plane, he kissed his palm, put it on the side of the plane, and said, "Goodbye, God, I'll see you when I get back from Vegas." But I digress . . . back to the raised stage.

One of the shows I convinced Danny to do was one that would go back to his early days in burlesque and vaudeville and my love of that kind of comedy. People think burlesque was all strippers and bawdy sketches. But it was so much more, and the plan was to pay tribute to that culture.

On NBC, Sunday night at 7:00 P.M. was reserved for *The Wonderful World of Disney,* except they would occasionally put a special in there. So we convinced NBC to allow us to air a show called *The Wonderful World of Burlesque,* whose name got us a lot of promotion and attention. Makes sense, let's replace Davy Crockett with Sally Rand and Jimmy Durante. But to do the special right, it would be necessary to actually re-create an old burlesque theater, which of course would involve building a raised stage that would make it appear as the old burlesque theaters had appeared. This was obviously going to cost a lot of money. I was nervous about it because I not only had to sell Danny, I had to convince his nephew Ronnie Jacobs and Abe Lastfogel, both of whom paid great attention to the profit factor.

So I laid the whole thing out for the group. They loved the idea. They even loved the idea of a raised stage, until Danny said, "How much is this going to cost?" That was the one question I was hoping no one would ask. I decided to break character and answer honestly. I told them we were raising the stage thirty inches, and the good news, it was only going to cost $20,000. Everybody went crazy. Danny said, "Are you nuts? We're going to raise the stage thirty inches and you are going to spend twenty thousand dollars?"

I realized I was losing the argument, and even worse, I was getting desperate because I had already ordered the stage. So I finally threw up my hands and said, "Okay, okay, okay. You win. Same money, we're raising the stage thirty-six inches." Then I said, "But I gotta go now," and I left. They sat there in stone silence, thinking I must be nuts because I didn't understand that it wasn't the height of the stage they were complaining about, it was the $20,000 cost of raising it at all. We did raise the stage. Thirty-six inches. That became the height that all raised stages at NBC were after that, including in the Bob Hope specials and a lot of other shows that followed our theatrical presentation of *The Wonderful World of Burlesque*. No one ever understood why those stages were all thirty-six inches high. Well, now you know.

It was a great show. Lee Remick did "Girl in the Moon" actually sitting in a large moon. Jim Nabors sang a straight song. Well, almost straight. Sheldon Leonard did a candy butcher up and down the aisles. And we did all the classic burlesque crossovers, with Danny standing in the middle of the stage looking for directions as various comics and star cameos crossed in front of him.

We also did the "Hospital Room" sketch. Danny was in bed. Mickey Rooney came in as the crazy doctor, put his hand on a lamp, and said, "Boy, you got some fever there." Edie Adams came in in a tight nurse's costume. Jack Benny came in the room, and Danny said, "What are you doing here?" Jack said, "Looking for a quarter that I lost in the basement. Danny, why are you up here?" Danny said, "There's more light up here."

Dean Martin, Frank Sinatra, Andy Griffith, Don Knotts, and a ton of other television and film stars walked through this show. It was one of the biggest, best, and funniest specials ever done at that time.

Danny went on to do many more burlesque shows, but that first show did a lot to establish my reputation in comedy because it was a kind of comedy that had not been seen on television at that point. We also explained a bit about burlesque and the candy butchers, the crossovers, and the classic burlesque bits of "Go Ahead and Sing," "Slowly I Turn," and "Electric Chair." All of these had been the center of Abbott and Costello's act, as well as the Ritz Brothers (google them) and a number of other classic comedy acts. I had a good time with Danny, and it was my first chance to work with Jimmy Durante, which made the whole experience worthwhile.

The only problem I ever had with Danny was cutting the monologues. His first love was as a monologist, telling stories. But Danny's stories ran ten, twelve, sometimes fifteen minutes. After we taped a show, I'd go into the dressing room. We would talk about the show and how wonderful it was. I knew I had about twenty minutes to cut out of each show. Danny's daughters, Marlo and Terre, and his son, Tony, and his wife, Rosemary, would come in the dressing room and tell Danny how wonderful he was. They'd say that the show was okay too, just so long as we did not touch the monologue. Danny would look at me as if to say, *I'm willing to cut it, but the family won't let me take any of that out because it's all gold.* Every time we did a show, it wound up that I had to convince Danny that time had to come out of the monologue, which always displeased him and the entire family. So that sums up my experience with Danny Thomas: I cut monologues and raised a stage.

AND THE WINNER IS . . .

In 1964, I received a call from a man by the name of Ted Bergmann who had sold Timex a show called *The Best on Record*, a celebration of the top recording artists. He thought I would be just the producer to head it up. It sounded like a good idea and that it could be a great television event.

Everyone was excited about it, including an obscure organization by the name of the National Academy of Recording Arts and Sciences (NARAS). However, I had two problems. First, no one knew what a Grammy Award was; second, NARAS had no idea what it was doing. Another problem was that no one was interested in attending a ceremony for an unknown award presented by an unknown organization for an unknown television show. Even worse, there were to be twelve awards presented, but since NARAS had no funds, we couldn't afford to make twelve actual awards. So we just kept handing out the same award to each winner and then took it back to hand to the next one.

Then I had another brilliant idea (and I assume it is too late for me to be hauled before a judge for this). My idea was to find out in advance who had won and see if the winners would be available to perform or to accept the award on camera. This practice would come under some scrutiny now, but it worked out fine back then. So somehow, with no money and knowing the winners in advance, I was there for the very first Grammy Awards.

FORGET THE THREE TENORS: I PRODUCED THE THREE DIVAS

Like Hep was a special I did with Dinah Shore, Lucille Ball, and Diana Ross. For one part of the program, I came up with the idea for a medley.

Three superstars, a great idea, and Diana was certainly used to singing with two other women. However, and this is a big however, Diana was used to being the star diva with the other Supremes as plus-one and other plus-one, not with two stars as big as her. And even though Diana was young and danced and sang like a dream with enormous energy and talent, she was taking the stage with two old pros. And because Diana was in awe of the two megastars she was working with, when they would tell her they were having trouble with "this dance step" or with "that lyric," she tried to be helpful and coach Lucy and Dinah.

I begged Diana to just forget about them, to do her own thing and not to worry about what they did, because if she wasn't careful, they would try every trick in the book to upstage her. Upstaging is a thing that actors do to divert attention away from the other actor and on to themselves. Watch *The Magnificent Seven*. Every time Steve McQueen is in a scene with Yul Brynner, who at the time was a much bigger star, Steve would tug his hat, make a face, pull down a tree branch, do anything to have you look at him instead of Yul. Well, these two ladies gave Diana Ross a master class in upstaging.

The way they did it was this: as we went to tape the number, Lucy and Dinah, who had said they were having trouble memorizing the steps and lyrics, came on with moves, and takes, and business, and dance steps that Diana had never seen before. They also took one step farther back than they had in rehearsal, which caused Diana to turn around and look back at them, meaning that all we were going to see was the side or back of Diana's head, while Lucy and Dinah continued to shine.

I stopped tape and pulled Diana aside. I said, "Diana, I believe I mentioned to you *not* to watch them. They are outrageous. They are killers. Piranhas. Land sharks. Don't look at them. Just do what you do." About four takes later, I finally convinced her to look forward so that it appeared that she was actually in the number. I'm going to go out on a limb and say Diana took that lesson and used it to her own effect for the next fifty years.

ME AND CHER, HAMMER AND NAILS

Disclaimer: The following material deals with my relationship with Cher, which was stormy, unpredictable, funny, and very successful. However, I do not want anything in my memories to indicate anything less than my absolute adoration of Cher, then and now. I love her and I remember fondly the many adventures we shared.

The first time Cher and I worked together, she started calling me "Hammer," which stuck with me throughout our relationship. It was a not too thinly disguised reference to what may be perceived as my somewhat less than gentle approach to people and problems, which stems from some genetic flaw in my Germanic genes.

In self-defense, I called Cher "Nails," because of her dedication to flawlessly manicured fingers and at least as flawlessly cared for toes. When we worked together, it always seemed that we would spend fifteen minutes rehearsing a sketch, and she would spend hours trimming, filing, scraping, buffing, and painlessly painting each and every finger and toenail. God forbid one of those nails ever got scratched or broken, because then they *all* had to be redone. I realize now that I may have become impatient and on occasion would indeed pound on any surface I could find, including a stage manager. Thus the name Hammer. And we became a team, Hammer and Nails.

Now this was not the first nickname Cher had. She and Sonny had been friends with Jolene and me for a number of years, and one night they came to pick us up from the house to go to dinner. Our daughter A.J., who was three years old at the time, looked at Cher and said, "Hello, Pookie Face." So Nails wasn't the first nickname she got from a Schlatter.

Another night, coming home from a party, Sonny asked if we could stop at a grocery store. He picked out about $30 worth of groceries, discovered he didn't have his wallet, and so asked if

I could loan him some money. I agreed and then announced to everyone in the store, "Ladies and gentlemen, this is Sonny Bono, world famous rock and roll singer. He doesn't have any money with him, but he would like to sell some autographs."

We stood in the middle of the grocery store, and I sold Sonny Bono autographs until we got the $30. He was mortified, but it wasn't long until he got even with me.

One morning I awoke and looked out the window. In our front yard there were six huge antique barbershop chairs sinking slowly into our front lawn, courtesy of Sonny Bono. I loved the look, but you can imagine how difficult it was to dispose of six barber chairs.

MAKING CHER SQUARE

When Cher was signed to do a special for CBS, which was going to be a pilot for her series, she called to ask me to run it, and I was there immediately. But this was going to be a big change for her. For years Cher's career had been under the guidance of Sonny Bono, who pretty much told her what to do. She would resist, but Sonny was in charge. Once Sonny and Cher split up, she made sure there was never going to be another man who would dominate her career . . . and considering it's still going strong over half a century later, she's done a pretty good job. But the learning curve was steep. It was a whole new world for her, because Cher was not used to standing onstage alone. She was a "re-actor," a "counter-puncher." Before, Sonny would talk and Cher would wait and throw a simple line. Now she had to be out there by herself.

At our first meeting, Cher wanted to know how I planned to open the show. My idea was to open with a simple bell note and a tiny spot way in the distance. Then I wanted Cher to begin to sing a ballad arrangement of "Let Me Entertain You." We would slowly move in, and the little spot would become a close-up of Cher, with her black hair and a white mink coat. As I was describing this to Cher, I could see that the store was closed. She looked at me and said, "Oh shit. That's the squarest thing I ever heard." I explained that I knew it was square, but that she was now a thirty-year-old divorcée with a child and that the whole world had experienced her troubled marriage, her split from Sonny, and was now witnessing her for the first time on her own. My thought was it would be vulnerable and compelling for her to have a moment singing "Let Me Entertain You" as a ballad for one chorus, then she would kick off the white fur and she could be wearing practically nothing, walk toward the camera and do a rock and roll version of whatever she thought would be hip, cool, trendy, funky, far out, and with it. In other words, to unsquare the shit.

Cher reluctantly agreed and then wanted to know how she would follow that. I said I wanted her to walk down, take the applause, and then say hello to the audience. I was about to continue when she said, "Hello? *Hello?* I'm not into that shit." It was at this exact moment that I realized 1) this was going to be a long ordeal, and 2) "hello" might mean my goodbye. But if I am one thing, I am stubborn, and in the end, I believe talent will recognize an idea that is good for them . . . usually. Cher is too smart to not latch on to an idea that showcased her in a good light. So on the show, she sang "Let Me Entertain You" and she said hello and she was terrific. But it was a tough sell all the way. Many times the harder Cher fought against an idea, the greater she was when she finally did it. It was the perfect opening, the audience loved it, and I loved it. I think secretly Cher loved it too . . . although she would never admit it.

Our first choice for guest stars on her show were Bette Midler and Elton John. We flew to New York and had a memorable, hysterical, and wonderful meeting at Bette Midler's apartment. Bette was concerned about working with Cher and how she would come off. Cher was thin. Bette was more full-figured, or as she put it, "great tits." We assured her she and her singing and her tits would be terrific, so she agreed to come on the show.

At that point, Cher was dating David Geffen. David had arranged for us to have a meeting with Elton John. We flew down on the shuttle to see Elton's concert in Washington, D.C. It was magic. Elton absolutely put us away. High energy, wonderful songs, great costumes, and an absolutely outrageous approach to show business. He was fabulous. Following the concert, we all flew back on Elton's private jet and discussed the possibility of a guest shot. This never would have happened without David Geffen, who could sell people in Phoenix space heaters in July. Both Cher and David did tell me, however, that I made Elton a little nervous, a nice way of saying he thought I was either a little crazy or, in the words of Judy Garland, an asshole; I opt for the former. So all future negotiations were going to have to go through David, who communicated with Elton much better than I did. They were right. It was perfect.

So Elton and Bette both agreed to do the show, and then CBS came up with the request that we add some comedy to the guest star list. Why we needed to add comedy when we had Cher and Bette, I will never know. But this was not the first time that a television network suit confused me. So we added Flip Wilson to the show.

We were all set to go. At this point, we unleashed the brilliant Bob Mackie, who proceeded to collect every bugle bead in Los Angeles and put them on everything in sight. He bugle-beaded Cher, Bette, Elton, and the set. I think he even put bugle beads on top of the bugle beads, but that sure was one exciting stage with Cher, Elton, and Bette in a sea of white and silver balloons, all of them covered in bugle beads. They did a medley of famous rock and roll songs, Elton did a solo, Cher did a solo, and Cher and Bette sang a whole medley about "trashy ladies" where they wore corsets, garters, and black stockings with what Bette called "fuck-me pumps" as they sang and writhed around on a settee. Flip did a comedy spot, and we did a piece with all four of them in an old folks' home. It was great. Suddenly Cher was a star on her own.

Bette's manager was a singularly offensive human being who really pissed me off with great frequency. He kept demanding that I give Bette a solo. I explained to him again and again that the show was already way over time and that we wanted Bette to be *with* Cher; also, it was Cher's pilot/special, and there would not be room for a Bette solo. I still can't figure out what part of it being Cher's show and not Bette's did he not understand. I finally got tired of listening to him and gave in—temporarily. I recorded Bette singing "Hello in There," which was a song for old people. It's a wonderful song, but when it was all through it was nothing you could put on a show that had the purpose of selling a series with Cher. Cher was great and she was funny, magical and exciting, but vocally, she was not up to Bette. I'm not going to let a network executive compare them. Let's be real, who is up to Bette? Streisand for one, but I digress. Geffen cut Bette's ballad, and I don't think Bette ever forgave me or Cher. She still talks about it. What's the statute of limitations on a grudge? In show business, there is none.

We finished the show, and it was a huge hit. Within a few days, Geffen had an order for a Cher series to go on the air in the fall. Sounds perfect, doesn't it? Not so fast. We had a concept problem, because Cher was now back to not wanting to do anything that would appear square. Cher thought of herself as a rock and roll queen. The audience thought of her as Sonny's wife, as Chastity's mother, and as a young woman whom they had grown up with. CBS thought of Cher as the new Carol Burnett/Lucille Ball/Dinah Shore. David Geffen was focused entirely on Cher's recording career, and Cher was sitting firmly in the middle of the fence. That was okay for Cher but not for me, the guy in the middle with one leg dangling down each side. Get it? Ouch! When you have to decide things, "I'll get back to you" is not a decision, it's a stall. "I'm still thinking about it" is a stall. "Maybe" is not an answer or a decision. The problem was that for years Sonny Bono made the decisions and told Cher what to wear, what to sing, what to do, and what to say. And the more I tried to make decisions for her or even with her, she shut down.

Now I have worked with some strong ladies: Dinah Shore, Judy Garland, Lena Horne, Doris Day, Betty Hutton, Lucille Ball, Pearl

Bailey, Shirley MacLaine, Sophie Tucker, Mae West, Bette Davis, and everybody in between. Cher was, in some ways, no more difficult except for the fact that Cher wanted to be a rock and roll princess. And so the adventure began.

CBS told me they had tested the *Cher* show and Fred Silverman sent me the results, which said she licked her lips too much (there's a great note from a suit) and should not be so sexy. The execs said she should wear more clothes, get her nose straightened, get her teeth capped, and be more ladylike . . . and oh, by the way . . . be *much more* ladylike. The test results puzzled me. So I sent them to a research institution to have the process reversed; I showed researchers these reactions and asked what questions could have generated those reactions. The research institution told me there had been no tests done, that these were opinions put in the form of research, and that CBS obviously felt this would be an easier way to convince Cher to take their suggestions than it would be if they just made them as network requests or demands. In other words, they lied.

Let me digress and talk about some other wonderful remarks made over the years by network suits.

- Mike Dann, upon canceling a show called *He & She*, said, "That is the finest show we have ever canceled."
- In the book *Only You, Dick Daring!*, there was a line where the network told the writer that "a Martian wouldn't say that."
- Lawrence Welk once told his band, "Don't play it fast, just play it half fast," and he told Arthur Duncan, "You get ready to dance while I beat off the band."

These are just a couple of the memorable TV executive remarks I remember. But "Cher licks her lips too much"? That's an all-time classic.

Somehow, we did some great shows with Cher continuing to lick her lips. We had guest stars like Art Carney, the Jackson 5, David Bowie, Ray Charles, and Jerry Lewis, none of whom noticed or cared that they were onstage with a notorious lip-licker. And we put them on in wonderful combinations, like having Cher, Tina Turner, and Kate Smith perform a medley. It was hysterical. Kate had never used a hand mike before and didn't know what to do with it, so she twirled it by holding on to the wire and swinging the microphone around, and she was still louder than Cher and Tina together. It was an exciting show and got big numbers on Sunday night at eight o'clock. Cher thought it was square; maybe it was, but it was what the audience loved. Not only that, Cher was upset that she had to follow *60 Minutes* because none of her friends watched *60 Minutes*. At that point, I didn't even try to explain to her that if we relied on just her friends, there wouldn't be much of a future.

But I would much rather rely on the insights of a star than of a network executive. Let me be clear: executives are not stupid or mean. They are just usually uninformed, inexperienced, and insecure . . . which is why they ended up putting their opinions in the form of surveys. I can remember vividly the network notes and complaints we received when we delivered *Laugh-In, Real People,* and the other specials I have done, most of which were legendary successes. I'm convinced that all producers should wear helmets, cups, and body armor—and, if you remember my onstage debut, chicken shit remover.

And it's even worse today. At least back in the '50s and '60s and '70s and '80s, we would have a meeting with one or two executives. Today, selling a show requires a meeting with at least ten people in the room and memos from each of them, all giving contradictory opinions. Television is not an exact science. Most of my successes are the opinions and the obsessions of one or two people, and most of my failures are the result of having compromised, which at my advanced age, I no longer have to do.

CHER, THE COCKATOOS, AND 350 LITTLE OLD LADIES

One of my favorite moments with Cher was during the first season. Bobby Kelly, who was our set designer, had set up a very elaborate look for her ballad. Onstage was a huge, tiered plywood wall that looked like steps going up about twenty-five feet. The top of the wall was a trough, into which we put dry ice, and when water was added to the dry ice, it made smoke that cascaded down the wall, a living waterfall of smoke. There were huge paper sculptures, a pond with floating lilies, and live cockatoos swinging on perches over the water. It was absolutely breathtaking. When Cher walked out through this dry ice waterfall, wearing not much except a jewel in her navel and her huge hair, it was something to behold. Obviously, this took a little time to set up and coordinate, but we were finally ready for a take. In the audience we had 350 little old ladies wearing sneakers and carrying shopping bags, because we had rounded them up from Farmers Market. They were so excited to see Chastity's mom: sweet, adorable Cher.

The music swelled. Cher walked through the wall of dry ice smoke. Fabulous! She came downstage, stopped, and said, "God-damn it, Hammer, I can't hear the fucking slapback." The 350 little old ladies did not know that "slapback" meant that she could not hear the orchestra; I'm not even sure they knew what "fucking" meant, but the tone gave them a pretty good idea.

I explained to Cher that when it came time to sing, she would hear the orchestra just like in rehearsal. I then addressed the audience: "Okay, folks, we are now going to take it again from the top." This meant more dry ice, more smoke, calming the cockatoos, getting some of the cockatoo doo-doo out of the water, and setting up to go again. (On the other hand, I would rather work with cockatoos than work with the Marquis Chimps . . . or with most network suits. Although both chimps and suits are responsible for a lot of crap.) It took about thirty minutes to reset everything, but we were ready to go. Cue the smoke . . . Cue Cher . . . Cue the slapback.

Cher came through with her big hair and the jewel in her navel and hit a honker like the world has never heard. Again, she stopped and said, "Goddamn it, Hammer, I hit the wrong fucking note." This, of course, was apparent to me and even to the audience of 350 little old ladies wearing sneakers and carrying shopping bags, who, so far, had heard one bad note, four "goddamn its," and two "fucks."

We rehearsed the music again. Cher went off the set while we prepared more dry ice, cleaned the cockatoo doo-doo off the water, calmed the cockatoos, set the paper sculpture in the right position, and begged the 350 little old ladies to stay and listen to the number. We were ready to go. The music swelled. Everything was perfect and . . . *Cher did not come out at all.*

I know you can't imagine this, but trust me, I was upset. Hammer was not happy. Calmly, I said, "Cher . . . Cher . . ." Then I yelled, "CHER?" Still nothing. If you can, imagine a man of my size and dimension, screaming, "CHER, WHERE ARE YOU?" and then hearing from a stage manager, "She went to look at a house." She had gotten in her little Ferrari, with the medium-sized jewel in her navel and the big hair, and driven off to Bel Air to look at a new house. And you wonder why I drink.

We had about a three-hour wait. The little old ladies went home, the cockatoos were back in their cages, but eventually, Cher returned, and we taped the number. Which, by the way, was quite magnificent, but a little bit frustrating. The season went like this. Good ideas occasionally well executed. Like Digby Wolfe's brilliant concept.

Since Cher was now divorced and starting to date again, Digby wrote a piece where every week Cher would come home from a Saturday night date and get undressed behind a screen. She would put on various kinds of nightwear ranging from sexy to silly and sit on her bed while she described the evening's activities. It was delightful, it was funny and warm, and it fit in with the idea of a recently divorced woman, back out there starting to date again.

It was a tough sell to Cher, until I realized that she would be more comfortable if we made the room look like her room at home. Expensive, but effective. We got the same curtains, the same bed-spread, and many of the same toys and stuffed animals. From then on, the piece went much better, unless, of course, one of the stuffed animals got lost, which meant we couldn't tape until it was found, at which time Cher would go out and look at another house. Did I tell you that sometimes stars can be difficult?

And the Emmy Does Not Go To

The first season of the *Cher* show, we were nominated for twelve Emmys, and I was sure we would win at least ten. My good friend Larry Gelbart was nominated for about twenty Emmys for *M.A.S.H.*, and we were sure that together we would win most of them. So we decided to go together in a stretch limo with a huge trunk, into which we would be able to put all our Emmys. We sat at the ceremony with Cher, who showed up with Gregg Allman. He was wearing a white suit, white shirt, and pink tie. During the ceremony I glanced down and noticed what looked like powdered sugar on his tie. I mentioned to Gregg that if the camera got a shot of this, we might all go to jail. So we did our best to get rid of the residue of his last sniff of what must have been powdered sugar from a doughnut.

As the evening went on, it became apparent that Larry and I were not winning many Emmys. Obviously, it was a disappointment, so none of us felt like waiting around for the Governors Ball after the Emmys to see all the winners holding their trophies, so we went to Chasen's, where everyone was supposed to meet up later for dessert. There was no one there when we got to Chasen's, but since we had missed the feast at the Governors Ball, we decided to send our limo driver to Fatburger to pick up dinner. Within half an hour, we were seated in the big center booth with a cardboard box full of burgers and big jars of ketchup, mustard, and mayonnaise that we had borrowed from Chasen's spread all over the table. Nothing like the odor of a $2 Double King Burger with chili and cheese overpowering the aroma of Chasen's $40 entrées. By the way, back then $40 was expensive.

One by one other Emmy losers arrived, none of whom had had dinner. Robert Blake ordered Italian food, probably from Vitello's, where he of course did not shoot his wife, Bonny Lee Bakley, despite what every bit of evidence indicated. One of the other tables ordered Chinese food. Here was one of the most elegant restaurants in the world with all this takeout spread out all over the choice tables as the celebrators arrived from the Governors Ball. All those boxes and aromas in the main room of Chasen's made the whole evening worthwhile. Although it would have been more worthwhile if I had won a few Emmys.

Despite being full, but Emmy-less, it was time to plan for the next season of Cher's show. Cher and I had a long talk, and I explained that she was thirty. Halfway to sixty (and you thought I couldn't do math). I told her that to get to the next level, she could not sit in her Bel Air mansion behind huge steel gates, eating candy bars, smoking cigarettes, filing her nails, and practicing her autograph. These activities, by the way, consumed much of her time. I explained that to make the show better, I had three requests. First was to get a vocal coach over the summer, so she could develop at least one, maybe two more notes at the top and one or two more notes at the bottom of her range, which would open up a wide variety of songs for her to perform that were not possible now. Second, I wanted her to enroll in a class in improvisation with people she liked, and three nights a week we would work out new characters and new situations so that she could hone her acting skills and develop some improv techniques. The third request was that we get a choreographer, who would work with her three times a week on exercises, karate, and aerobics that could be turned into dance routines. My idea was that by the end of the summer, she would have a whole new repertoire of music to sing, a whole new technique as far as her comedy, and a body that could handle six tough dance numbers. After a great deal of selling, Cher said, "Okay, Hammer, you got it." I thanked Nails. We were off and ready to start her summer of corrective show business.

The next night she met Gregg Allman, and the night after that she was playing in the sprinklers on Sunset Boulevard with the Hudson Brothers. Cher caught a cold, and the next time I saw her was three months later, three days before we were to tape our first show of the new season. No vocal coach. No improv. No dance routine. No rehearsal. No new notes, no new characters . . . but her nails looked great.

My adventure as producer of the *Cher* series was highlighted by one of our final encounters. Bob Mackie had designed the most spectacular Indian outfit for Cher. It was a huge white feather head-dress with a train that went all the way to the floor and little else. There were some crystal beads and a few well-placed feathers, but that was pretty much the outfit. When I saw that spectacular Bob Mackie creation, I got a brilliant idea. I called Irving Berlin and was amazed that he knew who I was. He was amazed when I told him what I wanted: to do a modern version of *Annie Get Your Gun* with Cher as Annie Oakley. There was a long pause on the phone, during which I'm sure he considered calling 911.

Anyhow, a few weeks and many calls later, Irving agreed to give it a shot. I think showing him the half-nude photo of Cher as Annie Oakley may have clinched it. I was thrilled because I thought this could really reinvent Cher on another level where she had never gone before. All I had to do now was convince Cher. When I made my pitch, she looked at me as if I had just arrived from Mars. She said, "Wow, Hammer. I'm not into that shit." How can you not be into Irving Berlin? Anyhow, the idea died there, but it would still have been a hell of a performance for Cher.

That was the capper. It was then that I realized that this would be a long series of conflicts between me wanting Cher to be more than she was and Cher wanting to be exactly what she was, just with more bugle beads and better nails. I left the show. We remained good friends, and I am still disappointed that Irving Berlin died without ever seeing Cher as a half-naked Annie Oakley, onstage, singing "You Can't Get a Man with a Gun."

REDD FOXX REMINDS PEARL BAILEY HOW SHE USED TO TAKE MONEY OFF TABLES WITHOUT USING HER HANDS

I had been watching friends like Sammy deal with racism their whole life. There are little ways you can make a difference. Frank did it in a big way—he of course only did things in a big way—in how he fought for Sammy to be treated fairly in Las Vegas; I did it in ways I could, whether by buying Sammy a house or my plan in 1969 to do an all-Black variety show, something that had never been done in this country. My idea was to book contemporary Black music artists like Joe Tex, the Chambers Brothers, and Martha Reeves and combine them with the variety talents of Gregory Hines and the comedy of Nipsey Russell, George Kirby, Slappy White, and the bad boy of the time, Redd Foxx.

Now Redd had trouble getting booked on network television . . . for good reason. His party records would have been considered obscene in a brothel. As a result, it wasn't possible even to discuss using Redd Foxx on a network television show. However, I somehow was able to convince the network to let me use Redd Foxx as part of our show. He was brilliant. It was on this show that Redd did his famous "What I Wish for the Grand Wizard of the Ku Klux Klan."

SLAPPY
Well, what do you think of the
Grand Wizard of the Klan, Reverend?

REDD
I'd like to wish the Grand Wizard
of the Klan a five-car accident

with no survivors, a slow ambulance
with four flat tires and no spares . . .
a junky doctor with an $800-a-day
habit with an orangutan on his back . . .
and a rusty scalpel in his hand as
he's operating on the Grand Wizard
in a hospital that's burning down on
top of the operating table and frozen fire
hydrants from Alabama to Nova Scotia . . .
if they even thaw out, muddy water in his
coffin. Other than that, Godspeed and may
lightning strike him in the heart 374 times
just before some hungry, hydrophobic-filled
possum chews through his expensive coffin
for something strange to eat . . . Amen.

The name of the show was *Soul*, and Lou Rawls was the host. All the breaks between acts were done by a line of dancers. *Soul* became the prototype for *In Living Color*. In fact, when Keenen Ivory Wayans was preparing *In Living Color*, I sent him a copy of *Soul* and that became their format. Keenen, you're welcome.

My experience with Redd Foxx can be described by the three *E*s: enlightening, endangering, and enrapturing. And one more *E*: exasperating. More on that one later.

Here I was, a very young midwestern white producer, and Redd was not any of those things. The only other white person involved in the show was Digby Wolfe. Digby was teaching a class at the Watts Writers Workshop, and he brought in some great young Black writers. We would have gone to the Writers Guild of America for names, but that would have been difficult, because at that time there were more dwarfs in the NBA than there were Black comedy writers in the guild.

So I had the talent I wanted and I had writers, but I still needed a director. So I called Sammy Davis Jr. to see if he knew of a Black comedy director. Sammy laughed and said, "There aren't any." The only one Sammy knew of was a young man working in Canada by the name of Mark Warren who primarily did musical shows.

I called Mark and said, "Are you Mark Warren?"

He said, "Yes."

I said, "Are you Black?"

He said, "Who is this?"

I said, "Do you know Sammy Davis?"

He said, "Yes."

I said, "I want you to come to Los Angeles and direct a television show." Mark thought I was kidding, and then I told him why. I said, "You're young, you're Black, you know Sammy, and that's what I need."

As we got onstage, I realized that the whole cast was looking at me like I was from Mars. What was I doing, producing a show that was going to be a comedic look at the Black experience? I sat down with Redd Foxx and explained my dilemma to him and that if the show was successful, it would open doors for him as well as other minority artists. Redd didn't care about that; he was interested in what doors it might open for him. He walked onstage, and just by his attitude he indicated that it was okay for everyone to work with this honky. We became good friends, the show was enormously successful, and Herb Schlosser, who was head of NBC at the time, said that the only reason they did not put it on as a series was because they were afraid they could never cancel it. It was huge. So, as always, the logic of a suit made no sense.

After that experience I wanted to keep working with Redd, and I got my chance after I bought the script of the play *Norman, Is That You?*, which had a very brief run on Broadway starring Lou Jacobi and Maureen Stapleton. It was one of the first plays ever to deal with a gay relationship. My first choice for the role of the father was George C. Scott. He loved the play, loved the idea of doing it as a movie, but he wanted a million dollars. At that point no motion picture star had ever gotten a million dollars. So goodbye, Patton.

STILL LAUGHING / 101

Then a lightning bolt hit: what if we changed the play's characters from Jewish to Black and cast Redd Foxx. Redd took one look at the script and loved it. I sent it to my agent, Tony Fantozzi, who showed it to Pearl Bailey, and she loved it. We now had two of our leads. I went in to MGM and they loved it. Then MGM discussed it with Sherry Lansing, who thought it was time in these days of the sexual revolution to take a shot at this subject matter. So everyone loved it, things were going smoothly, and a commitment was made to rewrite the script with Ron Clark and Sam Bobrick, who had done the original play on Broadway. The rewrite was done, and I was ready to go.

It was determined that we would shoot the movie on videotape, because by combining Redd's familiarity with video on *Sanford and Son* with multiple cameras, I would be able to deliver it in much less time than going with a single film camera. This was revolutionary because no one had ever shot a motion picture on a major motion picture lot using videotape.

I laid out a production schedule that would be under three weeks and a budget that would be about a million dollars, and we were off and running—except for just one little detail: we still needed Redd to sign his contract. I had been assured there was no problem, Redd was reviewing the contract with his lawyer and said he would send it back shortly. Shortly became longer, and while no one said there was any problem, the contract just did not come back. Eventually I called Redd and told him, "Look, we're going to shoot any day now, everything is in place, but I must have that signed contract." One delay led to another, but eventually the contract did indeed come back. I checked the contract to make sure Redd had signed it and then sent it to MGM.

About eight seconds after I sent the contract, I got a call from the president of MGM to come to his office . . . immediately. When I arrived, he was almost comatose, lying on the sofa with a towel over his head. I said almost comatose because he was screaming obscenities about Redd Foxx. As a matter of fact, some of the same obscenities were directed at me, instructing me to read the contract. I said, "I read it, I helped draw it up."

He said, "Did you read the signed contract?"

I said, "No, I just saw that it had been signed."

He directed me to the middle of the contract, where Redd Foxx had changed one word . . . only *one* word. He had drawn a line through the word "NET" in "NET PROFITS" and written in "GROSS." Of course, this seriously changed the structure of the deal, which was pointed out to me repeatedly in obscene phrases. I called Redd and mentioned to him that he had made a very important and unfortunate change in the contract, which caused Redd to start screaming obscenities at me. It was apparently Tell George to Go Fuck Himself Day. To paraphrase Redd's yelling, he was telling me that this was a white man's form of suppression of his rights. He had taken a three-hundred-page contract, thick as a motherfucking phone book, and he had changed one word, and everybody was all excited just because he was Black.

I pointed out to him that the word he changed was perhaps the worst one he could have tweaked, as it changed net profits to gross. Redd pointed out it was the best change he could have made for Redd. After prolonged discussions while sitting at Redd's home with the air thick enough that we both could have been arrested, I finally got the contract signed and we were ready to go.

I decided to shoot the film top to bottom so that the relationships between the characters could develop. Well, that was the plan, until Pearl announced that she was available for only five days, so we would have to shoot all her scenes first. That was a horrible idea, and I was totally against it . . . until I discovered the very awkward preexisting relationship between Pearl Bailey and Redd Foxx. What I had not known was that when Redd Foxx did an act with Slappy White, Slappy had been married to Pearl. She was a big star on Broadway, and Redd was still upset that Pearl had never done anything to help the careers of Slappy White and Redd Foxx. And he was also upset that he had never been able to coax, cajole, con, or convince Pearl to go to bed with him.

During that period of time, Pearl had just graduated from the gin mills where she used to work, where she was known for occasionally performing a bit of business called "takin' the money off the tables." If you can imagine a folded five-dollar bill sitting on the edge of a table and Pearl Bailey removing that bill from the table without using her hands, you can visualize the kind of clubs she worked in and how this must have gone over with the patrons. Years later when Pearl worked Ciro's, it was closing night and Pearl repeated the act of "takin' the money off the tables." I thought we were all going to go to jail.

First day of rehearsal for *Norman, Is That You?*, Redd reminded Pearl of this former part of her act; this began to create the kind of tension that could grow into major hand-to-hand combat.

Later that first day, on the lunch break, Pearl walked outside and saw Redd Foxx's red convertible with a license plate that featured a very inappropriate street word that Redd often used, which prompted Pearl to decide to "educate" Redd. She explained how the word was bad, how people of all races had to learn to live together, and to achieve this end, she had gone to Africa to visit the natives living there in grass huts with mud floors. She said she would sit cross-legged on the ground and explain the need for people to love each other and live together in harmony so that there would not be any more wars. At that point in the conversation, Redd lit a strange-looking cigarette, took a deep hit, and told Pearl, "There is no one living in Africa in a grass hut, on a mud floor, that was going to start a fucking war anyhow, so Africa and you can kiss my ass." Pearl went out to her dressing room, Redd continued to puff on his funny cigarette, and I was about to lose half of one of my precious five days with Pearl Bailey.

As you can imagine, it took quite a bit of time to get them back together again; in fact I think I invented shuttle diplomacy, not Henry Kissinger. Eventually, I convinced them to move forward, which did not stop Pearl from going through her entire peace and love speech again. She explained to Redd how she had become an

"Ambassador of Love" with the UN, and to prove her importance, she pulled out a Louis Vuitton wallet and began to shuffle through various cards. She had a card from the U.S. Senate, the House of Representatives, the UN, the CIA, the FBI, and the Supreme Court. She even showed Redd a card to get into the White House and other cards that would gain her access to places normally not frequented by entertainers. Midway through her speech, Redd dropped a wad of one-hundred-dollar bills on the floor. He said those were his "cards," which would get him a smile and a hello at the front door of the White House, whereas "those bullshit cards" she had wouldn't get, in Redd's words, her "big fat ass past the kitchen."

World War III broke out immediately, and it went on like that for all five days: Redd constantly teasing, and irritating, and aggravating Pearl while still trying to convince her to "give me a kiss in my mouth." Since the relationship within the play was adversarial, it helped their performances, but it aged me noticeably during the process.

Eventually the film was finished and everyone at MGM thought we had a major hit. I set up premieres in Chicago, LA, Harlem, and Redd's hometown of St. Louis, where we were going to have Redd Foxx Day. The plan was he would be met by both dignitaries and civic leaders as well as members of the gay community, who would praise Redd for what he had done to promote understanding with this wonderfully warm and hysterically funny film. A week before we were to leave on this extensive promotional tour, Redd wanted to know the whereabouts of his check. I reminded him he had already been paid for the film, which caused Redd to say, "No, my check for promotion." Of course, promotion had been part of the original deal, but Redd made it clear the original deal wasn't good enough, and he demanded $25,000 a day to go out and promote his film. I explained that Redd had 10 percent of the profits of our film, and he said *they* had 90 percent of the profits from *his* film. Redd never did any promotion, and the film opened well its first weekend and more than made back the cost of the film and the ads. But because Redd did nothing to promote the film, MGM would not continue to advertise it as hoped. The result: *Norman, Is That You?* is gone, resurfacing once or twice a year on cable.

Don't Worry, Be Mr. Happy

In addition to producing events aimed at making money for yours truly, I've done a lot of charity events helping raise money for causes big and small. One year the people at American Cinematheque asked me to produce the night they were honoring Robin Williams. Now booking guests for this was a piece of cake because everybody loved Robin, but instead of the normal presentational-type show, I decided to do a dais of all comics: Johnny Carson, Billy Crystal, Chevy Chase, Martin Mull, and eight more of the best and really outrageous stand-up comics of the day.

I felt that the best way to keep the evening from getting out of control would be to have the show hosted by a very dignified person with an unquestionable reputation who would be greatly respected and play the straight man. Someone who would keep the train running and at the same time wouldn't get in the way of the comics and their "funny" by trying to be funny. So naturally I pursued Michael Eisner, who agreed to host the evening. When you want "not funny," Michael is your man. But I knew he would want to be prepared, so to make him feel at ease I told him I would write some remarks for him as introductions. When we got to the Century Plaza Hotel, I gave him a stack of cards introducing each one of the comics in a very straight, lighthearted, but not "jokey," fashion. Mr. Eisner explained to me that he would read the cards; however, first he had some jokes he wanted to do. And then he reminded me he was funny.

Note: Whenever someone tells you they are funny, they are not. Especially executives whose staff laughs when they say "good morning." And when the staff says, "He's really funny, you should see him when he loosens his tie," I have two words for you: Al Gore.

Back to Eisner. I begged him to not do jokes. I said, "Michael, you are onstage with a dozen killer professional comedians who would like nothing better than to have you do jokes and be able to comment on both you and your jokes in this environment." He explained to me that he knew a lot about comedy and to trust him, it would just be wonderful.

The evening started out with the lawyer for the American Cinematheque explaining that he could not tell people yet what their goals were or what their accomplishments had been, but he promised they would announce them next year. For the time being, all they needed was a lot more money. That had a certain numbing effect on the crowd. Bottom line, the lawyer was human Ambien. And he was the opener for the comedy genius of Michael Eisner and his jokes.

As Eisner tried and failed to get a single laugh, I watched this killers' row of comics take the notes that we had carefully worked on for their performance, put them in their pockets, take out pencils and paper, and begin to write Eisner jokes.

Chevy Chase opened by asking Michael if it would be okay if he peed on his suit . . . and that was the high point, taste-wise, of the evening. Which brings me to Mr. Happy. A videotape had been put together about Robin's career and his preoccupation with Mr. Happy. Then the plan was for Billy Crystal to appear onstage. When we asked Billy to do the show, he said that he would, but he would like to appear as a phallus. A cock. A dick. A prick. A penis. That's right, he wanted to come out as MR. HAPPY. When I told Billy we might not be able to have his penis device built, he made it clear his participation depended entirely on coming onstage as Mr. Happy.

So I called my friend Ret Turner, who worked closely with Bob Mackie and Ray Aghayan. We're talking about the most brilliant, respected costume designers in the world. I explained to him that I needed a favor. His immediate response was they were all busy building an entire show for Vegas, plus they were doing a television series and a new line of clothes, and it would be impossible for them to accept any new assignment. But when I explained to him that Billy Crystal wanted to pay tribute to Robin Williams dressed as a dick, he said, "We'll be right over."

An hour later they arrived with a drawing of a Mr. Happy costume device. It was awe-inspiring. The next three weeks were spent with Billy Crystal going to an endless number of fittings for his penis costume. Cher never went for as many fittings. Mitzi Gaynor and Carol Burnett, added up, never went to as many fittings. Let's be honest, you don't want the wrong-sized penis. Plus Billy is Jewish, so it needed some trimming by a rabbi. However, eventually, the device was completed. It did, indeed, look quite real, and it did have a piece of monofilament rigged so that when Billy pulled it, the device would enlarge and become erect—much like the device many men over sixty used before Viagra.

A lovely, sweet, delightful, clean, wholesome, young woman by the name of Pam Dawber, who was Mindy to Robin's Mork, did a nice piece introducing Billy, who came out wearing the device, smoking a cigar, and announcing that he was Mr. Happy. It was hilarious. And according to people who have seen Milton Berle, life-sized. I never was asked to do an American Cinematheque event again.

Postscript: After Billy came home from a fitting wearing the device, he walked through the living room, and his children were playing on the floor in front of the television set. They barely noticed him, but his youngest daughter looked up, saw him wearing his obscene hat, and said, "Hi, Dad, are you working with Robin again?" and went back to watching television.

TAMING THE LION: ME AND JERRY LEWIS

One day I got a call from Joey Stabile, who was Jerry Lewis's manager. It was the twenty-fifth anniversary of the Jerry Lewis Muscular Dystrophy Telethon, and they wanted me to produce the show in hopes of giving it new energy, a new look, and to present a "new Jerry."

Now this was not going to be easy, because Jerry was . . . what's the word? A prick. So before I agreed I sat down and had a long talk with Jerry, who assured me that if I would do the show, he would be there to perform and do anything I wanted him to do. It sounded like a trick, but I went for it and agreed to do the show. Shortly thereafter, I discovered the reason I was brought in was because of my reputation for being somewhat firm with pricks . . . I mean performers.

Now everyone had an ulterior motive. Jerry's manager wanted me to make life easy for him. The Muscular Dystrophy Association hoped that I would tangle with Jerry and he would walk, since MDA had given me total authority over the program. But what they didn't understand was I was on Team Jerry because I understood Jerry's motive: the kids. Jerry devoted his life to the muscular dystrophy charity. He made no money—no salary, no expense reimbursement. In fact before I committed to do the show, I went through the budget and could find no fee paid to Jerry. So I explained to the MDA suits that without Jerry Lewis, they had no telethon, they had no charity, and they certainly didn't have me. As we know, later they got rid of Jerry, and guess what? Goodbye, telethon. It disappeared faster than a White House classified document. The suits finally understood what I was insisting on, meaning that we keep it the Twenty-Fifth Anniversary *Jerry Lewis* Muscular Dystrophy Telethon, but that we do it in a brand-new way. And we did.

For one thing, for the first time there actually was a script. We booked guest stars, had a schedule of who would go on and when, and everyone was deliriously happy with the entire preproduction process. I couldn't believe it. It was show business utopia.

The first day Jerry arrived at the old Aquarius Theatre on Sunset, everything was perfect. Perfect outside the theater. But then Jerry walked inside the theater and changed from the friendly, cuddly, adorable little pussycat I had been dealing with into Jerry the prick . . . I mean lion. He ranted and raved and roared: the home base was on the wrong side; the teleprompter was in the wrong place; he couldn't see the monitors; the lighting was all wrong. He was a real pain in the ass.

At this point, I asked him to come over and talk to me. As we stood, quietly talking, I placed his hand right between my legs. He jerked away and looked at me like I was crazy and wanted to know what the hell I was doing. I said, "If you're gonna act like a prick, I thought you ought to know what one felt like."

There was a moment of terrorized silence on that set. Everyone absolutely froze in position and nobody moved, nobody breathed . . . and we waited. Jerry looked at me for a long time and then began to laugh, and I began to laugh. We hugged and kissed, and I said, "Let me go and show you you're luxurious dressing room."

Jerry's dressing room for the telethon was a legend. It was big and lavish and elegant and well appointed. Until I got ahold of it. On the door I had the sign lettered like this:

JERILOUIS — HOST

When Jerry walked into the room, we had put little piles of dog crap all over the bright red carpeting. He started laughing and relaxed. The lion was a pussycat again.

The secret to Jerry was not unlike the key to Judy, Frank, Dinah, Lucy, or any of the other people whom I have worked with. If you can make them laugh, you relieve the tension, and everyone can then do what they do best. It is a dangerous activity sometimes, but it is effective.

I had decided to be ready for Jerry on show night if he got uptight, and of course, being Jerry, he was. We hadn't been on the air half an hour when he turned to me and in a somewhat intense tone said, "How long are we?"

I said, "Jerry, I really don't know. Call the booth."

He said, "What?"

I said, "Pick up the phone and call the booth."

Which he did. I had arranged for a recording, and Jerry heard this: "You have reached the booth for the Jerry Lewis telethon. There is no one available to take your call right now, but if you'll leave your name, your number, and a brief description of what you were calling about, we'll have someone get back to you as soon as possible. Have a nice day."

As Jerry heard this recording, which was played out over the air, he got hysterical. For him not to be able to place a call to his own director was a risky ploy, but it worked because it made him laugh.

Soon after that, Jerry said to me, "George, you haven't planned this schedule right. I need a bathroom break."

Instead of arguing with him or figuring out what I should do, I walked over and threw a large green plastic trash barrel out in front of him and said, "How's this?" On camera.

Throughout the telethon, he tried to see if I had run out of ways to surprise him. Fuhgeddaboudit. I had had a month to get ready for him, and I was not going to run out of schtick. He got upset at one point, and I said, "Please, Jerry, please don't yell at me. I get very upset, and I almost get sick to my stomach." At which point I bent over his plastic podium and spread out a sheet that is available in your local joke store that looks exactly like vomit. When he turned and saw this very real-looking puke, he broke up completely. Unfortunately, it happened right before a very serious part in the show, which kind of ruined the moment.

Later in the evening, he again asked me some question, and again I said, "I don't know, Jerry, call the booth." He did, expecting the same recording as earlier. Instead a very sexy voice came on and said, "Hi, Jerry, I bet right now a blow job would feel real good." Jerry was not sure if this had gone out on the air, so in a moment his laughter, or his glee at thinking about a blow job, turned to shock, terror, concern, and disbelief. All these emotions were, of course, exactly the desired reaction.

The list of these "events" that I had planned for Jerry was long and extremely effective. We had noisemakers, sound effects, props, sight gags; we even had a small remote-controlled speaker device that when triggered would emit a very loud but recognizable series of fart sounds. New farts, not the old Judy Garland farts. Hey, I don't recycle farts. Material, maybe. But not farts. My farts worked for Jerry Lewis. We had to be careful not to use that when he was on the air, but any time he was having a serious discussion with a member of the crew or staff, you can bet that the tension would be broken with a real "ripper."

In the middle of the night, he started talking about how tired he was, so we had Ed McMahon and Leeza Gibbons walk through behind him in pajamas and a nightgown and carrying teddy bears, telling him they were going to turn in, so he should stay there and lock up. None of this was planned, and it gave Jerry something to react to in a more improvisational way than the normal kind of set-up joke that they had been doing before. It was great fun, and it was an opportunity to have a lot of laughs in a show that for so many years meant so much to so many.

A few years later we wanted to honor Jerry with a Lifetime Achievement Award on the American Comedy Awards, and Jerry said, "Are you serious? But no jokes. And no farts."

I said, "Absolutely not."

My daughter Maria and Donn Hoyer, an absolutely genius editor, were putting together a retrospective. We took all of Jerry's tapes and films and put them together into a truly magnificent twelve-minute retrospective. Looking through those tapes, one realizes what a magnificent performer and creative genius Jerry really was. I gained a new and even greater respect for him. When we were almost finished, Jerry flew in to take a look at it. I had him picked up at the airport in the biggest, longest, whitest limousine that ever existed . . . and to make it even better, as he got off the plane, a beautiful blonde met him to carry his briefcase and hold the door open for him as he got into the limo. Knowing Jerry, I had her get in the limo with him. They drove to the offices of my production company, the Editing Co., where there was a red carpet leading from the car to the front door. As Jerry entered, we presented him with a five-pound box of chocolates for Valentine's Day. Jerry came upstairs to find we had laid out a buffet with all his favorite delicatessen foods. From the look on Jerry's face, you could tell that he thought that I had finally developed the proper respect for his career. Then we showed him the tape and he knew we all thought of him as the king.

Then Joey Stabile asked Jerry if he could have a bite of some of his chocolates. They opened the box and there were five pounds of candy, almost every piece with a big bite taken out of it. Some of them had a finger just pushed through, while other ones had lipstick on them. There was not one single piece of chocolate in that box that had not been mutilated or bitten into. Just trying to take the tension out of the coil.

The last episode of our long and wonderful relationship came when HBO wanted to honor Jerry at the Aspen Comedy Festival. I called and told him not to worry, it was going to be done with just as much real respect that the comedians showed him at the American Comedy Awards. All the comedians came to be part of it: Steve Martin, Mike Nichols, the Smothers Brothers, Robert Klein, Robin Williams, and many others. Just as the program was ending and Jerry had almost polished off a wonderful bottle of Petrus, someone asked him who he thought were the funny women in show business. Jerry, as a joke, kind of laughed and said, "I don't really think there are any funny women in television." The people there understood it was Jerry trying to make a joke and laughed, and everyone gave him a standing ovation. Unfortunately, there was a reporter there who took Jerry seriously and released the story that Jerry had said there were no funny women. That is not actually what he said, and it is certainly not what he meant, but the cry of outrage rang out through the media. Fortunately it blew over, and Jerry never really left his rightful position of respect and importance in an industry that he has contributed so much to.

I was and will always remain a big fan of Jerry Lewis. He was, without a doubt, one of the most talented people I have ever worked with or known. Even when the pussycat turned into a lion.

GOLDIE AND OPERATION SMILE

One of the causes I believe in is Operation Smile, an organization dedicated to helping children with cleft lips or palates. Their doctors arrive in a country, set up an operating room, and restore the faces of hundreds of children within a few days.

Goldie is who told me about it. She had been to Lima, Peru, to see their work up close. When she returned, she wanted to have a fund-raiser for Operation Smile, and she wanted me to produce it. Whenever Goldie calls me, it's not a question of yes or no, only when. Next thing I knew, I was at a meeting where I found out it had been already decided that the event would be at the Airplane Museum in Culver City. It would be the normal kind of fundraiser with a couple of acts and then some speakers asking for contributions. Very typical Hollywood fundraiser . . . but Goldie is anything but typical. She took a look at the plans for the Airplane Museum, called me, and said that she had been thinking about it and wondered what I thought of her giving the party in her backyard. Goldie's backyard is not an easy place to give a party or present a show. There is a sunken tennis court, a pool, different areas on different levels, and rock gardens, and none of that would lend itself to five hundred people coming to a fundraiser. I mentioned all this, which caused Goldie to say, "Well, figure it out, because it would be much more fun in my backyard."

So I went to Goldie's house with my team, and we found a way to cover the pool, raise the tennis court, and create different performance areas where people could mix without it looking like a normal event. We arranged for African chanters, salsa dancers, and sitar music so there would be a variety of ethnic and spiritual entertainment.

But in addition to entertainment, we needed to figure out a way to tug at the guests' heartstrings so they would write big checks. The key to that came when I saw the video of Goldie's trip to Lima, and I realized why Goldie was so passionate about this cause. When she was there, one of the children being operated on was older than the rest and was certainly more deformed than any of the other kids. He had traveled many days to get to Lima, even though he was told there was no way he would be chosen out of the hundreds of potential recipients of these complicated operations. This boy was eight years old and had been living on the street, eating out of dumpsters and sleeping in doorways. He had no family, no home, and no friends. Goldie met him and made sure he was chosen, and on the day of his operation, Goldie and Kurt Russell were there for him. Goldie was in the room with the doctors when they operated on him and next to his bed when he woke up. All of this was on the videotape that we looked at. I immediately called Operation Smile and said, "We must bring this young man to California to attend the fundraiser."

To set it up, I asked my daughter Maria to put together a piece about Operation Smile that showcased Juan and his successful operation. Meanwhile, the organization found the boy and got him to America. We brought Juan to LA and had him hide in the house during the event while we ran Maria's videotape. The tape was magnificent. Damn, that woman can put together emotionally packed videos. She could make a rock cry. Following the videotape, which absolutely thrilled everyone, Kurt came out and said, "Now you know why you are here. There are forms on your table so that you may fill them out. You should know that for every $750 you donate, a child can have a new face. We're going to need more of those forms. Would you ask that young man to bring them out and bring pencils?" Out from the house walked Juan, whom Goldie had not seen since she left him at the hospital. He had his new face, and he ran up to the stage. It was so powerful that even agents started writing checks.

THE NIGHT I THREATENED TO HURT GREGORY HINES

Sammy Davis Jr. and I had been buddies ever since I bought that house for him in a restricted neighborhood. We went back over thirty years. I saw his ups and downs, and in 1989, I knew that Sam was really hurting. He had friends but no money, and his career was far from hot. But I had a light bulb moment: What if we had a tele-vised tribute to Sammy? ABC liked it . . . but would not buy the show unless I guaranteed that I would deliver Eddie Murphy, Whit-ney Houston, Bill Cosby, Michael Jackson, and Frank Sinatra, none of whom was at that point available. But since this was for Sammy, I knew they'd come through. They were booked, and the deal was set to do the show. Everything was going great, and then a few days after the show was locked, Sammy's lawyer met me to tell me that Sammy had throat cancer and was undergoing radiation treatment, and that it did not look good. He asked if I wanted to continue with the special. I said if Sammy did, I did. Sammy gave his okay, and the *Sammy Davis Jr. 60th Anniversary Celebration* was under way.

It was touch and go whether Sammy was going to be healthy enough to actually come to the event, but his doctor said he could try. The challenge was that when the cancer was discovered, Sammy was given the choice of either removing the cancer, which would have meant taking out his voice box, or going for radiation. The sur-gery would almost certainly get rid of the cancer, but Sammy said if he couldn't sing, he didn't want to live. Would any of us have made that same choice? Who knows, but none of us are Sammy Davis Jr. By the time taping came around, Sam's throat was black from the radiation, the treatment wasn't working, he was very frail, and the clock was ticking. To make it as easy for him as we could, we arranged a box seat for him right in the orchestra pit, so Sammy could see both the show and the audience. But up until showtime, we had no idea if Sammy would make it there that night.

Eddie Murphy hosted the show. At that point, Eddie was red hot, but ABC was a little nervous about what he was going to do. When Eddie arrived for the afternoon rehearsal, I asked if I could talk to him for a few moments so that I could explain that the evening was going to be like a big living room, and that Sammy's family and friends would all be there, including his children, his wife, and his mother. Eddie looked at me and said, "So you don't want me to say 'mutherfucker,' do you?"

I explained that would be a really good start, because I didn't think "mutherfucker" would go down too well.

Eddie said, "Okay, I won't say 'mutherfucker,' is there anything else?"

I felt I was so far ahead with the elimination of "mutherfucker," I could live with the rest of his vocabulary.

Now one of my commitments with ABC had been that I would deliver Michael Jackson, but as we got closer to the show, I became more and more nervous, because I had no idea what Michael was going to sing. He was a bit skittish ever since he had been in that commercial where he had gotten burned. This was just one of the five hundred reasons we couldn't seem to nail Michael down. Our writer Buz Kohan and director Jeff Margolis and I had meeting after meeting with Michael as we got closer to the show. The meetings were great—Michael loved Sammy and was really enthused about performing—but we were getting nowhere in terms of him telling us what he would or could sing.

Then Buz Kohan came up with a brilliant idea. He wrote a wonderful poem for Michael to read called "You Were There." The poem references the many recent social changes that had been helped in a large way by the presence of Sammy Davis. Michael read the poem and loved it so much he asked if Buz thought we might be able to write a melody with the poem. Buz and I had worked together long enough that he would say yes to everything. I was real glad he said yes to this.

The night before the show, Michael arrived at the Shrine Auditorium at approximately nine o'clock. We were still camera blocking with a full orchestra. Michael, Buz, and I went in the Exposition Hall next door, and at that point the only things in the hall were the three of us and a grand piano . . . and I was leaving soon. The two of them stood in there for two hours and wrote a great song. The minute the song was completed, Buz gave it to Glen Roven, our musical director, who went home and wrote an arrangement. We continued to block the show and rehearse. At approximately 12:30 A.M., while everybody was on golden time, Glen Roven returned with the arrangement for "You Were There," and Michael began to rehearse it with the full orchestra. We were aware that if this could be done, it would be quite a moment. We also were aware that Michael Jackson rehearsed everything he did for months and months. He certainly never wrote a song, learned the song, and performed the song all within a space of thirty-six hours. But he did it for Sammy.

Someone else who did something special for Sammy was Goldie. Here was her video message to him:

When I was first starting out in show business, hmm. I was—oops! [*laughs*] What's this? [*GOLDIE is momentarily distracted before resuming.*] I was living in New York, and I was a dancer, and I auditioned for everything that came along. I even auditioned for *Golden Boy*, but I didn't get it. That's okay. I *did* meet a choreographer, however, and one day he gave me a call, and he told me that Sammy was throwing a big party at the Rainbow Room and he was looking for go-go dancers and, well, to liven things up, if I would like to do that. And so I said, "Well, yeah. I'd love to do that." I called my girlfriend, and I got all dressed up in my little nothings and fringe things and put on my makeup, and I went to this great party. Now I was up on this little platform . . . very little . . . and the music went nonstop, and I don't think I ever danced so hard before or since. At the end of the evening, Mr. Davis *himself* came up to me, and he thanked me *personally*, with all these other people around, for being so good and working so hard. No one had ever said that to me before then, and I just went home, I felt like a million bucks.

Years later, I was doing *Laugh-In*, and Sammy was a guest on the show. And at rehearsal he walked over, and I thought to myself, "Is he gonna remember me?" And he said, "I remember you. You're that girl who danced at

my party at the Rainbow Room . . . and you were terrific."
And, well, Sammy, I don't know how many hundreds of
times you have made people feel special in your lifetime,
but you can put me down for *two*.

It is strange how these productions come together. Many times
I will have some very clear idea, about which I am completely ada-
mant, and inflexible, and stubborn. As the show develops, I realize
how terribly wrong I was. My daughter Maria worked on the show
with editor Donn Hoyer and a staff of people, headed up by
Suzzanne Stangel, who collected the clips and helped put together
the tape packages. For this event, I had given strict instructions that
I wanted one videotape section of Sammy's dancing, a different one
of his singing, and a different one of his comedy, with nothing to
run over three or four minutes. I arrived one morning to see a piece
that Maria, Donn, and their team had edited that ran twelve
minutes. I was immediately upset because I didn't want, like, or
understand a twelve-minute piece in the middle of the tribute. I
told them there was no way I was going to ever air it. Then when I
saw the tape, I was thrilled. I told Maria, "You got me." That piece
is one of the reasons we won an Emmy for Outstanding Variety,
Music, or Comedy Special.

At one point we asked Whitney to sing to Sammy. She declined.
Maria pushed me to get her to do it, and I said, "You tell her." Maria
knew Whitney didn't want to sing directly to Sammy, but somehow, she convinced Whitney it was a good idea. Of course it was
one of the highlights of the show. (Just another example of where
my daughter made me look good.)

At one point as we were blocking the show, I got a tap on my
shoulder, and it was Mike Tyson. I said, "Hey, Mike, nice to see you.
How ya doin'?"

Mike said, "I want to be on the show."

I said, "What would you want to do?"

He said, "I want to mess with Eddie."

I did what any good friend would do. I went up onstage and explained this to Eddie. I confessed that I told Mike it was all up to Eddie. Eddie gulped, and we stood there looking at Mike Tyson, wondering what in the world we were going to do. We finally came up with this: Eddie would start an introduction doing an impression of Mike Tyson, and Mike, unannounced, would walk out behind him and stand listening to this impression, and then he'd "mess with Eddie." It was great.

Stevie Wonder showed up and as a surprise brought an eighty-voice choir with him. There goes the budget. Bill Cosby arrived and, for the only time I ever worked with him, read a piece that Buz had written word for word. That's how much respect everybody had for Sammy.

A show like this is very difficult to routine because everybody is an above-the-title, show-closing act. So I asked Frank Sinatra to open the show. I explained to Cheech (Italian from Francis) that if he went on first, he could then get it over with, have a couple of drinks, and take off. He opened the show but stayed until the end. Once Sinatra was the opening act, nobody cared where they were in the rundown, but closing was still a problem. So we decided to go with another legend: Ella Fitzgerald would close the show. Ella was somewhat frail, so during the show, I asked Eddie Murphy to walk out with her. As bold as Eddie is, he was afraid to stand there alone next to a legend like Ella, so I had both Michael Jackson and Eddie Murphy walk Ella out to the microphone to sing "Too Close for Comfort." If you have Frank to open with and Ella, escorted by Eddie Murphy and Michael Jackson, to close, the middle of the show is easy.

The highlight of the night was Gregory Hines doing a tap dance for Sammy. Before the show, I explained to Gregory that we had obtained Sammy's legendary tap shoes and that, following Gregory's performance, we wanted Gregory to show them to him, so that the audience could see shoes that to me are as iconic as Dorothy's ruby slippers. Gregory got more and more nervous as the evening went on and explained that there was no way he could show Sammy the shoes. I explained to Gregory that if he did not show the shoes to Sammy, I was going to come right out onstage and hurt him. You will learn over the course of this memoir that this is a go-to "suggestion" by me.

Gregory ended his performance, went down and hugged Sammy, got back up onstage, danced again, and then went back into the pit. Since I was standing there ready to inflict great bodily harm on his skinny little tap-dancing body, Gregory turned around, went back, and was handed Sammy's tap shoes. The audience went crazy. Sammy put on the shoes, and as Gregory walked up the stairs helping this very thin, very weak and dying Sammy, Gregory said, "Do you want to do a little shine?" (shine on your shoes).

Sammy, in a voice that was barely audible, said, "Make it easy on yourself." Greg, at that moment, realized that Sammy was going to dance . . . and dance they did. They did a challenge dance where they each did an impression of the other's style, and as it went on it kept getting better and better. At one point when Sammy did "shave and a haircut" followed by clicking his heels together, Gregory began to try to top it and gave up . . . dropped to his knees . . . and kissed Sammy's shoes.

That special meant so much to me and to so many. It was a night that we will all remember forever because it paid tribute to a friend whom we will never forget.

Sammy died just a few weeks later.

THE TIME DUSTIN HOFFMAN PLAYED MAGIC JOHNSON

One of the most exciting adventures in my life was producing Muhammad Ali's fiftieth birthday celebration for ABC. And unlike everyone else in show business, I am not going to take credit for an idea that was not mine—take that, Dan Rowan, who said he created *Laugh-In*—because this idea originated with Howard Bingham.

At this point who Howard was needs some explanation. Howard met Ali many years ago, became his best friend, and, through his photographs and recollections, chronicled the entire Ali career. To my knowledge, he was one of the few people other than Bernie Yuman who was deeply involved in Ali's life and career who never, ever, in any way, at any time, took advantage of their relationship. Which is a nice way of saying he was one of the few people who never ripped off Muhammad Ali. Lonnie Ali is the other one.

We went to John Hamlin at ABC, who was a big Ali fan, and he immediately saw the value in this. However, as always, to get a network commitment, you have to promise stars. You see, networks will agree to honor someone, but not because they deserve a tribute or because they had enjoyed a career that made them worthy enough to be honored. The tribute is really a booking device in order to obtain the services of a lot of major personalities. This happened in our tributes to Sammy Davis Jr., Frank Sinatra, Richard Pryor, and many others; however, that is the way the game is played, and if you want to be in the game, those are the rules.

To help get commitments of stars, Howard Bingham took me to see a man he called "the Godfather," Clarence Avant, a show business legend in both the Black and the white communities. We walked into Avant's corner office, which overlooked all of Los Angeles. Clarence was facing the window, talking on the telephone. When he got off the phone, he turned around and looked at Bingham and said, "What is that white mutherfucker doing in here?" I sensed that 1) he was talking about me, and 2) this might not be going very well. But Howard took charge. He explained to Clarence the purpose of our visit and that we needed him to put the word out that this was not another exploitation of Muhammad Ali, but rather something to raise money for the United Negro College Fund, and so it was something that the community should support. Clarence agreed.

Thanks to the Godfather, bookings began to be confirmed immediately. Show business is not what you know or who you know, it is who can get you to the people who know what to do and how to get you with the people who can do it. If that sounds mixed up, it's not nearly as mixed up as my meeting with Clarence Avant, but things began to work very well.

One of our ideas was to have May May Ali perform a rap number while famous clips of her father ran on a huge screen behind her. May May was just a tad bit mistrustful of the chubby white guy running the show, but as things went on, she actually began to like me. We rehearsed the number, which had rap lyrics and hip-hop choreography. The day before the show, I asked Muhammad Ali to look at it, and he said, "It's not a dance number, is it?" Warning bells started to go off. He explained that as a Muslim, he could not stay in the theater if his daughter was going to perform a dance number. Once again, my sphincter began to twitch as the tension began to build.

Buz Kohan was standing there and looked at me as if to say, *What now, chief?* At these moments, it is always good to take a deep breath to keep from fainting. Well, I took three to give me time to make up a kind of semitruthful explanation. Remember, a producer is not under oath. Here is what I came up with: I explained to Muhammad Ali that what his daughter was performing was *not* a dance number. It was an ethnic lyrical recap in rhythm and rhyme of his illustrious career while she performed aerobic exercises. So it wasn't really a dance number. Ali looked at me a long time, somewhat the same way he looked at Joe Frazier at the beginning of the fifteenth round. He asked me to explain it again. I decided rather than explain it again, it would be better to show him, so I had May May perform her ethnic review in rhythm and rhyme of Muhammad's career while she did her "aerobic exercises," similar to those that would be performed in a gymnasium. It was a stretch, but the reaction of the people encouraged Muhammad to accept it and my very flimsy explanation.

We also had Tony Danza performing a dance routine choreographed by the brilliant Antonia Christina Basilotta, aka Toni Basil, who had found four boxer-athlete dancers to perform while Danza tap-danced. So far so good, which is what the captain of the *Titanic* said before the iceberg. Then we hit the iceberg. The news had just come out that morning that Mike Tyson had been convicted of rape and sentenced to go to jail, and my four "dancers" were angry. They had stormed into the rehearsal hall and done permanent damage to a couple of walls and quite a bit of furniture. Tony Danza was petrified because he thought he could be the next thing to get broken. By the time I got down to the rehearsal hall it was handled by Toni—for those who don't know her, she's a singer, choreographer, dancer, actress, and director whose song "Mickey" was a huge hit. She's about five-foot-two, a hundred pounds, but a combination Philly tough and Vegas tough. So she explained to her dancers that she was not going to put up with any more of this craziness, otherwise she was just going to have to slap 'em upside the head. *That* they understood a lot better than Danza or me. The dance number proceeded.

We had booked Whitney Houston, who said she was doing the show for nothing because the proceeds were going to the United Negro College Fund, but by the time Whitney arrived with her musicians and entourage, it would have been cheaper to pay her.

We had a monologue laid out for Sinbad, which he didn't do any of (there's a shock, a comic going off the rails) but instead proceeded to talk about growing up in the neighborhood where Muhammad Ali used to live. All good until he told Ali he was glad to meet him because Ali had some "fine daughters." At that point I wasn't sure if Ali was going to rope-a-dope him or if the boxer-athlete dancers were going to use Sinbad to break up some furniture.

The show was all set to open with Magic Johnson as the host. Great basketball player, brilliant businessman, bad talk show host (his was the *Turn-On* of talk shows), and as far as hosting an Ali event . . . well, I'll never know. Because that day we heard that Magic could not be there. Dustin Hoffman had agreed to do the show, so—light bulb moment—I called Dustin and explained to him that Magic could not open the show, and I wanted him to replace Magic. I think much of my life has become a series of me saying something and then long pauses . . . and this was certainly one of them. Naturally Dustin said he wanted to know what we wanted him to say in his opening. After I explained that we would send the Magic Johnson script to him, he said he could not wait to see how the words written for a six-foot-nine Black basketball player was going to be performed by a five-foot-five (maybe) Jewish Academy Award winner. I admit, it may have sounded like a bit of a stretch, but when we sent the words to Dustin, he said he was surprised that it worked perfectly and agreed to open the show.

One of the highlights of the night was Billy Crystal performing a piece about the career of Muhammad Ali. Billy came to rehearsal, and when he and Ali looked at each other, it was one of the warmest, most wonderful, emotional moments I have ever seen. They both loved each other, and to see two men with that kind of mutual affection and respect was a moment I'll always cherish. Billy is a master of taking the audience to places of laughter and tears—remember *700 Sundays*—and the piece Billy performed did the same that night. And no wonder! It was a letter from Nelson Mandela, who had just gotten out of prison. The letter was hand carried by the attendants on several flights until it arrived in Los Angeles shortly before the show for Billy to read.

I loved it when I could make Ali laugh. One time at a wedding of a mutual friend, I went over to him, leaned over, and said, "Do you know who I just heard decided to be gay?" Ali looked at me and shook his head no. I leaned over and kissed him in the ear. A big wet one. He looked, he laughed, he put his fist up in the air, he looked at me again, leaned away, laughed again, and tried to kiss me in the ear. Throughout the rest of the party, I would look over from our table to his, and he would blow me a kiss or wave his fist in the air. It was extremely gratifying to know that I had gotten such a big chuckle out of the champ and, more important, that I was too far away from him to hit.

HAIL TO THE CHIEFS

I was not a big supporter of the first Gulf War. Any time there is a lot of oil and a lot of money involved, I get nervous. So in 1991, when

ABC's John Hamlin called and asked if I would like to produce a television special in connection with the fiftieth anniversary of the USO and celebrating the victory of the Gulf War, my initial reaction was that I did not want to do a show celebrating the victory. However, I told him that I would produce a show celebrating the USO and the American veterans of all past wars, including the Gulf War. John got it immediately and sold the idea to his bosses, Ted Harbert and Bob Iger. But then I added one more stipulation, and that was that President Bush would be there, as would President Reagan and President Ford, and that all the ex-presidents would be surrounded by enlisted men and women. Not officers, or brass, or suits. There was no way I was going to show President George H. W. Bush sitting there with his chief of staff, John Sununu, looking over his shoulder.

Of course my demand was a major stumbling block because, well, people at the White House naturally wondered who the hell was I to tell the leader of the free world whom he could sit with. Admittedly they had a good point, but if they wanted me there, the president had to be sitting with enlisted men and women from the Gulf War, as well as veterans from Vietnam, Korea, and World War II. I even wanted to include veterans from our very brief and very ridiculous war in Grenada, which, by the way, we won in an hour (but we made the point, as they have not attacked us since).

My demand caused, as they say in diplomatic terms, a shitstorm. They wouldn't budge, and I wouldn't budge. That's where Spencer Geissinger stepped in. Spencer worked with the White House as our conduit to 41, aka President Bush. He was a terrific-looking guy and had been trying to do naughty things to our talent booker, an adorable, little blond girl with a cute smile and all the accompanying attributes. I explained the situation to her, and she said she would try to have Spencer work it out. We had a meeting, and it still hadn't been resolved. Finally the Bushes were arriving at LAX with this one major issue still open. But then my talent booker called me and said she'd heard from her friend Spencer on board Air Force

One, and that Mrs. Bush understood the situation and had convinced the president that he should indeed be seated among the servicemen, not officers and suits. I don't know how my talent booker did it. But as we know, politics makes strange bedfellows. Or as sometimes has been said, bedfellows make strange politics.

This made me very happy, because we had laid out a hell of a show. We were going to open with Frank Sinatra singing "The House I Live In," and following him we had a terrific lineup of stars . . . but what truly mattered more than the lineup (forgive me, Frank) was the emotion of the night. Eight thousand men and women in uniform, plus three presidents (Bush, Reagan, and Ford), General Colin Powell, Secretary of Defense Dick Cheney, and various senators, governors, and celebrities all there to pay tribute to the U.S.A. and the people who had served.

Now as always with any show I've ever done, a problem arose. It was agreed that President Bush had to get out in time to be able to arrive at his next stop in Texas before the curfew on plane landings. Even Air Force One has problems with airport bureaucracy. That meant we had to start on time and there could be no retakes, delays, or stops. Not only that, but our rehearsal schedule was accelerated because we had to shut down the rehearsal early enough so police dogs could sweep the building and the Secret Service and a SWAT team could go through the entire Universal Amphitheatre complex to make sure there was nothing there dangerous to the president. They looked for everything from weapons to broccoli (41 hated broccoli).

Coming up to showtime, it looked like we were in pretty good shape, except for one small little fact: Frank Sinatra had not arrived. This was a cause for concern because Frank was never ever late . . . except that day. But he had an excuse. The reason he was late was because the president was coming in by helicopter, and all road traffic leading up to the Universal Amphitheatre had been stopped. How a car on the 101 affected a helicopter, I'm not sure. Regardless, you would think someone, namely me, would have anticipated this, but somehow I didn't. So Frank was in a limousine, it was stalled in traffic, and it was 102 degrees. Not a good situation. Now in terms of pecking order, most people would list the president first, then everyone else. Not Frank. After all, presidents come and go, but being Chairman of the Board is for life. So Frank kept trying to get out of the limousine to go back home because, president or no president, he was not going to sit in traffic and wait. I had to send people out there on foot to convince him to come in. Finally he arrived backstage after the theater had been shut down for the security sweep.

Frank's cheerful opening line to me as he watched the security was "I'm not the fucking enemy."

I said, "I know that, Francis, there was a mix-up. Come on in, say hello to a few presidents, and have a look around."

He came into the theater and then hit me with a new problem. Frank had changed the song he was going to sing. His first selection, the one we had prepared for, did not involve strings. When he arrived, he said he was going to perform a different song, and although we had the arrangements for it, the new song required a full string section that we had not counted on. This was a problem.

George's solution: I told Frank Jr., who was conducting, that since we didn't have any strings, he could use synths. Frank Jr., who knew his dad pretty well, raised the obvious by asking what would happen when Frank Sr. saw that there were no strings. I said, "Leave it to me, and we'll keep his attention directed out in front. He is so mad at me, and I'm the only one he's going to be looking at." Frank rehearsed and, while glaring at me, did not see that all the strings had been replaced by a synth player. After rehearsal Frank went backstage and we got ready to tape the show.

By then the president and Barbara Bush had arrived in their dressing room amid all the security, the guards, and the SWAT team standing by, and I had an opportunity to meet them. I have always been crazy about Mrs. Bush, so that was a thrill. After I exchanged a few pleasantries with 41, I had a moment to talk to the First Lady, and I thanked her so much for helping us out with the situation regarding them being seated surrounded by enlisted men. I went on to explain that the decision meant a great deal to us, and I was very grateful. So far so good. Then since she had been so nice, I asked if she would help me on one more tiny little thing. Being very polite, and also intrigued by this odd man standing in front of her, she asked me what I had in mind.

I said, "Well, when the president walks out we are going to play ruffles and flourishes and then 'Hail to the Chief.' So since the next person to come onstage is Frank Sinatra, how about if we play 'Hail to the Chief' for him too?"

The entire room went very quiet. No one spoke. No one moved. As I recall, no one even breathed, because this was as close to blasphemy as you can get in front of a president. I thought the Secret Service was going to tackle me. This was the political equivalent of farting in church, which I have never done because I don't go to church. Within three seconds of having made the suggestion, it became abundantly clear that I had, as they say in political circles, "fucked up." Instead of Mrs. Bush putting me down, she patted me on the cheek and said, "You are a very, very naughty boy, now behave yourself," as if she were my mother, but then to think about it, at that point she had become everybody's mom.

I withdrew the suggestion before they withdrew me, and we went out to pose for pictures of the full cast. By then Mrs. Bush had mentioned my suggestion to Frank, which he thought was amusing but was appropriately horrified. When the picture of the cast had been completed, Frank said, "George, come here and let's get a picture with you in it." That is where the photograph that appeared in *People* magazine originated, the one where I am standing in front of the cast. Frank had just put his hands over my eyes, and Mrs. Bush had taken two fingers and put them behind my head as an indication of either me being a devil or her just being playful.

A few days later, Jane and Jerry Weintraub had a party for the Bushes at My Blue Heaven, which was their magnificent estate in Malibu. In the reception line, for some strange reason, both President and Mrs. Bush recalled the suggestion of "Hail to the Chief" being played for Sinatra's entrance, and Mrs. Bush asked me, "Are you behaving yourself?"

I said, "Yes, a little better," and Barbara and George Bush posed for a photo with Jolene and me.

Then President Bush asked the photographers to take one more picture, and said to me, "Now, do it to her." So I did. For the second picture I put my hand up behind her head, with two fingers up exactly as she had done to me. Those pictures remain two of my treasured mementos.

HAIL TO THE CHIEFS PART TWO: THE SON ALSO RISES

New Year's Day 2001. Jolene and I were in Deer Valley. The skiing was great, even my old knees were great. Or is it that my great knees were old? I was having a wonderful time when my cell phone rang. Not on the slopes, at the bar. The call came in from Jerry Weintraub, a Hollywood icon and a legendary producer. Jerry was one of the closest people to the Bush family and to the new president-elect, George W. Bush, aka 43.

Jerry was a playful puppy who occasionally did a little herb. He enjoyed life as much as anyone I ever knew. He had always been full of surprises, but this was a real beauty. Jerry wanted me to do him a favor, so I said, "Whatever you want, Jerry. I will call you just as soon as I get home." He insisted he couldn't wait that long and that he needed to speak with me straightaway. He wanted me to produce the George W. Bush inauguration. I reminded Jerry that I had told him before to stay away from the medicine cabinet. He then explained that this was very important and that I really needed to do this favor for him. I reminded him that I was not a big fan of George W., and as a matter of fact, I didn't think that he had even won the election. So that should have ended that.

He then told me that I had to do it because the inauguration was only nineteen days away. There was no way I could produce an event like this in nineteen days. So that also should have ended that.

But I then started getting a lot of calls from some real "heavies" and a lot of financial coaxing (I can't be bought, but I can be leased and rented). I finally agreed to go to Washington for an initial meeting about the inauguration. When I arrived at the meeting, everyone in the room looked to be under driving age with sideburns cut well above the ears. You know the look. Each and every one of them had been president of their high school class and thought they would be one day running the country. Instead, they were in a room listening to someone they thought was an entertainment hack. I sat down at the head of the table and was introduced. For once in my life, I really did not quite know what to say. So I decided to speak my mind, which often is not a good thing. To break the ice, I noted that we were in a city with the largest percentage of Black people anywhere in the United States, but I did not see one person of color in the meeting. I also added that we might be three miles away from the nearest Jew, and that was counting Ruth Bader Ginsburg over at the Supreme Court. These young people started dropping their pencils and looking at each other. So then I explained that if we were going to move forward to the next meeting, I wanted to see a half dozen brothers and at least three Jews wearing yarmulkes, and if one of them was Lenny Kravitz, that counted only as one category, not two. The young man seated next to me said, "Mr. Schlatter, how do you spell the word 'yarmulke'?"

I looked at him and said, "Young man, this is going to be a tough experience for you. The learning curve may be a cliff."

I had done my homework and informed everyone in the meeting that $12 million had been spent on the Bill Clinton inauguration and asked what they had to spend on the George W. Bush inauguration. They told me they had $1.2 million. I said, "That's fine for my fee, but what about the rest of the event?" More coughing and sputtering all over the room. We almost had some spit takes.

I then said that if we were indeed going to proceed with this, we would need to find a way to communicate and to also have a good time. I did indeed have a good time—I always do—but we never quite established much communication. I spoke show business, and they spoke Brooks Brothers.

The next order of business in the meeting was the announcement of the entrance of Karl Rove with his big idea for the ceremony. He ran an eight-minute film, which was a tribute to the past Republican presidents. I then pulled an envelope out of my pocket. I asked everyone if they knew what it was. I told them it was an airline ticket home with an open date. I explained that *they* had to do this, *I* didn't, and if this was going to work, I was going to do a celebration of the presidency, not a victory celebration for the Republican Party. Mr. Rove's neck started getting thicker. Given he has a size 20 collar, that is pretty impressive. I then explained that I was not there for them to gloat over an election that many people felt was stolen. Again, there was a lot of coughing and stares across the room. We discussed further that the reason I was asked to come was because the Bush family had made no effort to establish contact with anyone in show business other than Jerry Weintraub and some country-western stars. This was not going to be an easy show to book. I reminded them again that I didn't ask to be there, but rather they asked me to be there, and I was ready to leave at any time so as to not be there.

But then a funny thing happened to lighten the mood a bit. No, I didn't play my famous fart tape. At one point I reached down to put some lip balm on. What I didn't realize was that I had swept a tube of glue across my lips. This made for a lot of laughs when I had problems getting my mouth open to speak. Poor Jolene—she had been praying for this to happen for years, and she wasn't even there to enjoy it.

Now came the biggest challenge: how to book a show with stars, most of whom, if they were any more left leaning, would be ten miles out in the Pacific Ocean. Luckily, my good friend and agent Sam Haskell, who was the head of the television division at the William Morris Agency, stepped in to help book the show. But as executive producer, I knew I had to call in some favors. So my first calls were to Muhammad Ali's wife, Lonnie, and to his manager, Bernie Yuman, to see if they could persuade Ali to attend the event. Ali and I had worked on some events together in the past, and once he agreed to appear at the inaugural, booking the rest of the show was much easier. When the press asked Lonnie why her husband rushed back from Europe to do this for George W. Bush, she explained that Muhammad was not doing this for George W. Bush; he was doing this for George Schlatter. You can only imagine how this went over with the Republican National Committee.

Upon arriving in Washington, I found out that the stage was six feet higher than we were told it would be, which meant that spectators in the first thirty rows would not even see the president. This made no sense; then again, very little does in Washington. I kept asking why this was done and I never got a good answer, until I discovered that Dick Cheney had bad knees and didn't want to walk up stairs. Bad knees, bad heart, bad judgment—he hit the bad trifecta.

Another speed bump we hit was that Andrew Lloyd Webber was originally approached to produce this gala. That was a problem as I didn't think he could book the talent; not only that, Andy, as I was tempted to call him, had planned the whole thing around a retrospective of the songs from his new musical, *The Beautiful Game*. Now this was not a great idea, as the musical had been showing in London for only a brief time and no one knew it. The way we worked it out was I told Andy he could play the piano on the song "Let Us Love in Peace," and he could have it performed by someone with range. I suggested Sarah Brightman, but he explained she didn't have the range. This made no sense, as Sarah can sing notes that aren't even on the damn piano. Turns out the real reason was that Andy and Sarah were divorced. I ended up booking Jessica Simpson, Josie Walker, and the Hoover Middle School Chorus. I guess Andy thought the Hoover kids had more range than Sarah.

Security was tight, and since I had a beard, I was looked upon suspiciously by security as well as by the Republicans. I guess they forgot Lincoln had a beard and he was a Republican—maybe they were still mad at that whole emancipation thing. This made it difficult to get past the security barriers so I could continue to put the show together. Democrats were much more flexible on the Clinton inauguration, but the Republicans really didn't care, so we had to go with a minimal staff and limited facilities.

As we got closer to January 20, we started to hit roadblocks again on booking talent. Even with Ali's participation, booking was a slog. With any show, as soon as you ask someone to be on, the first question is to find out who else is appearing. Big stars don't want to be with little stars, medium stars think they are big stars, little stars think they are medium stars, and 90 percent of them have no realistic view of where they fit in the pecking order. This is where the most important skill of a producer comes in: the half-lie exaggeration. "Yes, big star, we are very confident the pope, Madonna, Streisand, and Clooney are performing their big dance number . . . do you want to come onstage before that or after?"

And when that doesn't work, you go to old friends. One of them was Larry King. CNN gave him a lot of trouble for agreeing to appear, and John King said Larry made a mistake appearing for the president because it was partisan. And we all know no one on CNN has ever been partisan. Let me digress (like you have a choice at this point): in my opinion the inauguration for the president was not and should not ever be partisan. It should always—now more than ever—be a celebration of democracy and an attempt to (re) unite America. If that goal sounds unattainably lofty, so what? The most important things often seem impossible to attain . . . but they are worth fighting for. Once Larry agreed to do the show, he waved at CNN one finger at a time, and he promised me that he would be there.

My next call went out to Colin Powell, with whom we had worked on the ABC special *Welcome Home, America.* General Powell agreed to appear; however, when he arrived, he was very upset. His seat in the presidential box had been taken over by Dick Cheney's daughter and her significant other. Therefore, Colin Powell had to sit out in the audience in the seats that were reserved for my wife, Jolene. This meant that in addition to the other people I had upset, I now had an upset Colin Powell and an upset wife. I was worried that one of them might never forgive me.

I also wanted Arnold Schwarzenegger and his wife, Maria Shriver, to attend, but as I later found out, the Bush supporters did not want Arnold there because he would have taken too much attention away from the president.

Finally the show was coming into place. We had Larry King as master of ceremonies, plus Andrew Lloyd Webber, Jessica Simpson, Marilyn McCoo, Billy Davis Jr., Radio City Music Hall's Rockettes, Brooks & Dunn, Jon Secada, Charlotte Church, and the U.S. Army Parachute Team all agreeing to perform.

The last booking gave me another light bulb moment. I wanted a skydiver to land onstage in front of the president. The Secret Service would not allow this because they felt it was too risky. They also thought it was as dumb as when I wanted to play "Hail to the Chief" for Frank. 43 wasn't in office too long before we found out what the words "too risky" and "too dumb" actually meant . . . but again, I digress.

This was the biggest challenge: how to make an event exciting and entertaining while the Secret Service was telling me no skydivers and, in fact, no one could go anywhere near the presidential box. So naturally I had a solution. When Muhammad Ali took his bow and began to exit the stage, I gave him a little "nudge" so that he ended up walking into the presidential box. The president got up and hugged Muhammad, and from that moment on the event took on a different tone, although the Secret Service agents all noticeably seemed to reach for that lump under their coats. They would never have shot Ali, but they sure were looking at me.

It gets better. I knew that we needed some young stars, and one of the hottest people in the country at that time was Ricky Martin. Ricky had appeared for me at the Carousel of Hope Ball in Los

Angeles and was a huge hit. Getting Ricky to do the inaugural event was not easy, because not a lot of young people were enthused about our new president. But I knew it was important because Ricky bridged the gap ethnically and politically, so we moved heaven and earth to get him to cancel his appearance on the *Today* show. He agreed to fly to Washington to appear at the inauguration, but made it clear he had to leave immediately after the event to take a flight to Paris, where he was appearing the very next day. Since Ricky travels with an orchestra, all of this required an enormous amount of effort. Then in the midst of helping Ricky Martin's team work out the endless details of getting him to Washington and then on to his next event, we were told that a television producer by the name of David Gest had whined to the Republican leaders that I was interfering with booking one of his events by taking his commitments, which we later discovered he didn't even have. I know—shocking, a producer lying. Shouldn't there be a rule that only one producer can lie on any given show? Even worse, one of those commitments he claimed he had was Ricky Martin, whom I was told we now could not have because he was supposed to appear at a youth rally being put together by the Bush twins. This was a disaster—not the first disaster of the Bush years—because Ricky Martin was scheduled to be our final act. I then called Spencer Geissinger and explained that there was a flight back to Los Angeles at five o'clock, and I was going to be on it unless he got to the bottom of this. Notice I have threatened to quit everything over the last seventy years except my marriage. At that point Spencer set up another meeting with my new best friend, Karl Rove, to make sure that I didn't fly my ass back home.

I met Mr. Rove in a cold room facing the Washington Monument. It was a warm room until Karl entered, and then the temperature dropped 30 degrees. I bet his wife gets frostbite if they ever have sex. I explained my plight to Karl, who sat there, very calm, wearing one of the most expensive shirts I had ever seen. He stared right at me showing no emotion at all. Finally Karl spoke (and by the way, let me clear up a rumor—he sounds nothing like Darth Vader). To my amazement, my new BFF Karl said he understood what I was talking about and said to go ahead and proceed with my plans for Ricky Martin. I did.

Before Ricky went on, I explained to him that after he performed, he was to go over to the presidential box and shake hands with the president and invite him to come out onstage. Ricky said that the Secret Service had told him specifically he was not to go near the president. I said to Ricky, "The president asked me to tell you to invite him out onstage for a bow." It may have been a lie. I also told him that the president really liked to dance. That might have been another lie. Lastly, I explained to him that he was not to mention anything about this to the Secret Service, because they would be fine with it. That was also a lie.

At the end of the event, Ricky performed his hit "Livin' la Vida Loca." And being assured how much the president wanted to meet him, right after he took his bow, he walked over to 43, shook hands, and invited him out onstage. At that moment, the Secret Service looked as if they were going to shoot Ricky once and me twice.

The president joined Ricky, and we cued the orchestra for one more chorus, and the president performed sixteen bars of the dance, which was seen in newspapers and television screens across the world. It kind of turned the president into a nice guy.

Normally the story would end here. But in order to help get some of the stars to appear at the show, I had promised each of them a picture with the president. Getting the pictures taken was the easy part. It would seem like an easy task for the Office of the President to then forward those pictures to the cast. However, the wheels of government don't turn slowly; they fall off completely. No one could figure out how to get the photos mailed, FedExed, UPSed, or Pony Expressed. Finally, after six months of repeated calls to the White House, an envelope did indeed arrive one July morning from the Office of the President. It was paid for by the Republican Party, *not* taxpayers' dollars. When I took out the contents of the envelope, what did I see? It was an autographed picture of the president of the United States expressing his undying gratitude and devotion to George Schlatter for having worked so diligently to make this inaugural event a success. That was fine, but the photograph was not of me; it was of my head writer, Buz Kohan. So there it was, a photograph on my wall in my office with a lovely letter from President Bush to George Schlatter . . . shaking hands with Buz Kohan.

HAIL TO THE CHIEFS PART THREE: LIKE ARNOLD, I'LL BE BACK

You can image my surprise and amazement when, four years after driving the Secret Service crazy a second time, I received another call from the Office of the President. Turns out that the reviews we received on the 2001 inauguration special at the Lincoln Memorial were so positive, I was asked to produce an inaugural event following the election of 2004.

My initial instinct again was to say no. But the pressure for me to do it was huge, and so was the money. And as part of my deal, I was even promised a meeting with the secretary of the interior to discuss my project to reclaim the millions of logs lying on the shores of the Columbia River from clear-cutting.

As with the previous inauguration, Team 43 waited until the last minute to begin to put things together. This time my contact person was not Spencer Geissinger, the Republican male model with whom I had worked on the *Welcome Home, America* event and the 2001 Bush inauguration; it was a young man named Jason Recher, who was the special assistant to the president. He was a very white Republican, which is redundant—a very right-wing Protestant choirboy who actually turned out to be a pretty good guy with one annoying habit. He would say, "I've taken care of it." Which usually meant *Please don't bother me anymore.*

Even after four years in the White House with the opportunity to invite celebrities to their many functions, the Bush family had not formed any relationships with any celebrities. And there was probably no one under the age of dead who really cared about being involved in the 2005 Bush inauguration except me, and I was getting paid. But the show must go on.

We decided we wanted Ryan Seacrest to host the Celebration of Freedom concert at the Ellipse the night before the swearing in. A great choice—Ryan was the hottest guy in television at the time thanks to him hosting *American Idol*. But once again, a problem arose. Ryan was taping his show the night before our event. This meant to get him there in time, a private plane would have to pick him up in Burbank and fly him to Washington, D.C., by the next morning, Ryan having had little or no sleep. We would then rush him from the airport to the hotel, give him a few minutes to change his clothes, and then rush him over to host our outdoor show. As with everything to do with the Republican Party, this took longer to arrange than I ever dreamed possible.

It wasn't until 5:30 P.M. the evening before Ryan was to depart from Burbank that they finally found a private plane to take him to Washington, D.C. However, there was a problem. The charter company announced that they would not extend credit to the Republican National Committee. I guess you can imagine my displeasure with this announcement and some of the extensive vocabulary I utilized to demonstrate the urgency of the matter. It turned out that the only credit card in Washington, D.C., that the charter company would accept for a $53,000 charge was George Schlatter's American Express card. I should have left home without it. The reason they would not extend credit to the Republican National Committee was they had done so before, and I believe the word they used was "stiffed." It amazed me that I had more money and a better line of credit than the Republican National Committee.

When Ryan arrived in town on January 19, it was windy and 3 degrees above zero. My new best friend, Jason "I'm On It" Recher had not been able to arrange for heaters in the orchestra area, which meant that the space had not been heated at all. In fact, all the heaters had been installed in the presidential box. Now this is a problem. It's not that I have anything against a very warm president; it's just that I like a warm brass section. Any trombone, trumpet, or French horn player will tell you that their instruments when played will collect a large amount of moisture. They will frequently hit what's called a "spit valve" so that the air can continue on through the passageway of the instrument and keep it clear. This allows them to play wonderful, melodious music. Which brings me to the fact that water and spit freeze at 32 degrees, and without a heated environment . . . guess what? Visualize a group of horn players whose lips are frozen to their mouthpieces and the spit valves are now frozen solid with their saliva. Luckily my longtime colleagues Gary Necessary and Glen Roven decided that the way to solve this was to prerecord the entire orchestral portion of the show. A very good idea, except for the fact that there had been a terrorist threat and all the roads were now blocked. Somehow, and I will never understand how they arranged this, the entire orchestra was transported from the White House to a recording studio in Connecticut. The orchestra members were not happy about this. The only thing I could say was "C'mon, we're doing this for the goddamn president of the United States!"

The result of moving the orchestra to Connecticut was that we now had a group of musicians wrapped up in ski clothes so they would fit in with the crowd and weather, pretending to play their instruments for Patti LaBelle and Kenny Chesney. There were other artists there, but I can't remember because my eyelids had frozen shut. But if you believe the news reports, there were performances by Yolanda Adams, Andrea Bocelli, the Gatlin Brothers, Mary Haskell, Daniel Rodríguez, Ruben Studdard, and the Temptations.

As the temperature fell below zero, the Steinway Company announced that if any damage was done to their piano, I had bought it. Since I had already overdosed my American Express card by paying for the charter for Ryan Seacrest, I was not anxious to buy a nine-foot concert grand piano. It made me sad watching the great

Van Cliburn rehearsing in subzero weather. He would go over and place his body, hands, and arms against exhaust fans so that he could keep from freezing.

The show was scheduled to be broadcast at 5:00 P.M. worldwide, including to our troops in Iraq. At 4:00 P.M. sharp, a pack of young Republicans led by Jason Recher arrived onstage to announce that the event had been canceled. My reaction to this was predictable, with some more extensive vocabulary. I explained that we could not, should not, nor would not let our troops down in Iraq as they were waiting in 125-degree desert heat in anticipation of our show. All the plans had been made, and we were proceeding with the broadcast to Iraq to show the troops our gratitude for their sacrifice. This caused these East Coast suits (men in black chesterfield coats with black velvet collars and fedoras) to explain to the president that it was impossible to cancel the event, because the producer said it had gone too far and refused to back off. Not only that, they repeated my promise and threat that if they didn't agree to my terms, I would light the show with flashlights and broadcast it with bullhorns. At this moment, 43 arrived backstage at the production area and appeared somewhat perturbed. The last time he was that pissed off, he bombed Iraq.

So the show went on as scheduled, and afterward the president told us that to show there were no hard feelings, we should all come back to the White House to pose for photographs. Of course the president had heard about the snafu with the backstage photographs in the 2001 inauguration and made a point of posing for a picture with Jolene and me. It indeed was not of Buz Kohan.

Now comes the best part. After the show was over and the bill came from American Express for $53,000, no one in Washington, D.C., remembered that they had made a commitment to reimburse me for the transportation for Ryan Seacrest. Someone even had the "huevos" to suggest that it was my patriotic duty to pay the tab. Eventually the check did arrive, and wonder of wonders, it cleared. However, the real wonder of wonders is that since the inaugural event in January 2005, I've had numerous requests to produce other celebrations for the Republican Party. Are they nuts or what?

THE BEST JOKE I EVER TOLD RONALD REAGAN

It happened at Marvin and Barbara Davis's annual Christmas party. President Reagan was the VIP guest, and as usual at events like this, he gave a speech and told jokes for about an hour. After he was done, he said, "Well, George, do you have any funny jokes?" So I told the audience my favorite joke about him.

> When Gorbachev was in the United States meeting with President Reagan, he explained that there was a shortage of many consumer items in Russia and could the president be helpful. President Reagan assured Gorbachev that he could. One of the things that Gorbachev said they needed desperately was condoms, and could he get an order for one million condoms. The president assured him that he could. Then Gorbachev said, "Oh, by the way, could you make them ten inches long and two inches across." The next day President Reagan called the Trojan factory to see if it was possible to get an order for one million condoms, ten inches long and two inches across. The factory explained this was an awesome order and an unusual size, but yes, they could do it. Then President Reagan said, "Oh, and could you mark them 'U.S.A.—Medium.'"

Part 3
The Birth of *Laugh-In*

T he first line in my obituary is gonna say, "George Schlatter, creator of *Laugh-In . . .*" or it's gonna say, "No one will know to this day why 100-year-old George Schlatter decided to go bungee jumping after a fifth of scotch . . ."

So this is about the birth of *Laugh-In*, and like most births, it involves foreplay, conception, and, somewhere along the line, somebody gets fucked.

It was the winter of 1967. I was doing a ton of shows, and one of the biggest and most difficult shows was Radio City Music Hall at Christmastime, which would be the first and only time the stage production there had ever been televised. Part of the reason was no one could ever make a deal, and part of the reason was that it was impossible to shoot in Radio City Music Hall. Too big, too dark, too expensive, too many unions.

Ed Friendly was in charge of specials at NBC, and he sold *Radio City Christmas Spectacular* to Chrysler. His idea was to shoot the show late at night after the scheduled holiday performances at Radio City one year and then broadcast it during the holiday season the next year. We did the show, and it was moderately successful.

For three years I had been pitching an all-comedy idea to all the networks and advertisers under many different titles: *Straight Up and Turn Left*, *Put On*, *Send Up*, *Whoopie*, and *Wackie*. It was to be a free-form comedy show connecting satire with cartoon kind of visual blackouts that would be lightning fast. Bottom line, I wanted to take elements of Ernie Kovacs's show, sprinkle in some of the things I loved from burlesque and vaudeville, and fill it with non-stop jokes.

Around that same time, I met a young English writer/performer named Digby Wolfe. We hit it off immediately and began to develop ideas. Digby changed my life. He was a political activist, perhaps even a revolutionary. He was exciting. He was a ladies' man. He loved music. And, most important, he was funny.

Digby joined me in working on ideas for a program that would encompass some of the comedic ideas from all the many programs that he had been involved with in England and Australia, such as *The David Frost Show* and *That Was the Week That Was*. Eventually, it was Digby who came up with the title *Laugh-In*. The genesis of that title was inspired by all the "happenings" occurring in the American counterculture: sit-ins, be-ins, love-ins, and smoke-ins tied to protest movements, consciousness raising, and, of course, free love. Now, whether you were "in" or not didn't matter all that much, the title was perfect for the appetites of American culture at large and contributed in a huge way to the success of the show.

Unlike Jesus, Laugh-In Was Not an Immaculate Conception

Back to Ed Friendly. He and NBC had nothing to go on the air following the Miss America contest in September 1967. Combine their need with my three-year obsession with this free-form comedy show and Digby's ideas and title, and now we were getting somewhere. Ed then came up with a plan where if he could sell *Laugh-In* to Timex, I would agree to go into business with him and set up a production company using my power base and my financial foundation. The main thing that Ed pitched was that he could handle sales and the contracts, lawyers, and network negotiations, leaving me free to just produce, direct, and/or write specials and series. Ed was a great salesman. He sure sold me.

So, how did it end up being called *Rowan & Martin's Laugh-In*? Concurrent with all of Ed's negotiations, I was working on reviving *The Colgate Comedy Hour* as a special presenting all the comedians and acts who might have appeared on the original *Colgate Comedy Hour* had it stayed on the air. The comics included Carl Reiner and Mel Brooks doing "2,000-Year-Old Man," Bob Newhart with "Driving Instructor," Shelley Berman's "Phone Call," a Phyllis Diller monologue about Fang, a Nanette Fabray song, Nipsey Russell's "Black Astronaut," and an Allan Sherman performance of "Hello Muddah, Hello Fadduh." These may not sound like so much in 2023, but at the time they were the hottest comedy acts around, and to top it off, I convinced Jack Benny to host the show. In addition I booked the funniest nightclub act in existence, Rowan and Martin. They were amazing, hysterical, professional—and they did not get along at all. Although they appeared successfully together onstage, from the time they walked offstage at the close of one engagement until they walked onstage at their next engagement, they didn't see or speak to each other. But that didn't matter; I knew they'd be great as hosts of *Laugh-In*.

So now we had a title, a concept, and hosts, and Ed Friendly and I concluded our arrangements. Without Ed's salesmanship *Laugh-In* might never have gotten on the air, but since Ed was also the buyer for NBC, it was a slam dunk.

As part of our arrangement, button-down New York Ed said he would come to Hollywood . . . but he didn't go Hollywood. Ed flew right over Hollywood and went Hawaiian. The first day in LA he bought love beads, shades, Nehru jackets, and a pinkie ring. He grew sideburns, stopped wearing socks, and bought a purple Chrysler with a front seat that could turn around so he could have meetings in the car.

Ed Friendly's first accomplishment in LA was to change the title from *Laugh-In Starring Rowan & Martin* to the possessive *Rowan & Martin's Laugh-In*, which they immediately took seriously. Changing this title eventually brought the show down. As long as Dan Rowan and Dick Martin remained the comics, it worked, but the possessive title made them think they could go in another direction. Of course, they never produced anything before or since (not to mention they didn't speak off camera), but this was not the first show to crumble under performer ego and partner treachery. Remember, I said someone was gonna get fucked.

No one really had much faith in the concept. The West Coast network executives didn't even bother to come to the taping of the pilot. We did have a censor, but he also did not believe it had much of a chance, so he dropped his notes to us through the mail and headed toward the bar.

So what was the secret to the series' groundbreaking success? It was due to Digby's creative input, the phenomenal editing of Carolyn Raskin, fabulous writers, the best staff ever assembled—which included a very young Lorne Michaels—and a brilliant cast, who all worked together on a new concept where the idea, the format, and the philosophy were more important than any one element or person. And what did I do? What a producer does: lay out a vision for the show, bring together talent, fight the budget battles, say no without getting too many people mad at you at the same time, tell little lies to keep the whole project going, and keep the suits away from the stars.

BEFORE THEY WERE STARS

The auditions for *Laugh-In* consisted of calling up people whom I had seen or people sent to me by agents or suggested by Digby. The network suits didn't audition or approve any of them. That could never happen today. All the cast, except Goldie, had been around for years, and like Dan and Dick, they were good but had not made it to the top. The network didn't know them, Dan and Dick didn't know them, and Ed didn't know them. But I knew they had good credits and worked regularly; they were just waiting to "happen."

Digby Wolfe had known and worked with Judy Carne. When Digby brought her in, she was in a loose summer dress and was not wearing a bra. She sang sixteen bars from a Broadway musical, did some high kicks, and flashed me. I said, "Can you take a punch?" and she said, "Yeah." She was hired.

Arte Johnson was working selling suits. He had enjoyed a very successful career in New York in stage revues and shows, but things were going slow in La-La Land. It wasn't even going very well selling suits, because Arte would hide behind the counter so no one would recognize him. Digby knew him and loved him, so we went out to Easter brunch. Afterward Arte came back to the house and played with our daughter, pretending he was a giant chicken laying Easter eggs around the front yard. He spoke with many accents. One was a double-talking Swede and another was a German who said, "That's verrrry interesting." He also did a Russian rock and roll singer. He was hired.

Henry Gibson had done a number of talk shows. He came into my office carrying a little bouquet, did a stupid poem and a back flip, but he was sweet and gentle and adorable. He was hired.

Next I got a call from an agent who said, "Wait till you hear this." In his office he had Jo Anne Worley, who hit a couple of high notes and told two bawdy jokes. She was hired.

One day in the mail I received a picture of Ruth Buzzi in her Gladys Ormphby costume sitting in a wire mesh trash barrel. I had seen her work with Dom DeLuise on a TV series, and I could see she was great. I think I hired her because of my passion for Gladys Ormphby. I must admit that the hairnet and the rolled-down stockings did light my fire. My favorite Gladys line was when she announced that the day of the office Christmas party, they sent her home early.

One day I went to the men's room in the Smoke House, which was across the street from our offices in Burbank, and was standing at a urinal facing the wall when Gary Owens walked in. I knew him since he was an LA radio personality. As we were relieving ourselves—which didn't take as much time for me in 1967 as it does in 2023—I listened to Gary's voice, which was always magnificent, but in a men's room it was pure music. It struck me that he was a very "mod" version of an old-time radio announcer. I asked him, "Why do announcers put their finger in their ear?"

He said, "Because many times they don't have pockets." He stood there with his finger in his ear, doing an announcer—and he was hired.

There was an adorable girl doing Dodge commercials who looked a lot like the only other woman I was ever engaged to, the five-foot-tall blond coloratura whom I referred to earlier in the book. Her name was Pamela Austin. She was hired just because she was so sweet and gorgeous.

I wanted to have Black characters on the show that we would use without any reference to or casting restrictions on how they would be used. One of the dancers on that show was Chelsea Brown, who was a great dancer and a beautiful girl, and she had the most adorable little lisp you ever heard. I've always been a sucker for a lisp or a limp, so I hired her. The only problem was that between the time I hired her and when we started taping, she had gone to a speech therapist and cured the lisp. She was still adorable, and she was on the first season.

I had seen another awesome young performer who was an extremely exciting singer and dancer, and to top it off, she was outrageously funny. Her name was Teresa Graves, and she became a regular and an important part of the cast. After *Laugh-In*, she went on to star in her own show called *Get Christy Love!*, but on *Laugh-In* she added energy, beauty, and excitement. Eventually Teresa became a Jehovah's Witness and went around knocking on doors to raise money for the cause. I don't know how successful she was in raising money, but we were all sure glad that she knocked on our door.

Now about the real star of the show, Goldie Hawn . . . I could do a whole book on Goldie Hawn, without whom Jolene and I would still be living in the Valley. Into the life of every producer one Goldie Hawn should fall. She remains pure magic. Goldie, my friend, my love, and the reason for much of my success.

We had other "regulars" like Flip Wilson, who was on seven of the first fourteen shows. Tiny Tim was first seen on *Laugh-In*—a result of Digby Wolfe interrupting a meeting to tell me he had something I must see immediately. I said, "Dig, can it wait?" Digby said no, and he and record producer Richard Perry brought in a man with a polyester coat, long black curly hair, and a shopping bag from which he extracted a ukulele and went into a falsetto version of "Tiptoe through the Tulips." We put him on the next show. When NBC saw Tiny Tim, they were horrified. I had to explain to them that he was actually a very famous personality playing this outrageous character . . . and they allowed us to book him. Looking back, I think I lied. When Tim went on, the place went crazy. NBC said, "You said he was a famous character," and I told them to look at the reviews, because he was famous now. Tim appeared regularly, and as a result, he eventually went on *The Tonight Show Starring Johnny Carson* and on tour.

Another young lady came to an audition and our casting director, Susan Silver, looked at her and said, "You'll be fine, come in Wednesday." The young woman said, "Don't you want to see me dance?" She was told, "Don't bother, you are tall, dark hair, dark eyes, high cheekbones, full lips, and a great smile—you look just like his wife. You'll be perfect." The day the woman came in for the first time, I looked around, saw her, and said, "Now that's the kind of woman we should have in the cocktail party all of the time." And, of course, for the next year, she stood on top of a piano, waved her arms, and said, "Sock it to me." Now she has overcome these humble beginnings and become one of the most successful studio heads ever and perhaps the only woman to head up three studios. Her name is Sherry Lansing.

And now, time for some of my favorite memories.

The First Nipple on Prime-Time TV

To shoot the opening of the *Laugh-In* pilot, we went to a big park in the San Fernando Valley. It was 103 degrees, and we were shooting all kinds of sight gags in the park with three crews going all at once and toys, go-carts, huge weather balloons, and everything you can imagine in the way of props. We sent Judy Carne to one end of the park where there was a beautiful setting, and since it was very hot, Judy felt the need to remove her top. She felt that need on a regular basis. No one objected.

And this leads me to our iconic *Laugh-In* "body credits." That's where we would take a water-based paint and draw designs, graffiti, and cartoons on Goldie's and Judy's bodies. They then danced, making these words move in an exciting way that would not have been nearly as interesting if CBS News had done this on Walter Cronkite.

That 103-degree day, Judy had a great idea: she asked if someone could draw the petals of a daisy around her nipple. As you can imagine, this was not a tough sell to the crew, especially the body painter. It's the first time a member of the crew offered to pay me his day rate.

So we filmed an extreme close-up of Judy's nipple with the flower painted on it and then had her hold other flowers. Full disclosure: I didn't see this because I was at the other end of the park. I might have stopped it if I had been there—unlikely—because this was 1967, and even the crew realized that there might be some difference of opinion on the acceptability of a nipple shot in the middle of the family hour. Although it's seeing nipples that often leads to families being started. But I digress.

When we were editing the show, we decided to put in a half a second of this daisy shot. When we ran the tape, that half second was plenty of time to recognize that it was more than a daisy. Nevertheless, since I was so proud to have done the first Grammys on TV and to have invented the Las Vegas lounge act, I wanted to be responsible for the first prime-time nipple on the air, kind of making me the Jackie Robinson of breasts. At the same time, I knew it would have to be a lot shorter than half a second. Film runs at twenty-four frames a second. Eventually this shot was reduced from twelve frames to six frames, and even then, you could still see what it was. Its final version was three frames, which is one-eighth of a second. Even Stevie Wonder could see it was a nipple. But for some reason, the NBC censors could not. My guess is they had never seen a nipple.

So every time we ran the shot for NBC censors, they looked and said, "What is that picture?" and we all said we had no idea. Now if they could have paused it, they would have had a chance to identify it, but it went by unidentified because at that point in the technology of television you could not pause videotape. So it went on the air, and every single time it ran somebody would say, "What is that?" It went on. Stayed on. The shot was in all the repeats. Not until the technology had advanced far enough could anyone still-frame the tape and recognize the fact that it was part of Judy Carne's anatomy, but by then it was too late, and no one wanted to tell NBC what it was and how many times it had been on. Getting away with the Judy Carne nipple shot and putting a single hand clap under the NBC logo are two of my proudest moments. Wait, you want to know about the clap?

ME AND THE CLAP

No, not that clap. A TV clap. The year we did the pilot for *Laugh-In*, we finished the show at three o'clock in the morning, and we were all aware that we had done something really unusual and wonderful. We were standing out in the parking lot, feeling exhausted but fulfilled, when we ran into Carolyn Raskin. She was one of the brightest and most creative people I ever worked with, so I always asked her, "Well, what do you think, Carolyn?" She stood there quietly clapping alone in the parking lot. We looked at each other and realized that was the only fitting ending for this crazy comedy we had just completed. So we went back into the studio, reopened all the tracks, and added the single handclap.

Everyone thought it was very funny, but on the third show, NBC called a meeting and said we had to discontinue the single handclap. We could not understand why, but they then explained that the hand-clap took place at the same time as the NBC credits, and it appeared that only one person was clapping for NBC. You can imagine how the rest of that meeting went.

I unsuccessfully resisted the temptation to comment on the fact that before *Laugh-In* came along on Monday night at eight o'clock, opposite Lucille Ball, NBC didn't even have one person clapping. Of course, my comment was not met with great enthusiasm from the network, but by then we were such a big hit, and my head was too big to fit in a size 9 hat, the chance of talking me out of that single handclap was *really* slim.

The single handclap became a trademark, and it is one of those little things I am justifiably proud of.

GOODBYE, JUDY. HELLO, LILY.

During the third season of *Laugh-In*, Judy Carne began to have emo-tional problems due, no doubt, to increasingly frequent visits to the illegal medicine cabinet. We also were aware that Judy had become very popular and was getting offers from *Ed Sullivan* and other shows. The *Laugh-In* contracts restricted the number of outside ap-pearances that the cast could make, so Judy's agent set up a meeting to explain to me that Judy was tired and needed a rest. They asked if she could be released from her contract and make only occasional appearances. Normally, this would hit like a thud. However, I had a backup plan to replace her: a group of the most wonderful, funny, outrageous characters I had ever seen. Their name was Lily Tomlin.

I first fell in love with Lily on my last day in New York after *The Steve Lawrence Show*. I went to the Ed Sullivan Theater to say goodbye to some of the crew as they were preparing a new show. Onstage was Lily doing a barefoot tap dance. That's right. She was doing a barefoot dance with taps taped to the bottom of her feet. She was adorable, and the idea was hysterical.

A short time later I saw a piece of videotape of this very attractive girl sitting on a stool with her face all screwed up, confessing that she had been a rubber freak. She was hooked on eating rubber: galoshes, raincoats, and even tires. The final straw was when she was eating a typewriter eraser, and her husband came home and found her with bristles sticking out of her mouth. The piece was hysterical, and she was wonderful. That also was Lily Tomlin.

I had actually wanted Lily for the first season of *Laugh-In*, but she had already made a commitment to ABC to appear Sunday nights on the new *Dean Jones Variety Hour*. Fortunately for everyone except Dean Jones, the show did not last, and Lily became available.

My first meeting with Lily was supposed to be a half hour, but as I sat in a room absolutely mesmerized watching her become all these characters in the blink of an eye, I decided to cancel all my other appointments. I signed her, and she was now going to appear on *Laugh-In*.

When I think of legends who had total commitment to their characters, three names rise to the top: Gilda Radner, Ruth Buzzi, and Lily. Lily always told me she wanted her characters to "feedback on the culture," and while she was funny, I always enjoyed the fact that each performance had more than just a tinge of truth and reality in the humor.

The first day Lily was taping our show, she was dressed up as Ernestine with the slingback pumps and the high hairdo. I was so sure that Lily was going to be a star that in her dressing room, we talked about the fact that after we taped this first piece, her life would never be the same again. She had paid her dues, had perfected her craft, and was now about to explode onto the TV horizon. Ernestine became an instant hit . . . and Lily became a star.

The one thing I contributed to the character happened right before she began to tape. I asked Lily that instead of dialing with the normal index finger, to dial with her middle finger, as Don Quixote would use a lance. No one ever realized that in order to reach all the people Ernestine intimidated, she was actually using her middle finger on prime-time TV. Jonas Salk may have come up with the polio vaccine, but where would prime-time nipples, single handclaps, Las Vegas lounge acts, and middle fingers be without me?

FINDING PURE TV GOLDIE

When Goldie first started on *Laugh-In*, we didn't know quite what to do with her because she was not a comic, she was a go-go dancer, and she was not really an actress . . . yet. It would take her about three years to go from go-go dancer to body-painted dancer to Oscar winner. But that first year we had to find out what she could do on the show. Finally, I hit on the idea of having Goldie do some introductions. The very first introduction she did, Goldie blew the line . . . and it was adorable. Gordon Wiles, the director, yelled, "Cut!" and said we'd do another one. I raced to my phone to explain to Gordon that I never wanted to hear the word "cut" ever again when Goldie was onstage. By the time I got to the phone, she had already blown another take. So I told everyone to take five, and I had the words inverted on the cue card because I was sure that by now Goldie had memorized the correct version. When we started taping again, the cue card boy held up the cards with the wrong words, and Goldie reinverted them back into the proper order and did it perfectly. From that moment on I knew we had a major treasure. Of course, what went on the air were the two takes she had blown before she did it right.

You know the giggly dumb blonde image? Truth is, Goldie was the smartest member of the whole cast. Goldie didn't make mistakes from being dumb; Goldie was just always thinking about something else. But because it was so funny every time she made a mistake, I worked nonstop to come up with ways to confuse her. She would be on camera, and the moment she started to talk we would make rude sounds, have our shirttails coming out of our fly, snore, wink, wiggle, twitch, fart, and do anything else that might draw Goldie's attention away from the cards. When that happened it was magic. Pure magic and pure TV gold.

ROWAN AND MARTIN: FRENEMIES—A NON-LOVE STORY, PART ONE

Dan Rowan and Dick Martin were older than the rest of the *Laugh-In* cast, which meant they were our connection with the show business establishment. Dan was very cool, extremely attractive, well-spoken, and one of the best straight men who ever lived; Dick, who never did memorize a script, was one of the walking wounded, whose reaction to life was total bewilderment. He was the perfect com- bination of morally challenged and hysterically funny. You know how they say opposites attract? What they never tell you is that at first they do, but over time they get on each other's nerves as they try to change each other. Dan continually tried to keep Dick focused, while everyone else on the cast continually urged Dick to be himself. On the plus side, that growing conflict between them became a vital element in the success of the show.

One of my challenges was dealing with Rowan and Martin's talking pieces: simply put, they were a problem on a one-hour show because these pieces went on forever—eight, ten, even twelve minutes. This was one of the reasons the brilliance of our hand- cupped-around-his-ear announcer worked so well. We would always bank on Gary Owens saying, "At that very moment in another part of town . . ." or "Later that same day the Lone Ranger turned to his faithful Indian companion and said . . ." We would use these pieces to interrupt Dan and Dick so we could cut back to Dan's end line telling Dick it was time to go to the party. This got us around some of the censor problems and made it possible to shorten the Dan and Dick talking pieces. It was just one of the endless problems for which the solution made the show so much better.

Everything was great the first few episodes. Then the strains began as Dan and Dick became extremely jealous of the rest of the cast. They never realized that the cast was what the people loved. The audience loved Rowan and Martin for bringing that cast to us and for sharing them with us. So there was tension between Dan and Dick and tension between both of them and the cast—but what kept them together was this: Rowan and Martin had a common enemy: me. They resented my devotion to getting credit for the writers and for the cast. And they really hated the fact that they could not convince anyone that *Laugh-In* had been their idea. It wasn't.

How I Ruined Dan Rowan's Broadway Career

Dan Rowan was the perfect straight man. His biggest problem— okay, second-biggest problem other than the fact he was having an affair with Mob boss Sam Giancana's mistress, Phyllis McGuire, which led to Sam having the CIA bug his room and possibly putting out a contract on Dan—was that Dan had no humor about himself at all. One year we were doing the Halloween show, and one of the blackouts involved Dan dressed as Dracula with a black cape. When he turned around, you could see that he had a stake driven through his chest. He sang "Peg o' My Heart" with his fangs in.

Dan was not a singer and couldn't find a note with Google Maps, so it took quite a few takes even to get him to do a recognizable eight bars of "Peg o' My Heart." And when he could find the notes, he couldn't find the words. It was hysterical watching him do this, so we did what we had done with many of the mistakes by stars on the show. We edited all those outtakes together. When it went on the air, it was one of the funniest single moments of any *Laugh-In*. However, immediately after the show I got a call from his lawyer, Ed Hookstratten, who babbled that he had been on the phone for an hour with Dan, who had complained that I had ruined his "singing" career. He said Dan had been up for a Broadway musical, and by me making fun of him, he had lost his opportunity to star on Broadway. I didn't take it seriously then, and as a matter of fact, I don't take it seriously now. It was just more evidence of the very thin skin that Dan Rowan was wrapped up in. Under Rowan's Rules, it was cool to make fun of Dick, or President Johnson, or anyone else, but no one made fun of Dan. And by the way, can you see him as Tevye, wearing a tuxedo and smoking a pipe in Anatevka? I don't think so.

Rowan and Martin: Frenemies—A Non-Love Story, Part Two

At one point on *Laugh-In*, as a little perk we hired Floyd Jackson, the famous NBC shoeshine boy, to shine Rowan's and Martin's shoes each week. Dan then explained to everyone he had a valet who would shine his shoes, so he wanted to take the money instead. When Dick heard that Dan was taking the money away from Floyd, Dick got mad. His response? Dick began to bring his laundry to the studio every week. You can only imagine what the cost is of having the National Broadcasting Company handle your sheets, pillowcases, towels, napkins, handkerchiefs, and underwear. Just another example of the pettiness that big stars can have.

One week Dick got upset because someone got a line that he thought should have been his, so he refused to come into the studio at all. Since I wanted to continue taping, I went down the hall and asked Johnny Carson if he would come up and read something for us. He did. We put Johnny onstage with Dan Rowan, and Johnny did a cold reading of Dick's cards as if he were actually Dick Martin. I taped it, and it went on the air, and it was hysterical, because Dan actually read through it as if Johnny were Dick, neither one of them ever thinking we would put it on the air. We did, so you think they would have learned their lesson. Nope. Remember, they're stars, not geniuses.

Two weeks later, both Dan and Dick got upset about something else, and neither one came to the studio. This was a bit more
perplexing, and it took me almost a full two minutes to solve the
problem. My solution: I got Goldie and Teresa Graves to read the
Rowan and Martin cards as if they were Rowan and Martin. It was
the only time in the whole series when Dan's and Dick's words on
the cue cards matched the words that went out on the air. No one
ever knew that Rowan and Martin weren't there, because the rest
of the show was filled in with material we had in the bank. After
those two episodes, Dan and Dick decided not showing up wasn't
working, so they had to come up with other ways to annoy me.

ANOTHER REASON DAN ROWAN HATED ME: PETER SELLERS

Jolene and I went to England during a summer when Peter Sellers
was dating Liza Minnelli, and I went by Liza's apartment to see them.
They were very much in love, but I am not too sure if it was with
each other or with themselves. The two of them were so fried it
was difficult to know whether they realized I was actually visiting
them, or if they were visiting me, or if we were even there at all.

While Peter was floating, I convinced him to do *Laugh-In*.
That's always the best time to pitch a project: when someone is 1)
floating and 2) shooting a movie with Ringo Starr that involves
fifty topless women rowing an ancient galleon. Which he was.
Peter agreed to do the show with the only stipulation being that he
could get to work with Goldie Hawn, Arte Johnson, Ruth Buzzi,
and Teresa Graves, but not have to do any of the Rowan and
Martin conversational segments. I said, "Of course." I mean, what
would you have said?

When I got home, I described my trip and the events to Dan
and Dick. They both said it was terrific. Their only stipulation was
that they wanted to be the only people to work with Peter Sellers,
and under no circumstances did they want him to appear with any
of the other cast members.

I think the reason Peter had those demands was that he wanted to schtup Goldie Hawn and Teresa Graves, preferably both at the same time. Unfortunately for Peter, no one was about to get close to Goldie, and Teresa towered over Peter, so even if they had ever gotten together, she would have hurt him. For all I know, Peter might have just wanted to climb Teresa, but I do remember he was very eager (and, later, very disappointed).

Now once again, I was faced with a challenge based on my overpromising. I had promised Peter that he could work with Arte, Ruth, Goldie, and Teresa, and I had promised Rowan and Martin that Peter would not work with anybody but Rowan and Martin. You can see how this did present a bit of a dilemma, but I had plenty of time to work on it because Peter was not due for two weeks. Why worry today about what you can fix tomorrow?

Everything was good until Peter arrived in the studio. I have a wonderful picture of Peter Sellers looking at me and Rowan and Martin looking at each other, as Peter realized that he could not escape working with Rowan and Martin, and Dan and Dick realized that Peter actually wanted to work with only the people in the company.

In the end we did some wonderful bits with Peter—one involving me on the floor on my hands and knees, with Arte and Peter both as Germans. As one of them went up and the other went down, I would give them different things to say. It was purely improvisational with no rehearsal, but it didn't matter because they were both fantastic improvisational comedians. Peter also worked with Ruth as Gladys Ormphby and with Arte as Tyrone F. Horneigh. That tape is priceless—Peter was amazed at the talent of our *Laugh-In* cast, and they were thrilled they got to work with a legend.

Postscript: Years later when I was producing a series with Bill "He Whose Name Shall Not Be Uttered" Cosby, I called Peter to ask him to appear, but he made it clear he really only wanted to spend a couple of hours. Once more, I immediately made a firm commitment that he would be in and out in two hours. He knew better.

Enter Digby Wolfe, literally, who walked into my office with one of the best sketches ever. The sketch centered on a foreign embassy with Bill Cosby as a butler dealing with four separate ambassadors interacting with one another. All the ambassadors were played by Peter Sellers. This sketch on a motion picture lot would have taken four days to shoot. Peter had given us two hours. But once he was there, I had him, and he was brilliant.

On that same show, Peter also did a couple of sketches with Lily Tomlin. This drove Cosby up the wall, because Lily and Peter were totally prepared, and Bill never really rehearsed anything. I think he never liked to let the script get set early enough or the rehearsal go far enough as a way of keeping everyone on edge and keeping him in control. That show with Peter and Lily scared Bill. But it certainly delighted everyone else.

BOTH RANDY NEWMAN AND NBC DON'T LIKE SHORT PEOPLE

For the 2001 Emmys, Jon Macks wrote a great joke for Ellen DeGeneres. It was the Emmys after September 11, and in reference to the attacks, Ellen said, "I think it's important for us to be here tonight, because the terrorists can't take away our striving for excellence, our creativity, our joy—only network executives can do that."

Every great joke has truth within it. For proof of the above joke, you only have to look at how NBC handled the huge success of *Laugh-In*. First they demanded that we fire Henry Gibson and Arte Johnson because they were both short. That is a good note for a producer to pass along: "Arte and Henry, unless you grow, you're fired." If the NBC execs were NBA coaches, they would have demanded the Bulls fire Michael Jordan because he was too tall. Then the best network call came when we were taping our fourth show. They told me that the "little blond girl" hadn't gotten

Goldie, George and Lily — Reunited

Miss A.J. Schlatter posing with Cher

The whole family

Biker George

The Schlatter's 25th anniversary celebration in front of their wedding photo

The cast of *Soul*

Paul Keyes, Ruth Buzzi, Jack Lemmon and others

Redd Foxx

Frank Sinatra telling George to shape up

George surrounded by his Emmys

Diana Ross

Sammy Davis 60th Anniversairy Special

Berry Gordy, Jolene, Michael Jackson and George

Robin Williams pointing

Muhammad Ali

Quincy Jones, George and Richard Pryor

Barbara Bush bunny ears

George Clooney

David Foster and Jay Leno

Jolene + George + the star

The star itself

anything right yet and she better learn her lines or she would be replaced. Goldie Hawn stayed and became a legend. The executive was fired.

War Games

Barbara Eden's *I Dream of Jeannie* aired on the same night as *Laugh-In.* NBC thought it would be a wonderful idea if our cast went on *I Dream of Jeannie* and Barbara came on *Laugh-In* as a way to boost her ratings. At that time we had a fifty share, which meant 50 percent of all televisions in use at that time were watching *Laugh-In*—more than the combined shares of all the networks now. NBC knew that having Barbara (as Jeannie) appear on our show would do a lot for her, so as a favor to NBC, I agreed that our cast would go on *I Dream of Jeannie*, and then the next week, Barbara would come on *Laugh-In.*

But I thought we needed a hook . . . which is why we came up with the idea that when "Jeannie" came on our show, we would have the worldwide premiere of her navel. Up to that point, America had never seen her navel. Why? I still do not know what the problem was. Having worked with Barbara as a dancer, I was aware of the fact that she had an adorable navel. Everything was agreed to, but suddenly we got word from NBC that under no circumstance could we show Jeannie's navel. This was disappointing to me because I'd had a little tiny four-inch-wide proscenium built with a little tiny curtain. You'd pull a string, and the curtain would open, and there would be Jeannie's navel. Everyone loved the idea. I thought it was great. Barbara thought it was great. Claudio Guzmán, who was the director of *I Dream of Jeannie*, thought it was great, and Barbara's costar Larry Hagman was the biggest fan of the navel's coming out. Which raises a metaphysical question: If your navel is an "innie," can it be a coming out?

Again, with my fifty share I was more arrogant than anybody has a right to be. I thought I had been deceived, duped, tricked, conned, cajoled, screwed, and shat upon. It seemed to me that the network had conspired for the cast of *Laugh-In* to do *Jeannie*, and they had no intention of following through with the premiere of Jeannie's navel. What really upset me was the fact that they evidently did not approve of this from the beginning, and they had no intention of ever allowing Jeannie to go through with this outrageous, irreverent, tasteless, sexist exploitation, whereby a woman of the twentieth century would actually reveal her navel. What made it even funnier was that Goldie and Judy wore bikinis frequently during *Laugh-In*, and the Dean Martin "Dingalings" showed more navels than an orange grove. Yet the suits decided this was an unviewable area of Barbara's anatomy.

I go back a long way with Barbara Eden. She worked for me as a dancer at Ciro's when her name was Barbara Huffman. She was an adorable little girl with the cutest tush that resembled a little shelf at the bottom of her back. Talk about "Baby Got Back." Barbara was working at a bank at the time, and Jolene convinced her to come into Ciro's for an audition. When she walked up onstage and turned sideways, she had the job even if she couldn't dance at all. But, as a matter of fact, she danced quite well.

Barbara was certainly an asset (that's one word, not "ass set") to the line at Ciro's. But I wasn't her only fan. One day I received a call from Elvis Presley. I thought it was a gag, but when I got on the phone, it was Elvis. He wanted my permission to take Barbara out after the show. I thought it was a little weird to ask me, and then I suddenly realized this was quite a respectful, dignified, well-mannered young man. I must admit I felt a bit ancient for Elvis Presley to be asking me for permission to take one of the dancers out after the show. I asked her about it later, but she just smiled. I asked her again, and she smiled more. I guess she's still smiling. Someone must have loved someone tender . . . Stop with the suspicious minds . . . I wonder if he was a hound dog. I could go on and on and usually do, but time for the next story.

CLASSIC LAUGH-IN MOMENTS

CHER AND THE MOUNTIE: I had gotten a commitment from Cher to do *Laugh-In* as her first appearance away from Sonny. We also made a commitment for Sonny to do a later show, but this was to be Cher's first solo appearance. She came to the table read and absolutely loved the show. She was having a great time, but I noticed Sonny had a somewhat quizzical look. It was a different time in show business then, because there were no agents, managers, or network brass who came to the readings. We had just cast, and staff, and only a few of the writers who came to each reading because the other writers were off doing what we affectionately referred to as "feeding the monster." What does that mean? Every Tuesday night there would be another 150-page script to go through. "Feeding the monster" meant dumping an endless barrage of jokes humor, wit, comment, political observations, and silliness into a vast bottomless pit that devoured it all. The voracious appetite of that hungry monster left us with what was called our first draft.

After that first read through, I could see that Sonny was still perplexed. He said, "I loved the show, loved the jokes, Cher was great, but what about the songs?"

I suddenly realized that Sonny was not aware of the fact that there were to be no songs unless we were doing a parody. This was not a variety show or a musical show. *Laugh-In* was just jokes, all jokes, and only jokes.

Sonny was intensely concerned, so I said, "Oh, of course, the songs." And in that moment another light bulb went off. I turned to Billy Barnes, our composer/music director, and said, "Billy, where is the song?"

Billy Barnes was a sweet, gentle, kind, thoughtful person who was almost impossible to upset. He looked at me as if he had never seen me before and most certainly as if he had never heard anything about a Cher song. That was undoubtedly because we had never discussed a Cher song, thinking, of course, that everyone understood that this was an all-comedy show.

Next, I did what any producer in my shoes would do; I proceeded to scold Billy for not having played Cher her song. I will never forget the look of total disbelief on Billy's face that I had turned on him. I then said, "You remember, Billy, the Mountie number." I swear to you, I have no idea where the words "Mountie number" came from, but this confused Billy even more. In the silence that followed, I just started babbling, explaining to Sonny that this was a great song that Billy had been working on as a duet with Cher as an Indian and Tim Conway as a Mountie, and they were going to sing together. Sonny explained to me that Tim Conway was not a singer, and I said, "Well, he's not a Mountie either."

I took Billy into my office, at which point Billy turned to me and said, "What the hell are you talking about, there is no Mountie number."

I said, "Sure, there's no Mountie number *now*, but in ten minutes when you come out of this office, there will be a Mountie number."

So once again I did what every producer does in this situation after he's lied: I begged. I said, "Come on, Bill, I'm in trouble here, write me a Mountie number. You know, Cher's an Indian, Tim is a Mountie on one knee, and Cher lifts his hat and catches Tim's nose in the strap and then slips the hat off as his toupee slips and they continue singing."

Billy pointed out that these were not lyrics, these were jokes. I explained that I don't do lyrics, I do jokes, and, by the way, I needed a melody too. Somehow, in about twelve minutes, Billy Barnes came out of that office with one of the funniest numbers you ever heard. Sonny was thrilled. Cher was thrilled. The Mountie was thrilled. And Sonny and Cher both wanted to know if Billy would do some songs like that for their act. I am sure Billy went home that night bewildered by his own amazing talent and his ability to recover from what had been looking to be a very uncomfortable rehearsal. Sonny was so thrilled with Cher's song that he asked Billy to write a song for him when he appeared on *Laugh-In*, which of course Billy did. Sonny came out with three members of the cast—Arte, Henry, and

Alan Sues—singing, "We're four undertakers who welcome you to Happy Acres." Not quite Cole Porter, but close.

BOB HOPE: One day Bob Hope came on *Laugh-In* to do a monologue. At this point in his career, Hope was the king of television, and no one would think of interfering with the king while he was onstage. Except me. During his monologue, I sent Arte Johnson out as his "German with the cigarette" character, and in his accent he said, "Das is verrrry interesting, Mr. Hope, but every Christmas vee vaited for you in our bunker, but you never came to see us. Merry Christmas, Bobby." And he left. Hope almost died. The audience fell apart, and it became one of the classic *Laugh-In* moments.

THE GIRL SCOUT HOOKERS: Barbara Feldon, aka Agent 99 from *Get Smart*, appeared in one of the sexiest pieces we ever had on *Laugh-In*. And the best part—Barbara never realized that it was borderline obscene. In the sketch she performed an interview as the leader of a troop of Girl Scouts who were all twenty-eight years old and had been involved in at least two marriages. Each of her "girls" had a pup tent, a bedroll, and a flashlight and would go on field trips pitching their pup tents right outside Fort Dix. Barbara had no idea why those cookies sold so fast.

COFFIN NAILS: Truth is I have about five hundred classic *Laugh-In* moments and I could share them all now, but 1) that would turn this book into a manifesto, and 2) it would cut down on sales of the *Laugh-In* box set. But here is one that rises to the top.

When *Laugh-In* was the number one show with a fifty share, I was so cocky, and so arrogant, and such a pain in the ass that I was sure I could do and say anything that would support my commitment to the little guy. So on our first season, we put together a

"Salute to Smoking." Obviously, this was a tongue-in-cheek tribute to smoking, and it involved a lot of people coughing. It even featured Dan Rowan lying in an iron lung. He looked up into the camera and said, "Sure, I saved the coupons, how do you think I got this swell iron lung?" It should be noted that every time you saw Dan on camera, he was smoking a cigarette or a pipe, and he eventually did die of lung cancer. Surprise?

In the same show we sang a song, "Smoking Is Good for You No Matter What They Say, Smoking Is Good for You So Just Ignore the AMA." I remember at the end of the tribute was a shot of the old airbag that used to be in operating rooms that would inflate and, as the patient breathed, deflate. The bag inflated . . . deflated . . . inflated . . . deflated . . . and then it just stopped and we said, "Another smoker just quit." It was as big and strong an indictment of smoking as had ever been done on television.

Two of our sponsors were cigarette companies. So, quite naturally, the network was concerned, and the cigarette companies were concerned. First, they asked us not to do it, and you can imagine my reaction to that. They got a fast "fuck you" and a mighty "heigh-ho, Silver." I told you I was arrogant, cocky, and difficult.

They then asked if we could routine the show so that their commercials would not be next to the "Salute to Smoking." We said that would be impossible because the show had already been routined. We were secretly hoping that cigarette commercials would precede and follow our tribute to smoking, which they did, making it much more effective. When we went on the air, viewers saw a cigarette commercial, our "Salute to Smoking," and then another cigarette commercial. We were sure that the tobacco companies would pull out of the show. Guess what? They didn't. The ratings on *Laugh-In* were so high that the cigarette sponsors would rather stay on the show and sell their product to that many young people, even if it meant being subjected to rather strong ridicule and an obvious indictment of their product and their intentions. The cigarette company sponsors stayed on the show, and they stayed on the reruns.

That is how impenetrable the wall of commitment and intent was around the tobacco message.

That is why I hope people will always think of *Laugh-In* as one of the best and most innovative shows in the history of television. It is also credited for being very influential, which brings me to . . .

How *Laugh-In* Elected a President

Probably the number one question I've been asked over the years is this: "George, how did you get Richard Nixon to appear on *Laugh-In*?" Although the question should be "Why the hell did you put Richard Nixon on *Laugh-In*?"

The connection was this: one of Nixon's closest friends, at least one who didn't go to jail, was Paul Keyes, who was also a joke writer who worked on *Laugh-In*. Nixon and Paul were so close that at one time Paul actually had an office in the White House. So when I said, "Let's try to get Nixon." Paul talked him into it, and he did it.

Why did we want Nixon on the show? It was because he was somebody no one could get. *Laugh-In* was full of people you couldn't get to appear on television. From John Wayne saying "sock it to me" in a bunny suit to William Buckley Jr. doing one-liners, *Laugh-In* was all about people who wanted to be on youth-oriented "with it" television.

We had Nixon say "sock it to me," our catchphrase usually followed by the person getting hit with a bucket of water. Now Nixon was not a natural actor, although a born liar, so I knew it would take some coaching to get him to appear human. I got him in the studio and said, "Now, just turn to the camera and say 'sock it to me.'"

He went, "Sockittome."

I said, "No, Mr. Nixon. That's a little strong, could you just smile and say 'sock it to me'?"

He said, "Sockittome."

It took six takes to get him to say "sock it to me" and not look angry.

And here's where things went wrong—not for me but for the country. Nixon, in a strange way, was actually very charming, so when it went on the air, it was so unexpected, and people liked the fact that he was willing to make fun of himself. And showing him as a "good guy," as a politician involved in a show that was cutting edge, hip, and a trendy thing to do made Nixon appear to be part of the mainstream. What it did for him is the same thing it did for Clinton playing sax on *The Arsenio Hall Show* or appearing on MTV and announcing that he sometimes wears boxer shorts. It made Nixon seem to be a guy you could relate to. Before that you didn't. He was a suit. *Laugh-In* kind of helped Nixon take the hanger out of the suit.

When we realized what we had done, and that it could help elect Nixon, I chased Hubert Humphrey all over the country. I got him the message every way I could, telling him he had to answer this. But he never did. Hubert Humphrey later said that not appearing on *Laugh-In* may have cost him the election, because it did so much for Nixon. Hubert was right. It's been fifty-four years and I apologize every day.

The Best Show Ever Canceled—Fast

Laugh-In was such a huge success that I was more in demand than a hooker at a Shriners convention. I know, it's not fair to compare a producer with a hooker. There are some things a hooker won't do. But as a result of the show's success, I was able to produce dozens of specials and variety shows and create a few more series. Some were great, others pretty good . . . and a few were, well, not too memorable. What follows next are just a few of my favorites, and by that I mean those with the best stories.

Let me put in context how big *Laugh-In* was. With its fifty share, today I would be making Elon Musk money; back then it meant I was convinced I was a television genius. The next few months would prove I was the first half of an idiot savant. And the show

I'm about to describe *was* my fault . . . all my fault. I was cocky, arrogant, and, as time proved, probably semi-brain-dead, but I didn't know that, so Digby Wolfe and I decided to push the boundaries even further with *Turn-On*, which we promptly sold to Bristol Myers and to ABC for an on-the-air commitment of thirteen shows.

The original title of the show was *Section 8* (which in the military meant insane); it then was called *Kockamie* (which meant cockamamie . . . go figure), and then we went through a series of other titles, but *Turn-On* seemed perfect because of the evolutionary period we were going through in the development of recreational stimulants. Today it would change its name again, as it would be in TV witness protection.

The opening of the show featured a little old lady sitting on a Harley-Davidson, looking like Jonathan Winters's Maude Frickert, wearing a helmet and saying, "Hi, boys and girls, it's time to turn on." She gunned the Harley and went backward, right through a brick wall. From there on the show got weird.

One of the sketches on the first show featured Tim Conway trying to unsuccessfully commit suicide by lying down in front of a car so that it would roll over him. It missed. Then he tried again, sucking on the exhaust pipe and performing other strange and exotic attempts of self-eradication—all unsuccessful.

Another piece we did on the show was with Tim at the police station, having been arrested for making lewd phone calls. He asked the desk sergeant if he could make just one more call, which he used to make even more outrageous telephone contact with people, including even the desk sergeant.

We taped the first show, which we previewed for ABC, Bristol Myers, and AT&T. They all loved it and increased the commitment from thirteen to eighteen. *Turn-On* was going to open a whole new world of television. The show was shot on film using diopter lenses with split focus and high-speed cameras for special effects that intercut slow motion laid over high-speed shots to make layers of visual comedy. We also combined a totally white environment and shadowless light, a lot like commercials do now. We used the white as an optical devise so that images floated in and out through the air and could appear and disappear just as readily. We created multiple images, with three or four jokes happening simultaneously, which allowed us to do even shorter pieces of humor than we had done on *Laugh-In*.

Turn-On did not have any music but was scored by a synthesizer, which was groundbreaking back then. Now it is quite common. The audience reaction was created using sound effects, rather than a live audience or an applause machine. The whole show happened inside a computer, and the hosts of the show were two computer operators who would program the different pieces. Everyone who saw it was absolutely blown away by it.

February 5, 1969. Our premiere. A date that will live in show business infamy. We got everyone together to watch. The show went on at 9:00 P.M. on the East Coast, 6:00 P.M. in California. Cast, fans, friends, and press were at the Bistro celebrating what was to be my biggest success. I was already trying to decide between a yacht, a bigger mansion, and a new Bentley. Fifteen minutes after the show went on, the station manager in Cleveland, who was upset with ABC for canceling *Peyton Place*, went on television, interrupting the show, and announced that the remainder of *Turn-On* would not be seen that night . . . or *ever*. Something about hell freezing over. He then put on a test pattern, then a black screen with live organ music, and spent the next three hours calling all the other ABC affiliates to convince them to cancel the show as well. And you thought cancel culture was bad in 2023. This schmuck had not even watched any of the show. He claimed he had been swamped with calls from viewers saying how terrible the show was, but I still don't believe him. He just wanted *Peyton Place* back.

And although it has been fifty-four years, I never miss an opportunity to make a derogatory remark about this brain-dead, wing nut, Neanderthal, dipstick station manager in Cleveland who killed the show before he had ever seen it. He set innovative television back twenty years. *Turn-On* aired opposite a brilliant drama that had been highly touted for many weeks, so no one was ready to watch my show anyway, but when this putz went on the air and contacted station managers all over the country telling them how horrible it was, we had no chance.

As this was going on, I got ready to explain to ABC that this was all part of my master plan, to do a really wild show for the first week, and then to slowly back off of it in future weeks. The next morning, they informed me there would be no future weeks. *Turn-On* is in the Guinness World Records as the shortest television show in history. It was canceled before half the country even got to see the show. And you just know someone will mention that at my memorial service.

THE SEEDIEST PERSON I EVER HIRED

For *Turn-On*, I hired the seediest person I had ever seen in my life. His name was Bob Staats. I was crazy about Staats. He had a character named E. Eddie Edwards who had various personalities, all with bloodshot eyes, a mustache, ear and nose hairs, and a shiny black toupee. He would say to the girls in our office, "Come, child, put nature's poultice on my sore place and make your own Uncle E. Eddie feel better." He would also offer the girls in the office an opportunity to grab a glimpse of his male member, which he would explain was a legend and by actual measurement was about the same dimensions of the right sleeve of a size 46 navy peacoat. Today we would all be sued or at least arrested. Back then it was accepted. Wrong, but accepted.

E. Eddie was a real pitchman. One of his scams was selling "Lap Stallions" in four different sizes: small, medium, large, and the "Ebachenezer Model" for the girls who just couldn't get enough of the fabulous equine wonder. His pitch was this:

Each stallion comes complete with little leather booties, so that there are no unsightly hoof marks left on the mistress.

They are the friend of the lonely girl. A Lap Stallion in
your home, apartment, condo, or single, as we say in the
trade, will put a little color in your cheeks, a smile on your
face, a bounce in your booty, and lots of sparkle in your
bright little eyes. Hans has brought back twelve of these
legendary Lap Stallions, which can become yours for a
small, one-time-only price of $29.95, and for the first ten
people who call—you will get your own Lap Stallion riding
crop. You give that to your cowboy, your jockey, your
fellow who rides horse stuff, he'll thank you till the longest
day of his life, and you can tell *your* friends that you got
the "big one" from E. Eddie.

Staats also dressed up in full bridal gown with a veil over this
black plaster toupee and a wedding bouquet as he played the
"modern" bride selling marital aids that belonged in any suburban
dwelling. If we were not careful, E. Eddie also went into impas-
sioned pitches for salami, knockwurst, liverwurst, bologna, and
kielbasa that were enough to excite any young maiden. And yes, I
put him on television.

I heard later that he and his partner went to jail for what they
call "the EK" (as in Ecumenical Caper—no one cared about spelling, plus K is a funny letter unless there are three of them in a row).
The EK game involved going to the pastor of churches in the poor
areas of small towns. They would discuss the church's maintenance
and devotional needs with the reverend, who at first assured them
that the church didn't have any needs, didn't have any money, and
could not afford their service. Staats and his partner would then
explain that their service supplied everything from vestments,
candles, and choir robes to religious artifacts, Bibles, and even
pew wax, and that they had a very special offer. The reverend, by
now, would be bored and say he was not interested in the offer, or
in them, or in their pew wax. At this point, Staats would come in
for the clincher and explain that since the reverend was the best

judge of the needs of the community, 50 percent of any money that the reverend paid them for their goods and services would be returned, in cash, to the reverend to be distributed among the needy in his community. Cash?

It was failure-proof. The reverend's eyes would light up, and he would ask what kind of paperwork and bookkeeping would be involved, since as a matter of fact he was indeed about ready to run out of pew wax. Staats and his friend explained that there was no bookkeeping involved nor any reason for receipts, vouchers, checks, or records. They were trusting of a man of God, and they would promptly return, IN CASH, 50 percent of everything the religious leader spent on the needs of his church in the service of the Lord. There was a whole lot illegal about this, which I believe a magistrate in Michigan pointed out to Staats and his partner just before they began to live rent-free for about four to seven years.

The last time I saw him, he was driving around Manhattan in a darkened limousine with a six-pack of beer and a very, very bawdy-looking young lady as they toured the porno palaces of the Great White Way. E. Eddie sure did know how to live.

One of the Better Shows in TV History

Sometimes the TV gods taketh (*Turn-On*), sometimes the TV gods giveth, and one of the happiest periods of my life was the six seasons that we did *Real People* on NBC.

Real People was easily as important a show as *Laugh-In*. Not as big a hit, but it changed the way television looked at news and information and, well, real people. Today every network has its own version of our show.

Let's go back to December 1978, nine years after *Turn-On*, so I had somewhat recovered. I was skiing in Vail when I got a call from my agent, who informed me that Fred Silverman, then president and CEO at NBC, had asked if I thought I could do anything interesting and funny using "real people."

I skied for two days, thought about it, then called Fred to tell him that not only could I do a show about real people, but I thought it was an excellent title. Fred agreed to buy one special, then that became two, which became four, and when we went on the air, it became a series of six shows. Eventually it stayed on the air for six full seasons.

As with many hit television shows, the success of *Real People* was an accident. NBC had nothing to put on opposite ABC's *Eight Is Enough*, which was killing NBC every Wednesday night in its time slot, and they were basically looking for some cannon fodder until they could get a "real" show ready. (Note for young people: A time slot refers to a specific date and time when you could turn on the TV and watch a specific show. If you missed the time, you missed the show.)

So I had the title, the go-ahead, the time slot, and the concept . . . Now I had to put together the cast. One of my favorite shows at that time was *Fernwood Tonight*, where Martin Mull and Fred Willard interviewed unusual, bizarre, and eccentric characters. Fred was absolutely delightful on that show because he was a playful puppy who could be very funny but had the aura of an innocent. I leaned hard on Fred to get him to commit to the six shows. And I wanted Martin Mull because he once said that I meant as much to comedy as a banjo means to a symphony orchestra. Anyone who comes up with a line that good deserved to be rewarded.

I had seen a stand-up comic by the name of Skip Stephenson, who was from Nebraska. Pure Midwest, harmless, and seemed to me to be very straight and cooperative and would not get in the way. I was wrong on all counts, but he did have an audience appeal to the goyim. Skip was popular, but eventually put everything up his nose. They used to say when Skip drove down the street, the white line disappeared.

So now I had Fred, Martin, and Skip. While we were out shooting the first batch of stories, John Barbour came by to visit. I described the show to him, and he said he would very much like to be a part of it because he had interest in this area as well. So he became the fourth member of the cast.

So, you may ask, who was the real star of *Real People*? Of course the real people . . . but if I had to give out an MVP award to a cast member, it would go to a young woman I had seen doing news and weather in San Diego and who appeared regularly with Regis Philbin. I always thought Regis was boring, but she was terrific. We invited her in, had a meeting, and never even discussed anyone else for that role. Sarah Purcell became a big star and at one point was the highest-paid woman on NBC.

Sarah traveled all over the world for our stories and did everything I asked, whether riding with the Pony Express in Colorado or skydiving from twelve thousand feet over the Mojave Desert.

Sarah looked like such a lady, but underneath lurked the heart, mind, and mouth of a wonderful bawdy "lady broad." And I use that in the sense that one Frank Sinatra would use it, as the ultimate compliment.

One day we were getting ready to go on the air live, and she made a last-minute pit stop in the ladies' room on the way from her dressing room to the studio. Unfortunately, no one had remembered to turn off her microphone, so the entire audience got to listen in to the sounds of her bathroom activities. When Sarah left the bathroom and came out onstage, the entire audience applauded at having shared this rather private moment with our superstar. Sarah laughed so hard we almost never got on the air with the show.

One time I was on a plane, and the flight attendant saw my briefcase, which said REAL PEOPLE. She said, "Do you work on *Real People*?"

I said, "Yes."

She said, "Oh, you must work for Courtney Conte."

I said, "Why do you say that?"

She said, "Well, everybody on the show works for him. He's so young and so bright to be totally responsible for such a big show."

I explained to her that I too was very impressed with the young man. That horny bastard had told every flight attendant he met that we all worked for him. The rest of us were his "support team."

Perhaps Courtney's finest hour was when Sarah Purcell was getting married. We decided to do it aboard the *Constellation* luxury cruise ship in the Hawaiian Islands. My chief of everything, Gary Necessary, who has the greatest last name ever, had arranged for a beautiful ceremony and planned everything so that we would all be on board the ship at one o'clock in the afternoon for the wedding, with Hawaiian dancers and with petals being dropped from helicopters. That morning as we were making preparations, I became aware that every few minutes a navy jet took off right over the boat. Obviously this was going to spoil any attempt at a wedding. Also, it was equally obvious that we were under a lot of pressure to get this done in the prescribed amount of time. So Gary and I turned to Courtney and said, "Hey, hotshot stewardess schtupper, you gotta stop those planes." It's interesting to see someone when they are told they must do something that is impossible. Either they collapse and go into shock, or they say, "Okay." Courtney is the latter. He took two boxes of *Real People* T-shirts, jumped on a motorcycle, and went to the naval base. We had done a lot of stories on the military, and the powers in charge there were crazy about Sarah and our show. Courtney explained the problem to them and was back in about twenty minutes. He had bought us ten minutes of silence with no flyovers, from one o'clock until ten minutes after one.

We made all the preparations, and right up until one o'clock you never heard so many planes taking off, anywhere, at any time in your life. At 12:59 I gave Courtney my *if you're wrong, I'll kill you* look. We began the wedding procession, and at exactly one o'clock the flyovers stopped. We played the wedding march, we had the ceremony, we played the recessional, and at exactly ten after one, it sounded like Pearl Harbor all over again.

That team and the great stories are why we lasted for six years, airing twenty-six originals and about twenty repeats. For a long time it was NBC's top show. Many people today credit the increased interest in reality television to *Real People*. Again, I'm sorry. On the plus side, *Real People* had a real impact. Like our story about the Tuskegee Airmen, which was the all-Black air force unit that never received the recognition they deserved for their heroics during World War II, until we featured them on *Real People*. Eventually they did a motion picture about them.

But that wasn't the only story we did like that. We did one on Carl Brashear, who was the first African American to serve as a diver in the U.S. Navy. He lost one leg, and in spite of that, he learned to walk again and to swim. He went back into the navy and became the instructor for all the young divers. It was a hell of a story then, and a delight to see it was made into a movie in 2000 based on our story. The film is *Men of Honor* with Cuba Gooding Jr.

We also aimed our spotlight on the Navajo Code Talkers. For those who don't know the story, during World War II, the Japanese had been able to break every code the U.S. military had. A young marine who had lived on a reservation said a code they could never break was the official Navajo language, which could not be learned or taught unless you grew up as a Navajo. Marine Corps leadership selected twenty-nine Navajo men, who created a code based on the complex, unwritten Navajo language.

The chosen men went to the Pacific, each one with his own bodyguard, which the Navajos never knew was actually an assassin instructed to kill them if they were captured so that the Japanese could not break the code. When they came back after making a huge difference in the war effort, they never received recognition because the military never knew whether that code would have to be used again in the future. We did a story on them and went on the air live and said, "If the viewers feel as we did, that the Navajo Code Talkers should receive some recognition, they should perhaps do what we have done and send a letter to the White House."

The next day, the White House called my office. They were not happy with me. They were totally jammed with phone calls, telegrams, and letters asking for a presidential citation. We explained to them that we felt very strongly about it and were going to continue to do things on the Navajo Code Talkers up until they did get a presidential citation, which, by the way, they received within two weeks.

But of all the things I am most proud of with *Real People*, this rises to the top. For a long time there was no communication between the U.S. and Vietnamese governments. We were approached by the families of the MIAs and asked if we could try to get some attention focused on the fact that there had been no movement in this area, nor were there any discussions taking place. We did a story on the MIAs, and as a result, we began having conversations with the Vietnamese. There were still no talks going on between the U.S. government and Vietnam, so we were the only line of communication for many months. Since we were getting no place, we decided to go to New York to celebrate Veterans Day, and as part of our trip, we made an arrangement for the Staten Island Ferry to leave its normal run for the first time ever and travel up the river and park right outside of the Vietnamese mission. We had tried to set up a meeting, but they would not agree, so we told them we were coming anyway, and if they wouldn't meet with us, it would be an even better story than if they did.

We arranged for a tugboat to pick up Sarah Purcell, Bob Wynn, myself, and a female cameraperson (this really upset the Vietnamese), and we went ashore right at the Vietnamese mission. They knew we were coming and did, indeed, meet with us. In the room there were a couple of officials, an ambassador, and an interpreter. In the meeting we had the wives of some of the MIAs, and we said that we had proof that there were still some MIAs living in Vietnam, and we knew there were many remains that had not been returned.

A spokesman for the Vietnamese said that all the remains of the U.S. soldiers who had been "killed in captivity" had been returned. There was an intense flurry of activity, and then he explained that he had misspoken and meant to say "who had died in captivity," not "killed." At the end of the meeting, they did agree to look into some of the MIAs we had mentioned. We took the tape from that meeting and sent it to the Pentagon, who sent it to the CIA, who ran it through a voice stress analyzer. The answer came back that the ambassador was telling the truth as he knew it; however, the voice stress test showed that the interpreter, who was of higher rank than the ambassador, was not telling the truth.

While it was a frustrating experience, within a few weeks, the remains of the husbands of the women who accompanied us to the meeting were returned. No explanation, but they were later proven to be the actual remains of those servicemen. The Vietnamese in the meeting obviously had not told us the truth. Three weeks after the meeting, the remains of many of the MIAs were reluctantly returned by the representatives of Vietnam.

It always bothered me that we were in such conflict with NBC News because they were extremely envious of the fact that we could do a whole story. The format for the news allowed only for a minute or a minute and a half to be told, and they resented that we could go into such depth on a story. Now, of course, we have wall-to-wall news telling stories about everything under the sun. *Real People* was the catalyst for this. Again, I'm sorry.

One thing I'm not sorry for is happening to see Byron Allen on *The Tonight Show* when he was eighteen years old.

I called him for a meeting and was so impressed, I hired him to make six appearances on *Real People*. So he could learn the ropes I sent him out with a producer/director who was an ex-Green Beret, Bob Long. After Byron worked with him for two weeks, Bob called me and said he might kill him because he was already selling Byron Allen t-shirts and talking about Byron Allen projects. He had the three C's: confidence, chutzpah and cojones. Combine that with immense talent and you have a star. And over time, all of Byron's early predictions, hopes and desires came to pass.

Unfortunately, when Byron became an entrepreneur and launched his own media business, television lost a potentially great comic. Still, I am justifiably proud and willing to take a little credit for having given him his first major platform on *Real People*.

Part 4

Stories I Refuse to Tell . . .
and Some I Just Remembered

In a life filled with ten thousand stories, there are a few I refused to tell before—either because the statute of limitations hadn't passed, or because it would break up a marriage, or because the stars involved would have wanted me to wait until they were playing that big venue in the sky. These stories follow. Plus there are ones that I remembered as I was writing this book that, frankly, didn't really fit an earlier section, but that are worth sharing. Either way, all these stories make me laugh, help fill in the canvas of my show business career, or give you a glimpse of what things were like in earlier times.

I Knew Mork before He Was Mork

I first saw Robin Williams in March 1977 at the Comedy Store. Robin went on late, wearing a straw hat, no shirt, and overalls. He was barefoot, had a beard, and looked like he was homeless. I'm not sure that is a politically correct term anymore. What's better—"full-time outdoorsman"? But I digress.

Onto the stage Robin bounded and hung the microphone out over the audience. His first comment was that he was "fishing for assholes." That certainly got my attention. To this day I don't know why he was looking at me when he said it. Robin then proceeded to do fifteen hilarious and manic minutes that were scattered, very funny, and wildly inventive. He was like Jonathan Winters on speed—and since Jonathan Winters was already like Jonathan Winters on speed, you can imagine what Robin was like. After his set, I made sure to meet him and told him, "Look, if you ever want to clean up your act and get into mainstream show business, call me, and you've got a job on any show I'm doing."

Three days later, Robin showed up at my office, clean-shaven, looking great, and announced, "I'm ready to go to work, boss." And go to work he did. He did six of the funniest shows ever on the new *Laugh-In*. Robin had four set routines, including an impression of Nadia Comăneci, which he did in double-talk Russian, and a gay Shakespearean actor piece, which he called "Two Great Lovers from Santa Monica." All of this was brilliant and reflected the time he spent studying at Juilliard.

The show should have taken off and Robin should have become a big star immediately, rather than later on *Mork & Mindy*. The problem was that the head of NBC was Paul Klein. Those who are creative produce, direct, and act; those who aren't become agents; and those who are too unethical or stupid to become agents become network executives. Which brings me to Paul Klein. I'd call him a suit except he wore sweaters.

From the first moment he stepped onto our stage, Robin was a major star, and the show got a forty-five share; that means 45 percent of households or viewers actually watching TV at the time were watching Robin. As a result, Paul Klein was convinced that the new *Laugh-In* was invincible. So what did he do? He immediately reneged on our deal to do one show a month for six months on Monday night at eight o'clock, which is when the original *Laugh-In* had aired. Paul had an inane new technique of programming he called "stunting." We would tape the show, and then he would hold it back and wait until he saw what the other networks were going to program, and he would then, at the last minute, slot the new *Laugh-In* against the show he wanted to hurt. Eight o'clock, nine o'clock, ten o'clock, Monday through Sunday, he would wait until the last minute to make an announcement. As you can imagine, I went crazy. This was not our deal. This was not what I was promised, and this was not an intelligent way to proceed with a new hit show. But contract or no contract, promise or no promise, that's the way he scheduled the show, and it hurt it. NBC wanted me to continue to do six more next year, but I realized that Paul Klein's broadcasting technique and philosophy would kill the property once and for all.

In the meantime, ABC was negotiating with me to buy the new *Laugh-In*, which would have been great, but we then found out that they had seen a Robin Williams guest shot on *Happy Days* and were negotiating with me only to keep Robin off of NBC and to give him his own ABC show. So if you want to know how Robin ended up being Mork and going on to a career for the ages, it's all because of Paul Klein.

THE MANY STORIES I REFUSE TO TELL ABOUT TIM CONWAY

His real name was Tom Conway, but he changed it to Tim because there already was a Tom Conway. Tim was hysterically funny with Carol Burnett, with Harvey Korman, and with anyone else with whom he ever worked. And by himself, left to his own devices, the man was just as brilliant. Tim was funny. Always funny. And for me, he never missed.

Tim Conway had many personal misadventures, none of which I will tell you about, so there is no use going into when Tim visited a woman's house and, upon the arrival of her husband, went out the back door and wound up jumping into a doggy run. I'm not even going to get into that.

I also refuse to include the incident when Tim had a number of drinks and wound up escorting home a damsel in distress who lived in Redondo Beach. Tim spent some time consoling this lost soul. He woke up at four o'clock, and only someone who has been in Redondo Beach knows how cold it can be. Tim bent over to light one of those little gas stoves with briquettes in it to warm the room. Tim is not mechanically inclined. Obviously, he had the gas on longer than he should have, so when the gas ignited, it flared and blew up in Tim's face, which burned off his eyebrows, eyelashes, and most of the front of his hair. Tim then thought perhaps it would be best if he went home. On the way, he stopped at an all-night pharmacy to pick up some eyeliner and mascara. The plan was to restore his sideburns, eyebrows, and eyelashes. Of course, the owner of the all-night drugstore recognized immediately that this was Tim Conway, which he mentioned to Tim, who tried to deny that in fact he was Tim Conway. Which might have worked until he managed to knock over one of the display racks, causing various beverages to crash onto the floor. Tim eventually got home, went to bed, and woke up in the morning to find mascara and eyeliner all over his pillow. I can't remember if there was a Mrs. Conway at the time, but either way I am not going to tell that story.

And the other story I most certainly will not tell is the evening that Tim wound up detained until the wee small hours and realized he might be in trouble when he arrived at home just as it was getting light. The first Mrs. Conway, as first wives like to do, expressed a certain curiosity as to his whereabouts. Tim explained that his Jaguar, which had always given him trouble, had power failure, meaning that he would drive for a block or so and the lights would go out. Since it was dark, he had to wait there until the car cooled off and he could then resume his journey with headlights, which continued to go out once every block or so. This meant that it took Tim all night long to get from CBS to his house. That was Tim's story, and he was going to stick to it. Mrs. Conway was very understanding, quite sympathetic, and let Tim sleep until about twelve o'clock, when she woke him up to announce that they were going to go to a movie in the afternoon. She also mentioned that while they were in the movie, they could drop off the car at the Jaguar dealer,

where they could find out what the problem was with the headlights. Tim protested, but they went anyway.

When they got to the Jaguar dealer, Tim tried to explain to the
mechanic what the problem was, and then he and Mrs. Conway
went to the movie. When they went back to the dealer, the mechanic
presented Tim with a bill for $350 for repairing the wiring. Of
course, two people knew there was nothing wrong with the wiring:
Tim and the mechanic. But there was nothing Tim could say to the
mechanic other than, "Are you sure you fixed the problem?"

The mechanic responded that he was quite certain it would not
happen again. Mrs. Conway was pleased that Tim would never
again be detained all night long because of headlight problems. I'm
not going to get into that story or the mascara story . . . or the
doggy run . . . or any of the other episodes in Tim's life that were
just as funny when he told them over a drink to me as his legendary
sketches onstage.

A Story I Refuse to Tell about Richard Pryor

In the early '70s, I was producing *The New Bill Cosby Show*. (Disclaimer:
I didn't know back then that Bill was a great entertainer and a shit
human being.)

On our third show, one of the guest stars was Richard Pryor.
Richard and I had known each other for many years and were good
friends. The plan was to camera block the show, rehearse it, and
then in the afternoon we would do a dress rehearsal, have dinner,
and come back to do the final taping for broadcast. And because I
was not a trusting soul, and mainly because I knew Richard, I taped
the dress rehearsal . . . just in case.

The dress rehearsal was brilliant. Right afterward, I told Richard
I had to do something onstage, but I would meet him in a few minutes in his dressing room to go over a few notes that would make
this brilliant dress rehearsal into an even more brilliant television
show. It could not have been more than ten minutes before I arrived

in Richard's dressing room. I knocked, Richard said to come in, and as I entered, I saw Richard, naked, smoking a joint, sipping brandy, sniffing coke, and enjoying some spirited oral sex while listening to an album by the Chambers Brothers. As you picture this, please note he was receiving the oral sex, not giving it, because we had a conversation and that would have been very hard to do since Richard is not a ventriloquist . . . plus that might have created an echo. Take a moment and visualize that.

Richard kept doing what he was doing. I said, "Richard, I need to talk to you." Richard then became a bit perturbed and, with his best possible soul brother attitude, told this large white brother to go ahead and talk. I explained to Richard that what was going on made it difficult to talk to him, as it was a little distracting. Richard assured me that he was cool with me being there, and I assured him that I would appreciate any effort he could make to achieve his happy end as soon as he could and pull his sad ass away from all of these activities so I could talk about the show. Richard gave me his hurt *what do I do wrong?* look and promised to be good. The young lady also promised to be good. At least that's what I think she said. She kind of mumbled, and I could not see her face. I think she said, "I promise to be good," which prompted Richard to yell out, "Good hell, baby . . . You are great!!"

Eventually I got to give Richard my notes and he agreed to stick to the script. At eight o'clock, Quincy Jones and the orchestra played the overture, and Bill Cosby came out, did a short mono- logue, and introduced his special guest star Richard Pryor. Richard walked onstage, looked at the band and the audience, took a deep breath, smiled at me, and said, "I remember one day I was fucking this bitch in the back of a pickup truck."

Stunning! A comic gone rogue! Censors, network executives, advertisers, agents, managers, and Mrs. Schlatter all came jump- ing on me at once, as if it were something I recommended he say. Which was exactly why I taped the dress rehearsal, which was what actually aired. Although I'm sure to this day people in the audience are still wondering what happened to the bitch in the back of the pickup truck.

Many years after *The New Bill Cosby Show*, Eddie Murphy called me, having heard that Richard was suffering from MS. Eddie thought we should do a fundraising tribute, birthday party, and celebration of Richard Pryor. I immediately committed to it and sold it to CBS, and we were off and running with one of the great variety shows, made up of guest stars, all of whom had a relationship with and a love of Richard Pryor.

Eddie opened the show brilliantly and then introduced James Brown, who did "Sex Machine." Patti LaBelle sang to Richard and hit notes that I swear had never been heard before. Lily Tomlin did a great routine as Mrs. Beasley, who had once been trapped in an elevator with one of Richard's characters. And other performers, guest stars, and movie stars all arrived and took part in the celebration.

Before taping, we were all upstairs at the Beverly Hilton to pose for some photos of Richard and the various guest stars for a publicity shot. Everyone was assembled across the hall from Richard's room so that we could take this picture and then get downstairs. Richard arrived, and we took pictures for about four minutes, at which point Richard began to shake uncontrollably. I took him out of the room and across the hall and let him sit down to relax a little bit, and I said, "Richard, are you okay?" He explained that this was the way the disease MS had affected him.

I explained to Richard that I understood about the disease. I wanted him to know what to expect when we went downstairs, and I explained that we *were* going to go downstairs, because I did not look forward to Richard having me go in front of a room of eight hundred people to make some kind of an announcement pertaining to his not being able to join us. So I explained to Richard, "When we do go downstairs, if you have another episode like this and begin to shake uncontrollably, would you please hold your hands up so that people will think you are applauding?" Richard looked at me, stopped shaking, and started to laugh. And once again, that tight coil spring that creates such tension inside many performers opened up. Richard finished laughing and put on his tuxedo, we went downstairs, and he was perfect.

Tony Fantozzi and the Heineken Hotel Caper

My agent, Tony Fantozzi, had come to New York with Jolene and me when we were on a talent hunt; we were all staying at the Sherry-Netherland hotel. After an evening of auditioning performers at different clubs, we wound up back in my hotel suite. We had a wonderful time. Fantozzi, as usual, had contributed in a large way to the profits of the Heineken beer company. For a skinny guy, Fantozzi could drink more Heinekens than anybody I've ever known and still not have it affect his speech, his logic, or his motor skills.

Two thirty in the morning, we were having one more cold Heineken, at which point Tony asked me where I grew up. Jolene knew that this could lead to a much longer discussion than she wanted to have held in our suite. She said, "That's it. Everybody out. No more stories. No more beer. I'm going to bed. That's it." She went to bed, and Tony reluctantly departed.

Since I felt badly about his eviction, I went with him to walk to the elevator. I was barefoot in a sweatsuit, but it was just in the hallway. On the way to the elevator, Tony and I decided to continue our discussion, so I went up to Tony's room and walked him to his door. We finished talking and I went back to the elevator. It was at that moment as I looked at the elevator buttons that I realized I didn't remember which floor our suite was on.

No problem, right? I took the elevator to the lobby and went up to the desk clerk. Now remember, I was barefoot, in a sweatsuit, carrying a pretty good load of beer. Not only had I forgotten the floor,

I also hadn't taken a key. I asked the desk clerk, "Could I please have a key to my room?" Quite naturally, the desk clerk wanted to know my room number. I had no idea.

He said, "What floor was it on?"

I said, "I don't know that either, but my name is George Schlatter, S-C-H-L-A-T-T-E-R, now can I please have a key?"

He said, "Do you have any identification?"

I said, "No, I'm in a sweatsuit."

He said, "You don't have any identification. You don't know your floor. You don't know your room number. How do I know who you are?"

I said, "Because I'm telling you."

He said, "That's not good enough."

By then, we were surrounded by a couple of security guards who also had some doubts as to my identification. Then a light bulb moment. I told him to call Mrs. Schlatter in the room because she would vouch for me. He dialed our room and, of course, the phone had been put on "do not disturb." Solution number two: I told him to call Tony Fantozzi's room. Fortunately, Tony answered the phone.

The desk clerk said, "Mr. Fantozzi, there is a gentleman in the lobby who says he knows you, but he doesn't know his room number or the floor, but he says he knows you. His name is George Schlatter."

Fantozzi said, "I never heard of the bum," and hung up the phone.

I pressed onward and said, "All right, take the room registration when we checked in and look at that."

The desk clerk pulled out the registration, and of course, as luck would have it, when we arrived at the hotel, I had a meeting right away, so Jolene had checked us in, and the registration did not even have my signature.

It was now about three thirty in the morning. I was barefoot. Sleepy. Half ripped. Standing in the lobby of the Sherry-Netherland hotel with no identification and not a friend in the world. At that moment, Mickey Mantle, with whom I had become quite friendly, arrived in the hotel much later than he should have been up too. But as he arrived, he gave me a big hello and a hug and verified my identity. Had Mickey Mantle not been a bit of a night owl himself, I may still have been in that lobby or, worse yet, in the slammer.

BRUCE VILANCH AND CODE NAME LANCE

I have worked with a living Muppet. His name is Bruce Vilanch. You may have seen him on *Hollywood Squares*, or in *Hairspray*, or in a documentary called *Get Bruce*. He has blond curly hair and a big blond curly beard, is rather rotund, and wears outrageous T-shirts with even more outrageous sayings on them; one of my favorites is SEE DICK DRINK. SEE DICK DRIVE. SEE DICK DIE. DON'T BE A DICK. I love that.

One year at the American Comedy Awards, Bruce and I flew to New York to get a taped acceptance speech from Roseanne Barr Arnold, or whatever name she was using at that time. She was not available to join us at our scheduled hour, so we wound up taping her in a hotel suite at the Waldorf Towers around two o'clock in the morning. Normal, right? After which we had to feed her. So we all went out to breakfast, and I got back to the hotel at about four A.M. I went to my room and turned on the television set and wound up looking at channel 6, where a very attractive young couple were actively engaged in all kinds of wonderful heterosexual activities. I had never seen this on a hotel TV before, so I thought I'd best alert my buddy Bruce. I called his room, and as usual, Bruce answered the phone with "Hello, swimming pool." Sometimes he would answer with "orgy room." I said, "Bruce, quick, no jokes, have you seen what's on channel 6?" Just then I looked up, and the first couple had been replaced by two men performing many of the same activities that I had just seen between a man and a woman. Now I am not square and I am not a prude, but I must admit

I had never before seen men so occupied. Just as I said to Bruce "what's on channel 6," up came this somewhat startling image. Bruce, without skipping a beat, yelled, "Lance!"

I lost it. I could not believe it. Not only was Bruce not surprised to see this activity, but he knew at least one of the participants. He probably knew them both, but only one of them at that moment was recognizable. So "Lance" has become a code word between us ever since.

YOU CAN'T SPELL "DAVIS" WITHOUT *D-I-V-A*

When I was doing Bette Davis—let me rephrase that. When I was doing *Laugh-In with* Bette Davis, I was in awe of her. I mean, she was Apple Annie, Baby Jane, Queen Elizabeth, Catherine the Great, Regina Giddens, Judith Traherne, and Margo. And she was known for eating producers like me for lunch. The thing that really threw me off, however, was our first meeting, which was supposed to be at eleven o'clock. Bette arrived at ten twenty. Of course, this surprised me, and everyone thought that as usual, I had done something wrong. I got to her as fast as I could, throwing people out of my office like bales of straw off a hay wagon. Finally, I got to her at about ten forty-five and apologized for having kept her waiting. She reassured me that it was fine, that she had been early. During the next week, for every meeting I had with Bette Davis, she arrived a half an hour to forty-five minutes early, and it was truly disconcerting. It made me feel as if I were running late all the time.

Finally, the day of the shoot, her makeup call was at ten o'clock because we wanted her to get plenty of rest. When I arrived at the studio at nine forty-five, she was dressed, with her hair and make-up finished. She was in wardrobe, sitting in the center of the stage. I finally had to say something. I said, "Bette baby. What is it? You've been early every day. You're Bette Davis. You don't have to be here early. What is it with this obsession you have?"

Bette then gave me a lesson about the difference between an actress and a legend. She explained to me that when she was starting out on her first motion picture, one of the grips told her that if she got there early, she could see whose close-ups they were lighting. This meant that when the DP (director of photography) was hanging and focusing the lights, she would know where the key lights were and where her key light was going to be (or if she even had a key light). That way, when the scene began, she could move around to achieve the best possible position and benefit from the best possible lighting. Eighty years old, and she was still getting on set early to find out whose close-ups they were lighting. That, my friends, is a legend.

Here's another diva legend story. On one Grammy Awards, Barbra Streisand was supposed to sing "You Don't Send Me Flowers Anymore" with Neil Diamond. Barbra had arranged the number and explained to the director that they should have a minimal amount of lighting, which would direct the attention of the audience to the two performers. So they prepared the shot with key lighting on Neil from one side and key lighting on Barbra on the other side. Both had some backlight. Odd, but everyone thought, *This is Barbra Streisand. If that's what she wants, that's the way we'll shoot the number.*

I remember watching it being blocked, thinking what a strange way to light this, but it did have a certain intimacy to it, and I thought this might be very effective. However, when the number went on the air live, Barbra was aware that by moving her head only slightly, it put a shadow across Neil's face. This meant that the only shots that the director could use were a two-shot and then a close-up of Barbra Streisand. They could use only a few of Neil's close-ups because Bab's shadow was across his face. Neil might as well not have even been in the number. And the reason for it happening to him: he wasn't there when they were lighting. I don't know if Neil ever realized what had been done, but he sang almost the entire number with a dark shadow across most of his face. Streisand, on the other hand, looked fine and sang beautifully as always.

Another Barbra story. When her husband, James Brolin, started filming *Pensacola: Wings of Gold*, Barbra went to the set and personally told them how to light her husband's close-ups. Watch the show if you can catch it on some channel in the 300s. Everyone else on the show has a normal TV key light–backlight configuration . . . except for James Brolin. Every close-up of him leaps out on screen, indicating that someone had indeed spent an inordinate amount of time lighting Mr. Brolin's close-ups. Barbra did a great job.

Many times people in our business don't learn the fundamentals. No one will ever learn it as well as Bette Davis and Barbra Streisand, but learning those fundamentals is vital to the success and even survival of young artists. Knowing where the lights ought to be, where the mike should be, where the speakers are, where the sight lines are, is extremely important. These basics are not learned properly by show business newcomers, and as a result, their performances don't quite have the dynamic of other performers who have the knowledge or are surrounded with people who know lighting, sound, and staging. Trust me. It doesn't happen by accident. That's why some of the best cinematographers are as valuable to a project as the director, and sometimes even more so. Bad lighting can kill a performance faster than anything other than bad sound. No one can look out for you better than you can. Remember Bette Davis, an Academy Award winner who had done endless films, and who did a guest shot on *Laugh-In* and got there early to see whose close-ups they were lighting. It's called professionalism.

I once did a charity event with Julio Iglesias. Two weeks before the event, we had a complete list of everything in Julio's lighting package, and on the morning of the show, his crew showed up and hung his sound configuration with the speakers, the amplifiers, the slapbacks, and the soundboard. When Julio walked onstage for a full, complete rehearsal that afternoon, to just sing two numbers, he had the proper lighting and the proper sound: the speakers and the monitors so that he could hear himself were properly placed, and he had the microphone he always used.

And by the way, I learned before the show to never, ever, ever, ever shoot Julio's right side. Take only shots from camera left. He knows where the camera is, and he will turn all the way around. Why? Because he's a pro.

So what's the lesson from this section? Always be prepared, show up early, see where your key light is, and, if possible, have Barbra Streisand as your lighting director.

DIRECTING CARY GRANT

I know what you're thinking: Hitchcock directed Cary. So let's think of this as "Cary Grant, the Lost Episode."

Cary was a wonderful dramatic actor and a terrific comedy actor, and he was indeed a very private person. And behind that beautiful, suave, sophisticated, elegant movie star was a beautiful, suave, sophisticated, elegant, charming person. And strange as it seems, we did have something in common. Go figure that out—I mean, "beautiful," "suave," "sophisticated," and "elegant" are not the usual words associated with me. But here is the connection: when Cary was young, one of his first jobs was working at the St. Louis Municipal Opera under the name of Archie Leach. That is the same opera company where I got my start in show business as well, and I felt that would give us common ground, which I naturally tried to exploit the first time I met him.

Jolene and I had gone to a large charity event at the Beverly Hilton hotel, and there, in the lobby, was Cary. In a burst of enthusiasm, tinged with just the right amount of stupidity and chutzpah, I raced over to him and introduced myself, and it went something like this: "Mr. Grant, my name is George Schlatter."

With a big smile and a hearty handshake, he said, "Yes, yes."

I said, "We have something in common. I also worked at the St. Louis Municipal Opera."

I said, "And now I'm producing *Rowan & Martin's Laugh-In*. Do you know the show?"

He said, "Yes, yes."

I said, "Do you like the show?"

He said, "Oh yes, very much, yes, yes."

I said, "Would you like to appear on the show?"

He said, "NO, NO. Nice to meet you, George." And he was off. The "no" was equally as charming as the "yes," but said with just a bit more enthusiasm.

Despite that awkward first meeting, over the years we became friends, and Cary spent many enjoyable evenings at my house watching the fights on a TV screen we had in our living room. One night Cary and his wife, Barbara, invited us over to their house for dinner with Dudley Moore and his wife, Brogan. Dudley was about five-foot-three and Brogan was almost six feet tall, so it was already an interesting picture. He must have had to go up on her. Anyway, I couldn't wait to see this group together.

People in Beverly Hills have a deeply neurotic affliction called "earlyaphobia," a deep fear of being early. Not me. We arrived right on time, which is another one of my annoying habits. Barbara and Cary invited us into the living room, where there was a waiting dish of caviar and some Russian vodka in a block of ice. People often accused Cary of being cheap, which he was not. He may have been a little frugal, but he was not cheap. Although he did count the number of drinks I had. We sat down to await Dudley and Brogan.

Time went by. More vodka disappeared and still no Dudley and Brogan. To fill the time, Cary brought out a new Hi8 video camera he'd bought so he could take some home videos on a boat trip he and Barbara had made to Alaska. He complained that he just couldn't get it to work and asked me if I knew anything about cameras. I said, "Of course." By then, we were sitting in the kitchen, while Barbara was fixing bangers and mash. The vodka had almost disappeared. There was just Barbara, Cary, director Stanley Donen, Jolene, and me, and I was demonstrating to Cary how to work the camera. So I asked him to just pose for a minute, turned on the camera, and said, "Now, just say 'Judy, Judy, Judy.'" Cary explained that he had never said "Judy, Judy, Judy." I said, "Well, first of all, if we're going to work together, you're going to have to learn to take directions. Now say 'Judy, Judy, Judy.'" He started to laugh and said it. I said, "That is the worst impression of Cary Grant I have ever seen. Hold it, Cary . . . you're mugging. Don't look into the camera. Look at Stanley. Now, 'Judy, Judy, Judy.'" Yes, I was explaining to him how to be Cary Grant. I was on a roll, so I then asked him to say "In the name of Your Majesty, you are all under arrest" (which he had done in *Gunga Din*). He said it, and then I said, "That doesn't even sound like Cary Grant. You've got to be a bit more British. Now, Cary, just stand up and walk." I got him to stand up, walk, and do an impression of Cary Grant for about five minutes. It was hysterical. Somewhere there is a five-minute video of Cary Grant doing an impersonation of Cary Grant. One day that should air, because it showed what a charming, funny, cute guy this megastar rascal was, and as a director, it was my best work ever. My only disappointment was that I could never get him to appear on *Laugh-In*, but I guarantee if I ever find a copy of that 8mm tape of Cary in his kitchen doing "Cary Grant," I would have a real hit on my hands.

A STORY I REFUSE TO TELL ABOUT GROUCHO

Every star has a special ritual to get them ready before they go onstage. George Carlin used to do push-ups. Richard Pryor would get oral sex. Billy Crystal would practice oral hygiene. Let me explain. When Billy was growing up, he'd watch the Oscars with his parents, and since the Oscars went on so late back east, at some point his parents would make him go to bed. Before he did, he would pick up his toothbrush and pretend to give his own Oscar acceptance speech. Then when he started hosting the actual show, which he did nine amazing and innovative times, he'd carry a toothbrush in his pocket because he wanted that big auditorium to feel like the living room where he was so relaxed and comfortable. It worked for Billy. Now Groucho Marx, he had a different ritual, which I got to see firsthand.

I was producing a variety series starring Bill Cosby at CBS (the CBS slogan now is "Bill who?"). Groucho was getting very old and no longer working very much, but Bill and I thought it was worth one more shot to have him come on the show. We talked to Marvin Hamlisch, who was then Groucho's accompanist. Marvin set us up with a meeting with Groucho where I tried very hard to convince Groucho to do Cosby's show. He asked me, "Does this show pay money?" Before I could answer, he said, "That is not enough." Groucho wanted a *lot* of money. He also wanted some lines written for him, which he of course refused to do, and he wanted to do a number surrounded with girls. That he did get.

The woman living with Groucho at the time who was his "caretaker" was Erin Fleming. She was a minor actress who played a small part in Woody Allen's *Everything You Always Wanted to Know about Sex* (*But Were Afraid to Ask)*, although she is much better known for the major role she played in Groucho's final years and in the fight over his estate. Basically, she promised that she could deliver Groucho for this event if she was allowed to be with him and perform a song. Without ever having heard the woman sing, I said, "Sounds good to me." Since we were taping the show, I knew I could get rid of her song and still keep Groucho. You may have figured out by now: I will say yes and then think of a way out of it later.

I explained to Groucho that I would meet all his requirements and I would call him Tuesday, at which time Groucho said that I could call him whatever I wished, but that Tuesday was not his name.

The day of the show, Groucho arrived with Nurse Ratched—I mean Erin. He explained to me that he didn't need any rehearsal, and he went into his dressing room to get made up. What I didn't know was that part of the way Erin got Groucho alert and ready to go onstage was to dance in front of him . . . nude . . . while he was getting his makeup applied. That dressing room became quite a popular place, as Groucho continued to get his makeup on and his trousers pulled up, which under the circumstances was surprisingly easier than we thought it might be. Erin "handled" that too.

When the time arrived for the performance, the audience was excited, and we were ready for action. So was Groucho. Groucho came out onstage and sang "Hello, I Must Be Going," did some jokes about Dr. Cockenlocker—that's right, Dr. Cockenlocker—and sang "Show Me a Rose," which was one of his famous songs.

After Groucho's number came the interview where Bill sat down and talked to "the master." When Cosby asked Groucho if he had any unfulfilled wishes, Groucho said, "Yes, I do. My wish is to terminate this interview as soon as possible." Stupidly, Bill pressed on and talked about Groucho having had enormous success. Groucho explained, "I've had great success and tremendous failure. This is my first experience with humiliation." The interview went on and on like that.

We finished taping Groucho's songs, Erin's song, and Groucho's interview with Bill in about thirty-five minutes, after which Groucho was dismissed. At that point Erin came to me and said, "What do you mean dismissed? You can't send him home now."

I said, "Well, we're through with him. I wanted to get him in and out so that he wasn't tired."

She said, "Tired? You dumb son of a bitch, with what I've got in him he won't go to bed for the next twelve hours!"

Although it's been about fifty years, I can still describe rather accurately what Erin looked like dancing naked in the dressing room for Groucho. After watching her dance number, I was almost sad to have to cut her song. I would have left it in the show if she had worn the same outfit she was wearing when she danced for Groucho, which Groucho described as "two Band-Aids and a cork."

Postscript: Sometime after the taping with Groucho, we were remodeling the front of the office building I own on Beverly Boulevard. We tore up some carpet in the entry, and underneath it I discovered that Groucho, at one time, owned our office building along with producer John Guedel and TV host Art Linkletter. When they remodeled the front sidewalk on May 11, 1953, all three of them signed the cement, which we had been walking over the entire time we were working on the Bill Cosby program. There were the signatures of Groucho, Linkletter, and Guedel with the imprint of their hands and Guedel's pipe. I don't think I will ever move out of this office building. Not even if Erin Fleming were dancing nude in front of me.

A STORY I REFUSE TO TELL ABOUT PEGGY LEE

I've shared Richard Pryor's, George Carlin's, Billy Crystal's, and Groucho Marx's pre-performance rituals. Time to learn about Peggy Lee's. Peggy was a wonderful, exciting, inventive musical genius, but her preshow ritual was a little bit strange. Not quite at the level of having Erin Fleming dance nude in front of her, but every night before she would go on, the members of the band had to go into her dressing room and kiss her. Although I wasn't in the band, I felt left out, so I got in on that too by telling her I used to play C melody sax.

Another ritual: Peggy drank a little bit of brandy before every show and occasionally during her curtain calls. She might have done it during the show too. Regardless, she was an exciting performer, but she could get a little bit confused and confusing. She knew where she was, but it was not always easy to follow her.

The owner of Ciro's, Herman Hover, who was built like a refrigerator, would occasionally have a few drinks, get up, and tap-dance during the show. There but for the grace of God go I. He often told a story about how as a young man he wrote to the opera singer Enrico Caruso, saying that he heard Caruso had written some wonderful music and that since he was a very talented lyricist, he would like an opportunity to put some lyrics to the fabulous melodies that Caruso had written. Interestingly enough, no one knew that Caruso had written music, but Herman thought that anyone with the talent and the love of music of Caruso undoubtedly had some melodies of his own. Sure enough, Herman heard back from Caruso. They met. Caruso played him some of the melodies, and this young man became known as Caruso's lyricist. The story would be a lot better if that were true. Unfortunately, nobody ever heard any of Caruso's melodies, nor did they ever hear any of Herman's lyrics. Herman had quite a background, but he ran Ciro's and kept it open. Herman liked me because I had a relationship with the talent and, most of the time, could get them to do just about anything. I digress, back to Peggy.

The night that Peggy Lee was to open at Ciro's, there was a premiere that would be over at about ten thirty, so Herman wanted to make absolutely certain that Peggy Lee did a short show. To convince Peggy of this, her agents, managers, and Herman were waiting when she finished rehearsal. Herman motioned to me and said, "George, let's go over and just talk to her about doing a short show tonight."

I walked over to Peggy and said, "Peggy, we have to talk to you about doing a short show."

She looked at me and asked, "And who is we?"

I turned around and realized that all of them had taken off and decided to leave the entire negotiation up to me, which was a problem because Peggy could really be a handful in this kind of discussion. Actually, Peggy could be a handful in any number of situations, but this is not that kind of book.

I explained to Peggy that there was a premiere that night, it was very important that she do a short first show, and that this would leave us time to have some brandy between shows. Peggy liked this idea. She got all dressed up, the band and I kissed her just the way she liked before performing, and she came out and did one hell of a great show—"Lover," "Fever," "Mañana," and all her hits. She stayed on a little longer than we had hoped, so I was waiting for her right offstage in the hallway when she was taking her bow. My plan was to firmly take hold of her upper arm to prevent her from going back and doing any more encores. Peggy looked over, saw me, and realized she had been on longer than she should. This either a) did not bother her, or b) confused her, and she did what she was comfortable doing. So she never came entirely offstage, she just went back on and started the whole show over again . . . from the top.

Stars were all lined up on the sidewalk trying to get in, and my buddy—pretty, perky Peggy—did her entire show twice. Of course, the audience sitting there loved it, but as I recall the show ran slightly over two hours and Herman went nuts. It was, however, one hell of a show.

Gregory Peck and the Great Snooky Lanson

At one Sinatra event, Gregory Peck agreed to offer a toast to Frank, but was very concerned about the content of the toast we had written, in which we wanted him to say, "I would venture a guess that millions of people all over the world were conceived to the sounds of a Sinatra recording. As a matter of fact, probably half of the people in this room would never have been born if their parents had been fans of Snooky Lanson."

Snooky Lanson was a white-bread singer with Kay Kyser and His Orchestra in the '40s and *Your Hit Parade* in the '50s and a contemporary of Frank's. I knew the older fans in attendance would relate to a Snooky Lanson mention. Of course, like all of you reading this, including people named Lanson, Greg had never heard of Snooky and questioned the value of his name as a joke.

I assured Greg that the words "Snooky Lanson" coming from an Academy Award winner like Greg would invoke a certain level of mirth that was perhaps absent in *To Kill a Mockingbird* or *Gentleman's*

Agreement. Reluctantly, but obediently, Greg delivered the line, pronouncing Mr. Lanson's first name as "Snoooooky." He delivered this with almost Shakespearean importance. Of course, the audience was hysterical, and Gregory was so surprised he took a big step back. It was great. So if any of you reading this are Snooky Lanson fans, you're welcome.

STEVIE WONDER: MAKEUP ARTIST TO THE STARS

The Smokey Robinson Show was produced by Motown for ABC. Of course, I have always enjoyed all the people involved with Motown, especially Berry Gordy, so I agreed to help out as a consultant. Before I continue, I have to explain that I think Berry Gordy is one of the smartest people in the world, due in large part because he was able to con, cajole, or convince Suzanne de Passe to stay with him for years and to continue to amass even greater wealth. Berry can't argue with any of that. One of the other reasons I respect Berry so much, and I have told him this before, is the fact that he has been able to sell Motown no less than three times, and he still owns all the masters. That, I believe, in some states would go down as a felony, but in the Schlatter house, it is the cause for awesome respect and great affection mixed with an abundance of awe.

Smokey was the definition of cool and laid-back. He was wonderful to work with, and a lot of great performers appeared on the show. One of them was Little Stevie Wonder, when Little Stevie was no longer little. Because Stevie was a late booking and we needed to quickly figure out what he would do on the show, I got an urgent call from Berry Gordy and Suzanne de Passe to come in and say hello to Stevie.

We exchanged our hellos, and then Berry said to me, "George, tell Stevie about the sketch you guys have for him to do." They looked at me like . . . *Go ahead.* Suzanne gave me a little shrug and an *I don't know.* This ranks right up there with when I had to come up with the Cher and the Mountie sketch.

It is a little difficult sometimes to come up with a comedy sketch on a musical show for a blind singing pianist, particularly when you have no time to think about it. Sometimes, however, under those circumstances, I have come up with my best ideas. I said, "Oh, the Stevie Wonder sketch." Suzanne chimed in with a "Stevie, wait until you hear about this."

I said, "Yeah, Stevie . . . I think you're gonna like it. Now I don't know how much time you have to rehearse, and I'm not sure whether you will think this is funny, but I wanted to try it on you. We have some other ideas too."

That is me, stalling for time, trying to think of a funny sketch for Stevie. Stevie knew I was in trouble. I looked at Berry, I looked at Suzanne, and I looked at Smokey, who at this point was cracking up because he knew I had no idea for a sketch at all, and I was on the spot. After another deep breath I said, "Well, Stevie, you're the head of the ABC makeup department." All heads snapped back to Stevie. I said, "You are making up Smokey to get ready to go on and do his television show."

For some reason, Smokey was not quite as amused as he had been before he heard the idea; however, Stevie thought it was hysterical.

Then I said, "It's not like you're just fooling with him. You are really going to do the whole makeup with eyeliner, rouge, lipstick, and powder. It's possible, Stevie, that you may get the makeup mixed up—where it is supposed to go mixed up and the amount mixed up with the person you are making up."

Now everybody is cracking up because they can visualize what's going to happen when Stevie starts to put makeup on Smokey. Only Smokey indicated some reservations.

We pulled two cameras into the makeup room. Put Smokey in the chair. Gave Stevie eyeliner, lipstick, rouge, a hair dryer, a lot of white powder, and told him to just "work on Smokey." You have never seen anybody look as dumb as Smokey did by the time Stevie got done with him. It turned into a very funny sketch, and the best part: it was the last time that Suzanne de Passe, Berry Gordy, and Smokey Robinson ever tried to put me on the spot to come up with a sketch right away.

HENNY TEACHES ME NOT TO LOOK CHEAP

Henny Youngman would always tell me how much he liked me and about how he had told his family about me. He called one day to say he was having lunch at the Carnegie Deli in Beverly Hills with his entire family and asked me if I could come by just to say hello. I was in a meeting, and leaving the meeting to go and say hello to Henny Youngman's family was not at the top of my list of priorities. However, Henny kept begging and saying, "It will only take you a minute. Just come by. It means a great deal to me. I'm an old man, I may not see them again. Please, George, just come by for a minute and say hello to the family."

So I went to the Carnegie Deli. Sure enough, there was Henny with eleven people, his entire family, having lunch. I sat down. Henny said, "Have a Coke." I ordered a Coca-Cola. Said hello to the family. He had indeed told them a lot about me, and I left there feeling really glad that I had made an old man like Henny happy by saying hello to his family before he went to the great stage in the sky.

Two days later I got a bill for the lunch with an enormous tip for the waiter. He had signed my name. I said, "Henny, it's bad enough that I paid for the lunch, but what about this tip?"

Henny said, "George, I don't want you to look cheap."

A STORY I REFUSE TO TELL ABOUT JACK LEMMON AND HIS STIFFY

Jack Lemmon was over at my house one night for a few drinks, and since my car was in our driveway behind his car, he drove across my lawn to get out to the street. Naturally. That was bad enough, except for the fact Jack then called *Variety* columnist Army Archerd and told Army I had driven across his lawn. I had to call the gardener to fill in the deep ruts his Rolls-Royce had left across our recently sodded front yard. But being Jack, we decided to get together to have a good laugh over my lawn.

Sometime during that next drinking night, the Lemmons had a fight, and Jack said, "All right, that's it. I'm going home." I stayed at the bar with his wife, Felicia, and Jolene, because I really didn't want to risk walking at that hour. We were having a good time when Jolene asked, "Where is Jack?" Since none of us had the slightest idea, I thought it would be nice if I went to look for him. It was at that point I remembered that he had said he couldn't get his car, so he was going to walk home. Jolene said, "Well, you can't let him walk home, you have to go and find him." So, against all my better judgment, and the somewhat firm advice from the California Highway Patrol, I got in my black Mercedes to look for Jack Lemmon.

I drove up and down the street. He obviously wasn't there. I drove up and down the next street, and the next street. No sign of Jack. I drove all over Beverly Hills. Couldn't find him, so I came home and went to bed. Just as I was going to sleep, Jolene asked if I had found Jack and taken him home. I said, "No, I couldn't find him." This upset Mrs. Schlatter, who said, "You cannot get your friend drunk and then let him wander around Beverly Hills alone at three o'clock in the morning." Okay. Back out of bed. Got dressed. Started driving around the neighborhood again. Up one street. Down the other. I blanketed Beverly Hills a second time looking for Jack.

Since I was carrying a pretty good load myself, I was starting to nod off and I had had no success at all, so I came home. Got back into bed. Jolene asked, "Did you take Jack home?" And I did what any husband would do and lied. I told her I had found him and drove him home, and he was fine. It was the only way I was going to get any sleep.

In the morning, Jolene called Felicia to check on Jack. Felicia said it was a terrible evening because Jack had decided to walk home, and he suddenly became aware that someone was following him in a black car. Jack would walk a half block. The black car would come around again, and Jack would hide in the bushes until the car disappeared. She explained that Jack could only come home one block at a time between hiding and scurrying around trying to avoid the kidnapper in the black Mercedes. The black Mercedes was mine. The kidnapper was me. That search was a fruitless attempt I was making at the request of my loved one to protect my friend Jack Lemmon from real kidnappers.

Okay, how does this lead into Jack and his stiffy? It started when I asked Jack to appear on *Laugh-In*. Jack rarely did guest appearances, but he owed me for the lawn and my lost hours of sleep searching for him. After I made him feel guilty, Jack agreed to do the show, and as always, he was brilliant. He had a good time, and everybody wanted him to come back for a second appearance. Jack had had a good time doing the show, but just to give me trouble, he said he would do it again only if I could get his favorite line on the air, which was a comment that one of his professors in college used when the coeds came to class. The line was "Hey, would you like to sneak a peek at Stiffy?" Jack always thought that was hysterical and agreed that if I could get the line on the air, he would do the show again. This was not an easy task. By then, NBC was pretty much onto every trick, ploy, device, and bit of treachery that we had employed to get outrageous material on the air.

But I love a stiff challenge. A few weeks later, I had a dinner for Jack Lemmon at La Scala where we had invited some friends. I had brought in television sets so that Jack and I could watch what I had come up with. The sketch involved a graduation ceremony for undertakers conducted by Art Carney, who was giving out diplomas. At one point Art explained to one of the graduate undertakers that he was not going to receive his diploma because he had not completed the course. Art explained that they buried the dearly departed. They did not "plant them." When they lowered the casket into the ground, they did not say, "And away we go." And when they asked the relatives if they wished to view the remains, they did not say, "Hey, wanna sneak a peek at Stiffy?" The line got on the air! I had won! Then Jack explained to me that I didn't get the second half of the line on and that the deal was dependent upon the whole line. The part that, according to Jack, had been left off was "Or would you like to pop a peek at the pink part?" Well . . . the "sneak a peek at Stiffy" line caused such controversy that it was literally impossible to get the "pop a peek at the pink part" on the air. I tried it with flowers. I tried it with an artist painting a sunset. I tried it with a person having their eye examined, but the network was now aware of the attempt and had dug in their heels, refusing to allow anyone to say "would you like to pop a peek at the pink part." I bet Erin Fleming would have not only said it but shown it.

GEORGE BURNS DATED SHARON STONE

In 1993, I produced *The First Annual Comedy Hall of Fame*. It was a two-hour special airing on NBC in which we paid homage to various comedy performers. In the two shows we honored legends like Bob Hope, Milton Berle, George Carlin, Jonathan Winters, the Smothers Brothers, Richard Pryor, Walter Matthau, Jack Lemmon, Sid Caesar, and George Burns. For the George Burns tribute, I called Sharon Stone and asked her if she would be George Burns's date. This was the easiest booking I ever made in my life. Not only did she agree to be his date, she agreed to have the limousine pick her up first to go by George's house to have a martini with him and then come to the show. George Burns had two martinis every day of his life and smoked ten cigars. He said that's what kept him alive.

At the show, Sharon stood up and explained how happy she was to be there with George but admitted she had been worried that at the last moment his doctor might not allow this date to take place. Sharon explained that George's doctor had warned George to be careful, because a man of his age becoming romantically involved with a woman like Sharon could be very dangerous. And, of course, George replied, "Look, Doc, if she dies, she dies." Yes, it's an old joke, but no one in that room cared because Sharon delivered it like a gorgeous, latter-day Marilyn Monroe, with the innocence of Kay Kendall but the sexiness of Mae West. Another moment that I will cherish forever.

The last time I saw George Burns was at a party at Marvin Davis's mansion. Everyone had gone in to dinner, but George was still sitting in a position of honor in the lobby of the house. He was in a huge regal-looking upholstered, carved antique chair. I walked over to him, and I said, "Hello, George. George Schlatter. Don't get up!"

He looked at me, laughed, and said, "You finally said something funny."

That meant more to me than any great review I've ever received.

Part 5
Frank and Friends

H e was the biggest star I ever knew, and he would have been mad at me if he didn't get his own section of this book. What follows are just a few stories about the man (and a few of our Rat Pack circle of friends) who over the decades probably had the biggest impact on my career, and who I had the most fun with—the Voice, the Chairman of the Board, Frank Sinatra.

JAPAN'S THREE WORST NIGHTMARES: GODZILLA, MOTHRA, AND SINATRA

I got a call one day saying that Frank Sinatra had committed to do a series of commercials for a Japanese airline, and they wanted me to produce the ads. I explained to the ad agency that I was in the middle of a TV special and didn't really have time to do these commercials. However, they asked if I would just meet the people from Japan, because Sinatra was getting a large fee for doing these commercials. I did meet with them and was allowed to review what were the most complicated plans I had ever seen in my life. They involved having Frank for three entire days to shoot the commercials and two days to shoot the stills, for which the airline company was paying a huge price.

This was going to be a serious problem. None of the Japanese people in the room spoke any English, and at times I barely speak English, but I had to explain to them why this was not going to work. I said, "Frank will not give you five total days, or three days, or two days. I believe, to get Frank, you're looking at a total of forty-five minutes."

It was like they got a Rosetta Stone, because all of those Japanese ad people suddenly understood English when I repeated, "Look, there is no way Mr. S is going to sit there and do what you have laid out and spend three days with you—forget about it. You can do this in forty-five minutes." And then I told them how.

This was my idea: we would set up the commercial, light everything, and use a stand-in to go through and block and actually shoot everything that they wanted Frank to do in the completed commercial. I would then take the finished commercial featuring the stand-in to Frank's house and show him what the commercial would look like when it was completed. The Japanese were concerned about this approach, particularly since they were convinced that the entire problem was me and none of the problem was Mr. Sinatra. They were wrong.

The date approached. The set was installed. It was lit. We shot the commercial with a stand-in. Edited it. Dubbed it. Did the graphics, and it was ready to go on the air, except for the small fact that it did not have Frank Sinatra in it. I showed the commercial to Frank and told him what we had to do. He nodded. The next day at twelve o'clock, we had geishas lining the driveway with flowers awaiting Frank's arrival. As usual, he was exactly on time. Frank walked in, came up to me, and said, "Can I go home now?" I explained to him that we may need a little bit more time than that. When he started to get upset, I reminded him about all those zeros at the end of his fee.

Frank went into the dressing room to put on his tuxedo. I had everything ready to go so that when Frank walked out of the dressing room, he hit his mark and did the first section of the commercial. He then said to me, "Are we finished?"

I said, "Not quite, but we're getting there."

It went as planned. Frank went from one spot to another and said his lines, and in between spots we had areas set up where we could shoot the stills. At forty-two minutes into the shoot, Frank decided that he had had it and wanted to leave. I explained to him that I needed one more shot. Frank explained to me that if I needed the shot, I should do it myself because he had become bored and was leaving. He felt he had done the forty-five minutes I had promised. I then looked around at the Japanese people, who suddenly realized that this was not me, that this was the way the man worked. Frank was not being difficult; he was just Frank, and he felt that he had done what he had to do. I explained to Frank that it would be easier to just shoot this last bit, and he said no. I said, "PLEASE. I need this shot."

He said, "You are not going to get it."

I was desperate and I panicked. I took a deep breath and very quietly said, "Frank, don't make me hurt you." (Note: This is a phrase you will have noticed I have used a number of times throughout my career.) Sinatra looked at me like he had never seen me before. His mouth fell open and he mouthed the words, *Make me hurt you?* And I said, "Don't make me hurt you, Francis."

He said, "Well, okay, promise not to *hurt* me."

We shot the final lines of the commercial. He was charming. Said goodbye to everybody and was out in exactly forty-five minutes. The commercial went on to win awards and was the finest thing All Nippon Airways had ever done. Frank never forgot my "don't make me hurt you" comment.

The ad people came back to me later and said they wanted to do another commercial, and I asked them to please get someone else. But by then I was looking at some zeros on my fee too. I called Frank, and he agreed to do another commercial but made it clear this time he didn't want to hang around for a long forty-five minutes.

Everything was set to do it the same way we did before, and I told Frank we were going to pick him up at one o'clock. Then out of the blue his wife, Barbara, told me that Frank wasn't going to shave. He had grown a beard and decided he did not want to take the beard off. Since this commercial was going to intercut with the last commercial, having a beard for some shots and no beard for the other shots was not the best news I had ever heard. I explained all of this to Frank, and he said, "Well, you figure out something." Thirty minutes later I had a barber from the Beverly Hills Hotel at Frank's door with a sheet, a shaving mug, a brush in the mug with the lather already up, and a straight razor. At that moment I got Frank on the phone and told him that man was going to use that razor for one of two operations. One was a shave, and I told him I didn't want to discuss the other one. He said, "All right, all right, but . . . promise not to hurt me."

He got the shave and came to the studio. Before we shot the commercial, he wanted to know if anybody would like some photographs or autographs, which he proceeded to do for about forty-five minutes. He shot three different versions of the commercial. He was there for an hour and a half. We all had a wonderful time. And the Japanese thought that maybe this was a whole different person. The difference was that for the second commercial, Barbara was there with him because I had the brilliant idea of putting her in this commercial, which might make it go more smoothly. Smooth? This was glass. It was perfect. They were thrilled. I was thrilled. And I made a promise to myself: no more commercials.

No more commercials until I got a call from the Sands in Atlantic City saying Sinatra had committed to doing a commercial for them, and all I had to do was show up and be there so Frank could see me. They said everything was all set, and if I was just there, it would make it nicer for him. I explained that I was busy and not a chance. They then mentioned the fee. I said, "You can't buy me!"

A week later, I'm in Atlantic City ready to help shoot the commercial. As noted, I can't be bought, but I can be rented and leased. I asked for the script. They said, "There is no script, we haven't laid it out yet."

I said, "Guys, wait a minute. This afternoon at one o'clock, Francis Albert Sinatra is coming downstairs to shoot the commercial, and you mean you haven't figured out what it's going to be yet?"

They said, "No, there's been some confusion."

I explained that the confusion was in me bringing my sorry ass all the way to Atlantic City to be embarrassed in front of Sinatra, or, worse than that, to get to know Jilly Rizzo's knuckles better than I had gotten to know them over a period of many years. Out of desperation, I went upstairs wearing a hard hat and a tool belt and carrying a large megaphone. I went into Frank's bathroom, where he was shaving, and into the megaphone I said, "All right, now hear this: all boy singers get into the limo. Let's see if this turkey will fly." I scared him so much I thought he might have cut himself, but he did get dressed and he did get into a limo.

Then the next part of my plan kicked in. My plan was to keep him amused from the moment he got into the limo until we were ready to shoot.

The first thing I did was to have the parking lot attendant open the wrong door of the limousine. Frank was being his most cooperative, and he let that go. But then the front door attendant opened the wrong door and went in ahead of Frank, which began to perturb my friend. Then as Frank entered the hotel, two little old ladies walked up to him and said, "Mr. Sinatra, can we get a picture, just one picture?" He agreed because he was always charming with little old ladies. Instead of taking the picture with him, they handed the camera *to* Frank and asked him to take a picture of them. He'd never had that happen before, so he found this amusing. As he walked through the hotel to where the cameras were set, I had arranged for similar things to happen to him. My favorite was a gorgeous girl approaching him and asking, "How about an autograph, just one autograph?"

Frank said, "Okay."

She signed a piece of paper and handed it to him. He stood there looking at me, looking at that piece of paper, and realized what I was doing to him and broke into laughter.

When Frank finally arrived onstage, all the hotel employees were assembled and applauding. Frank did the ad, and to celebrate after we wrapped, we headed to the bar and we both proceeded to do irreparable damage to various body parts that did not react well to the poison contained in Jack Daniel's.

SINATRA HIJACKS A PLANE

Back in the early 1980s, the Golden Globes named Pia Zadora "the most promising star of the year." Her husband, Meshulam Riklis, was an older wealthy man (go figure, fifty-five-year-old rich guy with a twenty-one-year-old) who owned the Riviera in Las Vegas, and *he* convinced Frank that if Pia Zadora could go on the road with him, they could use Riklis's plane. Since Frank never saw the opening act anyway, he thought this might be a good way to save a lot of money and to have a very luxurious plane to travel in.

Things went pretty well for the first five dates. It was always the same procedure. The opening act would go on; usually Frank would stay in the wings and tell them to cut five minutes. Frank would walk out unannounced. He would do his performance, sing a couple of extra encores, and when he went into "New York, New York" our row, which included Jolene, Barbara Sinatra, some of Barbara's friends, and a couple of Frank's friends, would quietly go out the door on the right side of the theater and get into limousines, which were parked with doors open and engines running. Frank would come offstage. He never stopped for a beat. He stepped into the limousine, the car doors closed, the garage doors opened, and we would roar out with a police escort. While the orchestra was still playing, we would be headed to the airport. There were times Frank wouldn't work at a venue if it was too far from the airport because he hated to ride in cars, especially after the time I had him stuck waiting for a president's helicopter.

It was always the same ritual for Frank. Finish a show. Walk offstage. Bow. Encore "New York, New York." One more bow. Out the door. Into the limo. Police escort to the airport. Up the steps onto the plane to be greeted by an awaiting flight attendant with a Jack Daniel's over ice and a Camel cigarette in her hand. Both the J.D. and the Camel would be consumed before we were wheels up.

As you can imagine, it was important to stay ahead of Frank through this entire experience. On one memorable evening, Frank got on the plane and said, "Let's get out of here."

The pilot turned to him and said, "Mr. Sinatra, Pia Zadora and her husband are not here yet."

Frank said, "I don't care where they are, we're taking off." And they did. Frank hijacked the plane.

So here is the Riklis plane, just becoming airborne as the Riklis limousine drives up and Pia and her husband see their plane taking off for the next town. It was never even mentioned that night, the next day, or ever after that. I think they felt they were lucky to be traveling with him even if their plane had to make two trips.

ONE TIME WITH FRANK AND DEAN

I was lucky. I spent years hanging out with Frank, Sammy, and Dean. And to explain why I loved every minute with Dean, let me preface it by saying I love a great quote. Like the writer who put on his tombstone FINALLY, MY OWN PLOT.

I think one of my favorites is from Abraham Lincoln, who said, "If I were two-faced, would I be wearing this one?"

Pearl Bailey used to say, "If I can't sell it, I'm gonna sit down on it, because I ain't givin' nothin' away."

But my favorite quotes came right out of Dean Martin's act. He used to say, "You are not drunk if you can lie on the floor without holding on." He often said that he had been "overserved," and that is why he walked with his head tilted back, so that he wouldn't spill any. He said his doctor told him to stop smoking because the doctor was afraid Dean might explode. Dean would also say he was robbed last night—when driving home, he put out his arm to make a left turn and somebody stole his olive.

Dean was, without question, one of the funniest men in show business, and many of my favorite memories are of the wonderful times Jolene and I had with Dean and his wife. The Martins had a great house in Beverly Hills on Mountain Drive with a tennis court and a huge living room. On Saturday nights, Jeanne Martin would have a party for all of her younger friends. Yes, it's true, at one point this ninety-three-year-old was considered someone's "younger friend." Everybody would come and sit around the big living room and bar, while Dean would walk around the room with a martini and a bottle of beer. Around nine o'clock, Dean would suddenly vanish. Shortly thereafter, there would invariably be a knock at the front door. The police had arrived and would announce to Mrs. Martin that one of the neighbors had turned her in for having a loud party, and the neighbors weren't able to sleep. Of course, the police would then indicate, by pointing upstairs, that the complaint had come from Dean, who wanted to go to bed. He had turned in his own wife. By the time the police got there, Dean was watching *Gunsmoke* and couldn't care less about any noise covering up the sound of gun shots. Dean would then be asleep by ten o'clock so he could get to the golf course early the next morning.

Dean could not have possibly drank as much as people said. In fact, he could never even have had as much to drink as *he* said. Here's the difference between two legends of the Rat Pack: Frank loved to stay up late and party; Dean loved to *talk* about it.

This may be my favorite Dean quote. One night he brought Frank Sinatra home for dinner. Dean's huge family ate together at six o'clock every night in a gigantic dining room that seated twenty people. On this particular night, all of his kids brought all of their friends. Dean and Frank arrived, and the room was absolutely full. Dean looked around, saw there was no place for him to sit, turned to Frank, and said, "How do you like that, Paley, I fucked myself out of a seat at the dining room table."

DEAN MARTIN WAS OUR DEALER

No, not drugs—cards. Let me explain.

Dean Martin's first job was as a dealer in a gambling joint in Steubenville, Ohio. He never forgot that skill; Dean could do better stuff with a deck of cards than any magician. Plus he could deal all night long.

Between shows in the old days at the Sands in Vegas, Dean and Frank and I would go out into the casino, and Dean would deal blackjack. Dean would deal, and even if he didn't deal twenty-one, it didn't matter, because Frank would pay on everything. A customer would have eighteen and Frank would demand that they hit it. Dean would give them a ten and say, "Look at that . . . twenty-eight . . . Looks like we have a winner." Of course, if Dean had twenty, he would hit it. The payouts were outrageous.

You would think that the hotel would be upset, but on the contrary, they loved it. When Dean and Frank were appearing in Vegas, the place was jammed, in hopes that they would let one more customer into the room or that Dean and Frank would hit the casino after their show. The hotels made more money on that possibility than they could have ever paid out even if Dean Martin was dealing at every table in the joint.

After Dean got finished dealing, we would go into the Sands lounge. Sometimes he would get up and sing, and then we would go to see the late show at the Sahara. Nobody ever went to bed until dawn.

JILLY RIZZO AND RUDYARD KIPLING

Jilly Rizzo was not only Frank Sinatra's best friend, he was loved by everyone whom he had never hit. While major stars usually show up with huge entourages (in fact, some very minor stars show up with big entourages, or as Freud would call it, compensation), Frank would go anyplace with just his one-man security detail: Jilly.

I loved Jilly, so each week we featured Jilly at the end of *Laugh-In*. All he would say was "See yuz next week." No one knew why he was there, and NBC always tried to attach some sinister meaning to my fondness for Jilly. There was none. Having him at the end of the show was just one of many things on *Laugh-In* that not everyone understood. And I didn't care. My philosophy is that no one understands everything, but everything was understood by someone.

One time we were doing a celebration of Frank's career, and I wrote a speech for Jilly. When he was introduced and stood up, he got enormous applause. The speech went like this: "Thank yuz. It's a pleasure to be here at this suspicious occasion, and I hope yuz is all havin' a good time. It is only apropos that I read a short passage from my favorite composers, Rudolph Kipling." (At the sound of "Rudolph Kipling," Frank almost lost it, but Jilly continued.) "If yuz can keep your head when all about yuz is losing theirs, yuz must be some kind of schmuck."

Jilly bowed and sat down to thunderous applause.

One more Jilly story. When Pat Henry died, Jilly called his good friend Tony O. and said, "Tony, relax, I got some bad news for youse."

Tony said, "Oh my God, what happened?"

Jilly said, "Well . . . it's about Pat Henry. This morning he woke up dead." What Jilly meant was he had died in his sleep, but his way of expressing it was more colorful than just "he died in his sleep."

EVEN LEGENDS HAVE IDOLS

One of my favorite evenings spent with Frank Sinatra was during one of his last appearances at the Greek Theatre. We had decided to invite a lot of our friends who had not ever seen Sinatra in concert before to go to the show and then come back to our house for a party afterward. The guest list included Chevy Chase and his wife, Jayni, but since his wife could not go that night, Chevy's date was

Marty Short. Marty is a comedy legend, but even legends idolized Frank. Marty had never seen him in concert, had never met him, and was very excited to go.

We all met at our house and had a drink, then loaded onto a bus with a bartender for our ride to the Greek Theatre. Even Barbara and Marvin Davis came with us on the bus, and their bodyguards and security followed behind the bus in a limousine. I always thought that was kind of chic.

Appearing with Frank was Shirley MacLaine. Of course, some of the younger people in the audience knew Shirley only from her motion pictures and had never seen her onstage. They were totally amazed by this film actress who was able to sing and dance. After all, she started on Broadway. That set a great tone for the evening, but then Ole Blue Eyes came out and, indeed, blew everyone away.

After the show we arrived back at our house, and one by one, each guest paid homage to "his greatness." Finally, after most of the group had gone in to eat dinner, I was left at the bar with Frank, and I finally had a chance to introduce him to Marty Short. It was always interesting to see the awe that people had the first time they met Frank and how quickly he was able to put them at ease. I introduced them, and Marty said, "Mr. Sinatra, you just don't know what a thrill it is to meet you."

Frank smiled and said, "I think I do."

Frank then said, "What are you drinking?" Martin explained that he didn't really drink. So Frank turned to the bartender and said, "Give my friend a Jack Daniel's on the rocks." He turned to Marty and said, "I know your work and you're marvelous."

Marty was so thrilled with this that he did make a serious dent in that glass full of Jack Daniel's. Then Frank ordered him a second drink. Marty sat down on the barstool and prepared for a nice long chat with his idol and new friend, Frank Sinatra, who started to talk about various appearances of Marty Short that he had enjoyed. Just as Marty was reveling in this new relationship, a horn started honking out front of my house because Chevy, who had already met Frank, wanted to go home to join his wife and their daughter. All Marty wanted to do was hang out with his new BFF, but he had come as Chevy's date and had to leave with him. I got a kick out of it, because Marty told this story on the *Late Show* to David Letterman a few nights later, and both he and Letterman discussed the magic of Sinatra. It was great to hear. I sent a copy of it to Frank, who also got a big kick out of it.

Sinatra could come out in front of a crowd of twenty thousand people and feel the love, respect, and adoration of fans who had grown up on Sinatra music, many of them, as we've said before, having been conceived while their parents listened to Sinatra music. And I've yet to hear anyone who was conceived listening to the music of Snooky Lanson. I bet even Snooky Lanson fucked to Sinatra.

FRANK'S EULOGY

Frank died in 1998. I was terrified when Barbara Sinatra asked me to speak at his funeral, because I felt if I looked down at the coffin, he'd sit up and say, "Come on, crazy. Let's cut this short . . . and you only have one take." Not only that, the church was full of A-list, above-the-title friends who went back many years, and I'm not A-list, so to ease my nerves Barbara promised me that I would not have to follow a star like Gregory Peck. Welcome to show business, people lie. Here is the speech I gave right after Greg's:

Eulogy—May 20, 1998
Frank would have loved the idea of me making a speech in a cathedral standing in front of a full cardinal. I almost took Communion so I could tell Frank that we kind of had lunch together. Sorry, Your Honor . . . it was just a joke.
[Jolene looked very upset at me calling the cardinal "Your Honor."]
   I wonder what will happen in Heaven when Jilly tells God that he is no longer in charge.

Our friend had many names . . . He was known as . . .
the Leader . . . the Crooner . . . the Voice . . . the Man . . .
the Chairman . . . Ole Blue Eyes . . . Frank . . . Frankie . . .
Frances . . . Cheech and . . . pally. But *most* people were
safer just calling him . . . Mr. Sinatra.

Sammy Davis SENIOR called him "Buttah" . . . Buttah
stood for butter on the table . . . Sam said that when they
were working with Frank they could afford butter on the
table . . . Well, Frances put a *lot* of butter . . . on a *lot* of tables.

Great myths surround the man. Most of them incomplete . . . Many of them . . . un*true*.

Even now the media continually refers to him as the
"late . . . great . . . Frank Sinatra."

Great? Definitely . . . But . . . *late*? Never.

It's true that two of his most favorite words were . . .
"Jack" . . . and "Daniel's" . . . That is TRUE . . .

It's also true his two *least* favorite words were . . . "Take
two."

And it's true, with all of his fame, he was never *fully*
understood.

It was *rumored* that Frank had a rather *short* fuse and
little patience . . . NOT TRUE . . .

He had a *very short* fuse and *no patience*.

And it is true . . . that he *did* get a little upset at times
and he *did* occasionally become displeased and . . . somewhat . . . *intense*. But it wasn't *always* his fault.

Quite often Frank was a victim of his own fame . . .

That's right . . . *Frank was a victim*.

I'll illustrate with this short *TRUE* story . . .

Jolene and I were with Frank and Barbara on a concert
tour in the Orient. He was a smash in Japan, and then we
flew on to Hong Kong . . . There was a weather problem,
and the plane was an hour late . . .

NOT his fault.

It was a very bumpy ride . . . *not his fault* . . . and when we arrived in Hong Kong both Frank and I had somehow managed to become a little . . . "overserved" . . . due, I think, to some . . . bad ice . . . clearly not his fault.

They told him *not* to drink the water . . . but they never mentioned . . . *the ice.*

Our arrival at the hotel had been anticipated. The street and the lobby were full of fans, reporters, and photographers. It was a zoo. *No problem* . . . Frank was COOL.

You see . . . Frank *never* arrived through a lobby *anyway.* The most famous man in the world . . . never *saw* a lobby. As usual we came in through the loading dock . . . which was okay because we were both just a little loaded . . . and we went up the *freight* elevator.

Barbara and the people around Frank were meticulous in their planning, so his favorite suite had been ordered . . . However . . . an oil sheik was in the suite earlier . . . had a party and trashed it. The redecorating was not yet complete, so the accommodations were not what Frank expected . . . Again, *not* his fault.

He was a . . . little . . . DISPLEASED.

He didn't like the new suite, which overlooked the patio attached to the lovely suite he was *supposed* to have had.

Because of the confusion, the hotel operator put *all* of his calls through to the suite. Frank went room to room saying "He's not here" and hanging up the phones. Then Frank tried to throw the phone out of the window, but it just bounced off.

At *that* moment the door buzzer sounded.

When Barbara opened the door, a man was standing there explaining that he had made a suit for Frank thirty years before . . . and he was there to make him another suit NOW . . . which he would have ready in two days. He was carrying an armful of swatches of sample fabrics with a tape measure around his neck.

That was it . . . Frank became *even more* displeased . . . He was *REALLY DISPLEASED*.

Now . . . earlier that day, Jolene had ordered an elegant Chinese dinner for our group, to be served in the suite, and Barbara and Jolene thought it would be *nice* if all of us wore kimonos for our first evening of celebration in Hong Kong. Now just imagine this . . .

A hallway full of waiters carrying large serving trays of Chinese delicacies to our group, who were all wearing kimonos and were huddled fearfully in the corner . . . There was a tailor trying to measure Frank's inseam . . . Jilly in a kimono with a power saw, trying to carry out Frank's instruction to enlarge the suite . . . A very upset Frances *ready* to throw *bodies* off of the *balcony* but unable to get the sliding door open . . . All the while the phones continued to ring with the press calling up from the lobby . . . As Frank is ordering the waiters to get out . . . and Jolene and Barbara are coaxing the waiters to come back with our Chinese dinner . . . events clearly got out of hand . . . *not* his fault . . . Once again . . .

Frank was a *victim*.

Anyway, you get the picture . . . To his close friends, some of it may even sound . . . familiar.

At about three A.M. with this wonderful lady . . . his beloved Barbara . . . hiding under the blankets . . . an exhausted superstar sat down on the corner of the bed and said . . . "Well, Barbara, one thing you don't have to worry about . . . I'll never get an ulcer." And Barbara quietly mumbled under the blankets, "*You'll* never *get* one . . . but you're a carrier."

The next afternoon Frank *leapt* out of bed at the crack of three P.M. . . . had tea, toast, and bacon. We all went

224 / GEORGE SCHLATTER

shopping and had some laughs. Another day . . . another adventure, with our often misunderstood . . . but always exciting . . . Chairman of the Board.

While the world is mourning his death . . . we should all continue to *celebrate* his life.

Norm Crosby quoted Frank by saying . . . "Live every day like it's your last and sooner or later you'll be right." Well, that's what "Buttah on the Table" did.

Every day was special . . . every song was unique and meaningful . . . and every relationship was valuable.

When you were with Frank . . . you were transported to a different place . . . you were "in the zone."

It would be difficult to come up with any words that were not already used in Frank's lyrics . . . or have not been spoken by Frank's fans.

The only words I would like to add are plain and simple . . . Thank you . . .

THANK YOU for the MUSIC . . . thank you for the LAUGHS . . . and thank you for being such an important and irreplaceable part of all of our lives.

And thank you, BARBARA, for taking such good care of our friend.

"Sleep Warm" . . . dear friend . . .

Say hi to Jilly, Dean, and Sammy . . .

We'll "Put [Our] Dreams Away for Another Day" . . . but we'll be . . . "Close to You," "From Here to Eternity."

Delivering this eulogy was the most difficult moment of my life, but I will always be glad that I did.

Epilogue
Still Laugh-In

W hat you just read are just a few of my favorite moments from a seventy-plus-year show business career. There are a lot more stories, but either fear from the living or respect for the dead prevents me from sharing all of them . . . at this time. Or maybe it was just a rare burst of good taste.

I know this book is about my career, but I would have no show business career without Jolene. In fact she had a show business career and could have gone on to big things, but chose, instead, to have some babies, decorate some houses, make very profitable investments, and generally try to keep my ass gainfully employed and out of jail. She is my wife, my girlfriend, my roommate, my second mate, and I do occasionally refer to her as my "first" wife.

This has worked out for almost seventy years despite me breaking a few promises. One broken promise was when I was doing a lot of shows in New York. Jolene was getting a little tired of me being gone so often, and I had promised to stay here in LA. Then suddenly, a real opportunity came up. I didn't know quite how to tell her about it.

I should have realized that Jolene is always about six months ahead of me and somehow already knew about the show in New York. When I went to tell her, she said, "Not now, darling, I want to take you and show you something. I found those earrings."

226 / GEORGE SCHLATTER

Well, I had never heard the word "earring" or "those earrings" before. She made it sound like we had been discussing earrings for some time, which we had not. However, since I realized I might be in trouble with this "one more" trip to New York, I knew I had to go along with wherever this led.

She said, "Would you just look at them and see if you like them, and whether they are what *we* have been looking for?"

As I said, I wasn't aware that *we* had been looking for earrings. Nevertheless, we drove over the canyon to a place called California Jewelrysmith, which seemed to me an innocent enough name of an establishment. In the car, Jolene asked me to please not discuss money because she had been working on a very special deal with "our" jeweler because the earrings were VVVF, which I later found out means very, very, very fine. I am sure you are aware of what I could do with those initials. It might even turn into very, very, very . . . fucked.

We went in, and it was quite obvious that Jolene and the jeweler were best friends. Jolene's new best friend brought out a pair of earrings that were very impressive. When we finally left, I said, "Jolene, tell me how much the earrings *we've* been looking for cost."

She gave me a number that was also very impressive, but not totally out of the question, since I thought I could at least make up part of the money by accepting this one more special in New York. So it was agreed that we would get the earrings *we* had been looking for and I would do the special.

I went to New York on a survey, and when I came home and was going through the mail, I noticed a bill from California Jewelrysmith. I opened the bill, and the amount was exactly double the amount that Jolene had told to me. That evening after cocktails, I showed the bill to Jolene and said, "Honey, this bill is double what you told me it was. What's the deal?" She explained to me that the bill was indeed correct. I expressed my concern that it was twice the amount she had told me it would be. Jolene then gave me the greatest answer of all. She said, "That's easy. Two earrings."

After I got my breath, I expressed my opinion that "they don't charge per earring." Then came the beauty, the haymaker, the uppercut, the right cross, the knee in the nuts. Jolene said, "Goody for you, you know more about jewelry than I do."

So what's next for me? Clearly not becoming a jeweler. And we can rule out running a network, running a marathon, or running for president—although I would know how to plan the inauguration. Instead I'm spending my time focused on two things. First is the creation of the George and Jolene Brand Schlatter Theatre at the National Comedy Center in Jamestown, New York. Think of it as a key part of a hall of fame for comedians—and to make this what it can and should be, I've made a substantial donation (gulp!) and have also donated videotapes of my own comedy efforts and variety shows from over the decades. When you go there and see the range of brilliance in American comedy, I know it will make you laugh.

And that brings me to my second mission until that long dirt nap begins: to keep sharing jokes and stories that make you laugh and that make me laugh. I've been blessed to have worked with so many funny people for so long, and I can't thank them enough for the joy they've given me. And if two martinis and ten cigars a day kept George Burns going till a hundred, two good stories and ten good jokes a day are enough for me.

And you can be assured of one thing. When it's time to go to my next gig, my final words will not be goodbye. They'll be "Look at me, I'm still laughin'."

Afterword
by Goldie Hawn

I hope after reading this book you love George Schlatter as much as I do…or at least you wish you could have spent as much time with him as I have. So how did I end up with George? I know he talks about it in this book but here is how I see our story.

It was the '60s, and I was on a show. It went pretty well, but we only had 26 weeks, and I always saw myself as a dancer…and then I met George. We met in the offices at NBC. I sat down in this big red chair across from George who started things off with, "So Goldie, tell me about yourself."

I said, "Well, I'm a dancer."

He said, "No, you just were acting."

We talked a little bit about this, that and the other. I had no idea why I was there. The next thing I heard was that I got three shows, which was confusing because I wasn't really a singer and I wasn't a joke teller. I wasn't sure what I was going to do.

George put me on the stage and gave me the lines; something that wasn't funny. It was the introduction to Dan Rowan and the News of the Future. There were all these cue cards, and I mixed up the words. I put one word before the other so I asked if I could try it again. George told me it was fine. I think the little person in George saw the little girl in me, and that made all the difference.

That started my career. It blew up. I didn't know what happened to me. I didn't know why. I didn't think I was funny; and then all of a sudden, after I got used to understanding that, I mixed the cards up myself...which made it a little harder to figure out where I was going to mess up. I ended up not reading any scripts because I realized if I read the script, I couldn't learn it at all. I had to know how to be the dumbest, craziest, airhead, happy person. And George allowed that, he encouraged that just like he encouraged all of us. He is one of the great gurus of joy, and because of the team he put together he changed television, and in his own way he changed the world.

We need more George Schlatters with their positivity and optimism. But there's only one, the OG: George Schlatter.

Acknowledgments

In the acknowledgment section of most books, the author references and thanks all the people who helped in getting the book published. That's a very small list with this book. A much larger list follows: it is my shout-out to those who deserve special thanks for giving me the life and laughs I've enjoyed for these past ninety-three years.

This book would not exist without the support of my wife, Jolene. In fact, I wouldn't exist without Jolene. She had a great career ahead of her in show business with all her talent, but she put that aside when she realized what being married to me entailed. For the past sixty-six years she has guided me, tolerated me, and corrected me. And far too many times she has had to apologize for me. And so the least I can do is promise to buy her two new earrings.

Along with all the love she has given me, Jolene also gave me two amazing daughters, Maria and A.J., both of whom, in everything they do, make me enormously proud.

I have to thank Jon Macks for wading through this mountain of memories and adding some wit, wisdom, and order to this collection. And when I say I have to thank him, I mean that it was in his contract. In either 1999 or 2000, I called Jay Leno and mentioned I was doing another American Comedy Awards special and asked who would be a good writer to add to the team. Jay recommended

Jon, and for over twenty years we have been friends and collaborators. When the time came to write this book, I turned to Jon to lend a hand and his laptop.

Far too many of the people who follow have left us . . . but their work endures, and they will never leave my memory.

I'll start with the writers. At the top of the list is Digby Wolfe, who contributed so much to *Laugh-In* and to many of the other projects for which I took more credit than I deserved. Buz Kohan is another one of the creative geniuses who has played such a major role in many of my projects. He's at times grumpy, but always patient with me and creative with everything he does. Paul Keyes worked as a writer on *Laugh-In* and later became producer and stayed on the show after I left. Billy Barnes wrote so much of my special musical material, and Don Reo and Allan Katz both went on from our collaboration to long and great careers.

Next are those advisers essential to a life in show business. Tony Fantozzi was my agent with William Morris. Without Tony, I'd still be living in the Valley, and by that, I mean Death Valley. Sonny Golden was my business manager for many years and arranged for the investments that have contributed so much to Jolene and my security. Bob Finkelstein is my attorney; Bob started out working with Mickey Rudin and went on to become a major contributor to the Sinatra family and others. David Roth and Barry Gumerove, a lawyer for our trust and our business manager, respectively, add so much to our security and sanity.

Without the people at my production company, I would not have been able to put any shows on the air. Gary Necessary has been a part of my life for over forty years, supervising every production I have been involved in. He started as a prop man on *Laugh-In* and has guided me through and protected me in many of my adventures. Martha Boes joined me many years ago and has never managed to escape. She plans and manages my future as well as attempts to conceal much of my past, and she has played an enormous role not just in everything I do but in reviewing everything I wrote in this book, doing her best to make me sound smarter and to not end up being sued, shot, or both. Judy Pastore is the amazing producer who has made my work available on today's platforms. Oscar Moreno started with me as a valet and now has his own very successful valet company. He also manages my real estate and keeps the buildings leased out; and proving I do not have a "no dating at work" policy, his wife, Margaret, provides all the administrative support anyone could ask for. And Diana Moreno can call up any of our shows or clips at the touch of a button. I know this will come as a shock, but the last tech advancement I mastered was the fax machine.

Chris Coronado started out as a driver and caregiver and has taken such good care of me that I may even make it through the end of my nineties. Chris is now producing and directing a biographical video collection, including clips of most of my shows and interviews with many of the people I have worked with. It is an awesome undertaking.

The key to much of my success was my involvement with Ed Friendly. Ed was a major executive with NBC who was responsible for including me as producer in many of his projects. *Laugh-In* and *Real People* would not have been accepted by the network without its confidence in Ed as an executive. And thanks to Ed, I met Joseph Natalie, who had been Ed's assistant and wound up working for me for a long time.

Carolyn Raskin started out as a typist, became a brilliant production assistant, and eventually graduated to the producer of *Laugh-In*. During her career she created many of the editing techniques that were responsible for the kind of flash-cut, fragmented style of shows I did. Simply put, without Carolyn's expertise, *Laugh-In* would not have been possible.

Three more *Laugh-In* mentions. Hugh Lambert was our brilliant choreographer, and Ian Bernard wrote the arrangements and conducted our orchestra, and the brilliantly creative Michael Travis designed many of the costumes.

If I were a woman, I would have begged Bob Mackie to be my full-time designer, but because as a man I do not look good in gowns, I had him design the wardrobes for so many of my shows.

Paula Chaltas started with me as a typist and shortly after that became involved in staffing and promotion in the office. For fifteen years she organized the American Comedy Awards journal we had for each show.

Courtney Conte started as a page at NBC and went on to produce many projects with me and others, including the Carsey-Werner Company.

Bob Long was an ex-marine who produced and directed many of our most important *Real People* stories. There are so many things I should thank Bob for, but perhaps the biggest two are convincing Sarah Purcell to participate in some outrageous events on *Real People* and for having Byron Allen join our team.

I first saw Byron on *The Tonight Show* when he was only 18 years old. We did a number of shows together, including *Real People,* and he has gone on to phenomenal success. It is rumored he is worth $1 billion.

Bob Wynn was another vital associate, not just on *Real People* but on a number of my specials. He is also responsible for taking me on a horseback ride from which I still have barely recovered. Neither has the horse.

There are many people I've worked with over the years who deserve to be mentioned, but I am saving them for my next book.

And last but not least, a special thanks to the bartenders at Chasen's, Patsy's, and at least a hundred other saloons where I spent so many hours laughin' with friends. To quote Winston Churchill, "I have taken more out of alcohol than alcohol has taken out of me."

In Gratitude: An Appendix!
(A Not-so-partial List of the Talented People I've Worked With (In Alphabetical Order))

Paula Abdul, Kareem Abdul-Jabbar, Edie Adams, Jack Albertson, Buzz Aldrin, Jason Alexander, Joey Alfidi, Muhammad Ali, Byron Allen, Debbie Allen, Dennis Allen, Steve Allen, Tim Allen, Woody Allen, Kirstie Alley, Herb Alpert, Loni Anderson, Louie Anderson, Ursula Andress, Mario Andretti, Julie Andrews, Paul Anka, Sergio Aragonés, Army Archerd, Eve Arden, Louis Armstrong, Neal Armstrong, Desi Arnaz, Eddy Arnold, Tom Arnold, Bea Arthur, Ed Asner, Chet Atkins, Frankie Avalon, Dan Aykroyd,

Catherine Bach, Burt Bacharach, Jim Backus, Kevin Bacon, Pearl Bailey, Anita Baker, Kathy Baker, Lucille Ball, Maria Bamford, Anne Bancroft, Tyra Banks, Christine Baranski, John Barbour, Roseanne Barr, Rona Barrett, Kenya Barris, J.J. Barry, Drew Barrymore, Count Basie, Kathy Bates, Rhonda Bates, Elgin Baylor, Warren Beatty, Ed Begley, Jr., Harry Belafonte, Richard Belzer, Annette Bening, Tony Bennett, Jack Benny, Candice Bergen, Edgar Bergen, Polly Bergen, Milton Berle, Shelley Berman, Elmer Bernstein, Halle Berry, Ken Berry, Beyonce, Peter Billingsley, Larry Bird, David Birney, Joey Bishop, Lewis Black, Dan Blocker, Andrea Bocelli, Michael Bolton, Erma Bombeck, Lisa Bonet, Sonny Bono, Chastity Bono, Pat Boone, Elayne Boosler, Victor Borge, Ernest Borgnine, Alex Borstein, Brian Bosworth, Chris Botti, Wayne Brady, Eileen Brennan, Beau Bridges, Jeff Bridges, Tom Brokaw, James Brolin, Lois Bromfield, Foster Brooks, Garth Brooks, Mel Brooks, Chelsea Brown, Georgia Brown, Johnny Brown, Kobe Bryant, Betty Buckley, William F. Buckley, Sandra Bullock, Carol Burnett, George Burns, LeVar Burton, George W. Bush, Laura Bush, President George Bush, Sam Butera, Brett Butler, Red Buttons, Pat Buttram, Ruth Buzzi, John Byner,

James Caan, Sid Caesar, Michael Caine, Godfrey Cambridge, Kirk Cameron, Glen Campbell, John Candy, Dyan Cannon, John Caponera, Truman Capote, Charles Cappleman, Drew Carey, Mariah Carey, George Carlin, Judy Carne, Art Carney, Vikki Carr, Jim Carrey, Diahann Carroll, Leo G. Carroll, Carrot Top, Johnny Carson, Jack Carter, Nell Carter, Angela Cartwright, Dana Carvey, Johnny Cash, Dick Cavett, Wilt Chamberlain, Carol Channing, Cyd Charisse, Ray Charles, Charo, Chevy Chase, Dick Cheney, Lynne Cheney, Cher, Kenny Chesney, Margaret Cho, Dick Clark, Petula Clark, John Cleese, George Clooney, Rosemary Clooney, Imogene Coca, Nat King Cole, Jerry Collins, Perry Como, Sean Connery, Harry Connick, Jr., Billy Connolly, Chuck Connors, Jimmy Connors, William Conrad, Tim Conway, Rita Coolidge, Howard Cosell, Kevin Costner, Bryan Cranston, Richard Crenna, Walter Cronkite, Bing Crosby, Norm Crosby, Tom Cruise, Billy Crystal, Macaulay Culkin, Jane Curtin, Jamie Lee Curtis, Tony Curtis,

Bill Dana, Rodney Dangerfield, Ted Danson, Tony Danza, Bobby Darin, Barbara Davis, Bette Davis, Clive Davis, Geena Davis, Mac Davis, Marvin Davis, Sammy Davis, Jr., Richard "Dickie" Dawson, Doris Day, Oscar De La Hoya, Robert De Niro, Jimmy Dean, Ellen DeGeneres, Dom DeLuise, John Denver, Danny DeVito, Joyce DeWitt, Neil Diamond, Cameron Diaz, Angie Dickinson, Taye Diggs, Phyllis Diller, Celine Dion, Snoop Dogg, Fats Domino, Tommy Dorsey, Anne Douglas, Kirk Douglas, Michael Douglas, Robert Downey, Jr., Tom Dreesen, Fran Drescher, David Duchovny, Julia Duffy, Olympia Dukakis, Faye Dunaway, Jeff Dunham, Dick Van Dyke, Bob Dylan,

Clint Eastwood, Barbara Eden, Kenneth "Babyface" Edmonds, Blake Edwards, Jenna Elfman, Duke Ellington, Cass Elliot, Bill Engvall, Gloria Estefan, Robert Evans, Peter Falk, Barbara Feldon, Will Ferrell, Sally Field, Tote Fields, Carrie Fisher, Joely Fisher, Ella FItzgerald, Fannie Flagg, Henry Fonda, Jane Fonda, Betty Ford, Gerald Ford, Harrison Ford, Tennessee Ernie Ford, President Gerald Ford, George Foreman, John Forsythe, Bob Fosse, David Foster, Michael J. Fox, Jeff Foxworthy, Jamie Foxx, Redd Foxx, Connie Francis, Al Franken, Aretha Franklin, David Frost,

Zsa Zsa Gabor, Andy Garcia, Art Garfunkel, Judy Garland, James Garner, Teri Garr, Brad Garrett, Greer Garson, Mitzi Gaynor, Will Geer, Estelle Getty, Stan Getz, Leeza Gibbons, Henry Gibson, Mel Gibson, Melissa Gilbert, Sara Gilbert, Jackie Gleason, Danny Glover, George Gobel, Arthur Godfrey, Whoopi Goldberg,

Bobcat Goldthwait, Senator Barry Goldwater, Cuba Gooding Jr., John Goodman, Berry Gordy, Eydie Gormé, Frank Gorshin, Marjoe Gortner, Louis Gossett Jr., Gilbert Gottfried, Robert Goulet, Betty Grable, Billy Graham, Kelsey Grammer, Lee Grant, Teresa Graves, Brian Austin Green, Lorne Greene, Shecky Greene, Dick Gregory, Wayne Gretzky, David Alan Grier, Kathy Griffin, Merv Griffin, Andy Griffith, Josh Groban, Christopher Guest,

Buddy Hackett, Tiffany Haddish, Arsenio Hall, Monte Hall, Argus Hamilton, George Hamilton, M.C. Hammer, Chelsea Handler, Tom Hanks, Harlem Globetrotters, Angie Harmon, Mark Harmon, Tom Harmon, Valerie Harper, Woody Harrelson, Neil Patrick Harris, Phil Harris, Mary Hart, Lisa Hartman, Steve Harvey, Goldie Hawn, Isaac Hayes, Sean Hayes, Rita Hayworth, Hugh Hefner, Katharine Hepburn, Orel Hershiser, Gregory Hines, Al Hirt, Don Ho, Dustin Hoffman, Hulk Hogan, Evander Holyfield, Bob Hope, Lena Horne, Louis J. Horvitz, Whitney Houston, Jennifer Hudson, Kate Hudson, Rock Hudson, Engelbert Humperdinck, Helen Hunt, Holly Hunter, Anjelica Huston, Eric Idle,

Anne Jackson, Rev. Jesse Jackson, Michael Jackson, Samuel L. Jackson, Jameela Jamil, Elton John, Arte Johnson, Coslough Johnson, Magic Johnson, Shane Johnson, Van Johnson, Dean Jones, Jack Jones, James Earl Jones, Quincy Jones, Shirley Jones, Tom Jones, Louis Jourdan, Jane Kaczmarek, Carol Kane, Jann Karam, Boris Karloff, Alex Karras, Danny Kaye, Stubby Kaye, Lainie Kazan, Jayne Kennedy, Kenny G., Madeline Khan, Jimmy Kimmel, Alan King, B.B. King, Don King, Larry King, Shawn King, George Kirby, Robert Klein, Werner Klemperer, Jack Klugman, Evel Kneivel, Gladys Knight, Don Knotts, Buz Kohan, Harvey Korman, Ernie Kovacs, Jane Krakowski, Kris Kristofferson, Marty Krofft, Sid Krofft, Lisa Kudrow,

L.A. Raiders, Julius La Rosa, Patti LaBelle, Cheryl Ladd, Frankie Laine, Hugh Lambert, Martin Landau, Muriel Landers, Steve Landesberg, Michael Landon, Murray Langston, Angela Lansbury, Sherry Lansing, Tommy Lasorda, Peter Lawford, Steve Lawrence, Cloris Leachman, Norman Lear, Peggy Lee, Natasha Leggero, John Leguizamo, Carol Leifer, Janet Leigh, Jack Lemmon, Jay Leno, Sheldon Leonard, Sugar Ray Leonard, David Letterman, Jerry Lewis, Liberace, Licassi & Siegel, Wendy Liebman, Hal Linden, John Lithgow, Rich Little, Little Richard, LL Cool J, Kenny Loggins, Shelley Long, Jennifer Lopez, Trini Lopez, Sophia Loren, Gloria Loring, Julia Louis-Dreyfus, Jon Lovitz, George Lucas,

Bob Mackie, Jon Macks, Shirley MacLaine, Fred MacMurray, Sheila MacRae, Dave Madden, Madonna, Bill Maher, Ginny Mancini, Henry Mancini, Howie Mandel, Nelson Mandela, Barbara Mandrell, Barry Manilow, Rose Marie, Pigmeat Markham, Garry Marshall, Penny Marshall, Peter Marshall, Dean Martin, Dick Martin, Steve Martin, Groucho Marx, Jerry Mathers, Marlee Matlin, Walter Matthau, MC Hammer, Charlie McCarthy, Rue McClanahan, Marilyn McCoo, Eric McCormack, Reba McEntire, Ed McMahon, Katharine McPhee, Audrey Meadows, Anne Meara, Sérgio Mendes, Idina Menzel, Johnny Mercer, Robert Merrill, Debra Messing, Bette Midler, Luis Miguel, Martin Milner, Liza Minnelli, Don Mischer, Martha Mitchell, Les Moonves, Dudley Moore, Mary Tyler Moore, Roger Moore, Agnes Moorehead, Rita Moreno, Pat Morita, Zero Mostel, Bill Moyers, Martin Mull, Megan Mullally, Eddie Murphy, Mike Myers,

Jim Nabors, Ralph Nader, Kathy Najimy, Joe Namath, Kevin Nealon, Inga Neilsen, Craig T. Nelson, Willie Nelson, Bob Newhart, Anthony Newley, Paul Newman, Wayne Newton, Mike Nichols, Leonard Nimoy, Richard Nixon, Michael Nouri, Louis Nye, Hugh O'Brian, Donald O'Connor, Carroll O'Connor, Ann-Margaret Olsson, Shaquille O'Neal, Tatum O'Neal, Tony Orlando, Marie Osmond, Osmond Brothers, Cheri Oteri, Gary Owens, Frank Oz, Al Pacino, Chazz Palminteri, Dolly Parton, Suzanne de Passe, Luciano Pavarotti, Minnie Pearl, Gregory Peck, Rhea Perlman, Luke Perry, Matthew Perry, Joe Pesci, Peter, Paul & Mary, Regis Philbin, David Hyde Pierce, Bronson Pinchot, Joe Piscopo, Peter Pitofsky, Brad Pitt, Sidney Poitier, Paula Poundstone, General Colin Powell, Stefanie Powers, Robert Preston, Vincent Price, Jason Priestley, Louis Prima, Freddie Prinze, Paul Provenza, Juliet Prowse, Richard Pryor, Rain Pryor, Sarah Purcell,

Anthony Quinn, Radio City Music Hall Rockettes, George Raft, Tommy Raft, John Raitt, Sheryl Lee Ralph, Tony Randall, Phylicia Rashad, Dan Rather, Lou Rawls, Martha Raye, President Ronald Reagan, Nancy Reagan, Lynn Redgrave, Sumner Redstone, Carl Reiner, Rob Reiner, Paul Reiser, Lee Remick, Burt Reynolds, Debbie Reynolds, Caroline Rhea, Lionel Richie, Don Rickles, Rob Riggle, Bobby Riggs, John Ritter, Chita Rivera, Joan Rivers, Jilly Rizzo, Doris Roberts, Edward G. Robinson, Smokey Robinson, Sugar Ray Robinson, Chris Rock, Ginger Rogers, Kenny Rogers, Wayne Rogers, Ray Romano, Linda Ronstadt, Mickey Rooney, Diana Ross, Glen Roven, Dan Rowan, Rita Rudner, Bill Russell, Kurt Russell, Mark Russell, Nipsey Russell, Meg Ryan,

Katey Sagal, Carole Bayer Sager, Bob Saget, Mort Sahl, Soupy Sales, Salt-N-Pepa, Fred Savage, Arnold Schwarzenegger, David Schwimmer, Peter Scolari, Vin Scully, Ryan Seacrest, Jerry Seinfeld, Monica Seles, Tom Selleck, Peter Sellers, Rod Serling, Jane Seymour, Garry Shandling, Robert Shapiro, Dick Shawn, Judith Sheindlin, Cybill Shepard, Allan Sherman, Brooke Shields, Willie Shoemaker, Dinah Shore, Pauly Shore, Martin Short, Wil Shriner, Maria Shriver, Caesar Sid, Siegfried & Roy, Phil Silvers, Alicia Silverstone, Neil Simon, Paul Simon, Jessica Simpson, Frank Sinatra, Nancy Sinatra, Frank Sinatra, Jr., Red Skelton, Jada Pinkett Smith, Kate Smith, Katie Smith, Keely Smith, Will Smith, J.B. Smoove, Dick Smothers, Tommy Smothers, Suzanne Somers, Elke Sommer, Bono Sonny, Steven Spielberg, Bruce Springsteen, Jill St. John, Jo Stafford, Sylvester Stallone, Jean Stapleton, Kay Starr, Ringo Starr, Mary Steenburgen, David Steinberg, Skip Stephenson, Connie Stevens, McLean Stevenson, Jon Stewart, Gloria Stewart, Rod Stewart, Jerry Stiller, Stephen Stills, Sting, Sharon Stone, Meryl Streep, Barbra Streisand, Sally Struthers, Ruben Studdard, Alan Sues,

James Taylor, Rip Taylor, Toni Tennille, Judy Tenuta, The 5th Dimension, The Beatles, The Bee Gees, The Gatlin Brothers, The Hi-Lo's, The Jackson 5, The Jonas Brothers, The Jordanaires, The Lennon Sisters, The Manhattan Transfer, The McGuire Sisters, The Mills Brothers, The Muppets, The Oak Ridge Boys, The Osmond Brothers, The Pointer Sisters, The Temptations, Alan Thicke, Danny Thomas, Marlo Thomas, Terry Thomas, Tiny Tim, Lily Tomlin, Rip Torn, Liz Torres, John Travolta, Forrest Tucker, Ike Turner, Tina Turner, Mike Tyson, Tracey Ullman, Brenda Vaccaro, Dick Van Dyke, Luther Vandross, Ben Vereen, Gore Vidal, Bruce Vilanch,

Robert Wagner, Christopher Walken, Jimmie Walker, Nancy Walker, George Wallace, Marcia Wallace, Eli Wallach, Barbara Walters, Marsha Warfield, Malcolm-Jamal Warner, Dionne Warwick, Denzel Washington, Sam Waterston, Shawn Wayans, Damon Wayans, Keenen Ivory Wayans, John Wayne, Dennis Weaver, Andrew Lloyd Webber, Steven Weber, Jerry Weintraub, Wiere Brothers, Raquel Welch, Orson Welles, Paul Weston, Betty White, Slappy White, Dick Whittington, Gene Wilder, Fred Willard, Dick Williams, Andy Williams, Joe Williams, Paul Williams, Robin Williams, Bruce Willis, Flip Wilson, Meredith Wilson, Nancy Wilson, Rita Wilson, Oprah Winfrey, Henry Winkler, Jonathan Winters, Shelley Winters, Stevie Wonder, James Woods, JoAnne Worley, Trisha Yearwood, Michael York, Henny Youngman, Pia Zadora, Bob Zany

George Schlatter still goes to the office every day. He is the founder of the American Comedy Awards and for his work on television, he has a star on the Hollywood Walk of Fame (at 7030 Hollywood Blvd.). An immersive multimedia theater at the National Comedy Museum in Lucille Ball's hometown of Jamestown, NY is to be named in honor of George and Jolene Schlatter in 2023. The Center has collaborated with dozens of artists and estates to preserve materials that represent comedy's significant artistic, social, and political contributions to American culture.

Jon Macks is a comedy writer and award show writer who continues to work as a political consultant and speech writer. He wrote all 22 years on *The Tonight Show* with Jay Leno, has been a writer or head writer on 25 Academy Awards, which is the all time record; and writes speeches and special material projects for a wide range of clients including Helen Mirren, Michael Douglas, Hugh Jackman, Chris Rock, Billy Crystal, Martin Short, Steve Martin, Terry Bradshaw and Terry Fator. He has written five books with the latest being *Monologue: What Makes America Laugh Before Bed*.

Printed in the USA
CPSIA information can be obtained
at www.ICGtesting.com
JSHW021932270324
60054JS00002B/116

9 781961 884212